PROJECT
AZORIAN

PROJECT

THE CIA AND THE RAISING OF THE *K-129*

AZORIAN

NORMAN POLMAR and MICHAEL WHITE

NAVAL INSTITUTE PRESS
Annapolis, Maryland

This book was brought to publication with the generous assistance of Maura C. and Martin J. Bollinger.

Naval Institute Press
291 Wood Road
Annapolis, MD 21402

Library of Congress Cataloging-in-Publication Data
Polmar, Norman.
  Project Azorian : the CIA and the raising of the K-129 / by Norman Polmar and Michael White.
    p. cm.
  Includes bibliographical references and index.
  ISBN 978-1-59114-690-2 (hardcover : alk. paper) 1. Jennifer Project. 2. K-129 (Submarine) 3. Glomar Explorer (Ship) 4. Submarine disasters—Soviet Union. 5. Soviet Union. Voenno-Morskoi Flot—Submarine forces—History. 6. United States. Central Intelligence Agency—History. I. White, Michael II. Title.

  VB231.U54P65 2010
  910.9164'9—dc22

                                              2010037220

Printed in the United States of America on acid-free paper.

14 13 12 11 10   9 8 7 6 5 4 3 2
First printing

Dedicated to the
Parents, wives, and children
of the Officers and Enlisted Men
Lost in the submarine *K-129*.

Liberty cannot be preserved without a general knowledge among the people. Let us dare to read, think, speak, and write.
—*John Adams*

CONTENTS

PERSPECTIVE

"If you go back there it would mean war." Those words, spoken by a Soviet naval officer, demonstrated the concern of Soviet officials as they learned that the Central Intelligence Agency had salvaged part—and possibly all—of a Soviet ballistic missile submarine. The CIA had in fact raised a portion of the sunken missile submarine *K-129*, using a cover story that actually attracted world-wide attention, and undertaken with Soviet ships closely watching the lift ship without knowing that the salvage operation was underway.

During the first week of August 1974 a portion of the wreckage of a Soviet ballistic missile submarine was raised three miles, from the ocean floor up into the hull of a U.S. salvage ship. Although only a 38-foot section of the submarine *K-129* was recovered, Project Azorian was unquestionably the most ambitious and the most audacious ocean engineering effort ever attempted.

The "engineering" challenge was to recover an object, estimated to weigh up to 2,000 tons, from more than 16,000 feet. Previously, the only object known to have been picked up from such a depth was a satellite package, or "bucket," recovered by the U.S. Navy bathyscaph *Trieste II* on April 25, 1972. That object weighed several hundred pounds. And, prior to Project Azorian, the deepest ocean salvage of a ship was the raising of the U.S. submarine *Squalus* from a depth of 245 feet off the New England coast in 1939.

The *Trieste II* recovery and the *Squalus* salvage effort were undertaken in the "open," with the latter being reported in real time in the press. Even though the *Trieste II* effort was not publicized, the necessity for surface support by the floating dry dock *White Sands* and an ocean-going tug made it obvious that a deep recovery operation was under way.

Project Azorian was carried out under intensive press scrutiny because the "cover" for the salvage was a seafloor-mining project sponsored by the notorious Howard Hughes. Thus, the salvage of the *K-129*, besides being of unprecedented scope and depth, was conducted in the public view *and* with intensive Soviet naval surveillance *and* with the Soviet Embassy in Washington, D.C., having been previously notified by an anonymous source that the United States was planning to salvage a submarine.

The story of Project Azorian—incorrectly called Project Jennifer in the press—has been told and retold in the press and in books since it was first publicly revealed in February 1975. However, this book contains the accurate account of the location and salvage of the remains of the *K-129*, with details that have never before been revealed in the open literature. It is the first published account to be based on interviews with key participants in Project Azorian, official documents not previously available, extensive commentary by Soviet naval officers directly involved with the *K-129*, and photographs and other illustrations not previously seen in the open press. Perhaps most significant, this book explains for the first time information derived from analysis of the actual acoustic signals received from the events causing the sinking of the *K-129*, which were recorded by a U.S. Air Force hydrophone system in March 1968.

Although Project Azorian occurred more than three decades ago, U.S. law makes it a criminal offense to "out" a secret agent, i.e., to identify him or her using the person's real name. Accordingly, we have avoided linking codenames to real names of the undercover CIA officials and operatives involved in Project Azorian activities although they were made available to us by many of the participants and appear in reports provided to us.

■ ■ ■

The authors have sought to avoid abbreviations, acronyms, and jargon to the extent possible. Technical and naval terms are explained when first used. Three terms used extensively throughout the book are

- *Sail*: The upper appendage or "fairwater" of a submarine. The sail structure replaced the "conning tower" of earlier submarines, which was a watertight compartment placed on top of the hull, usually serving as the attack center. There is a small bridge atop the sail, with the structure serving as a streamlined housing for periscopes, masts, and snorkel induction tube; in some submarines the forward diving planes are mounted on the sail. It is also called "bridge fairwater" (i.e., a streamlined structure to support the bridge); it is called "fin" in the Royal Navy.

- *Snorkel*: An air intake tube that can be raised from the sail to permit the operation of diesel engines in a submerged submarine (operating at periscope depth). This permits the recharging of batteries to enable fully submerged operation with electric motors.

- *Project Numbers*. Beginning in 1936 all Soviet ship designs were assigned a sequential project number. The first, i.e., Project 1, was the large destroyers of the *Leningrad* class; the first submarine design was Project 6, the *Dekabrist* class. In this scheme Project 629 was the diesel-electric ballistic missile submarine class beginning with the submarine *K-96* (originally designated *B*-92). The *K-129* was of this class. A major design change would add a suffix letter such as 629A, or the letter M for modified. Not knowing most Soviet project numbers—and those acquired mostly were from highly classified sources—the North Atlantic Treaty Organization (NATO) navies established their own submarine designation scheme that was alphabetical, with phonetic words assigned to Soviet submarines. Thus, Project 629 had the NATO designation "Golf," and the modified Project 629A had the designation "Golf II."

Norman Polmar
Michael White

ACKNOWLEDGMENTS

The authors are in debt to many individuals who have helped us with this project, several of whom—with regret—cannot be publicly acknowledged at this time. First and foremost, we are in debt to Martin and Maura Bollinger for their encouragement and their support of this project.

Throughout the writing of this book, as well as during production of the documentary film "Azorian: The Raising of the *K-129*," we have benefited from a "team of experts" that provided peer reviews of our work and was an invaluable source of information. The team consisted of

Thomas J. Dougherty, PhD, technical story analyst.

Lee J. Mathers, former naval intelligence briefing officer in the Pentagon.

Bruce Rule, for 42 years the leading acoustics analyst for the Office of Naval Intelligence. Rule's analyses of acoustic data determined the cause of the loss of the submarines *Thresher* in 1963 and *Scorpion* in 1968.

Other individuals who have provided assistance or were interviewed for this effort are listed below; asterisks indicate persons interviewed for the film "Azorian" whose interview transcripts also were used as sources for this work. "H.G.E." indicates individuals who were aboard the *Hughes Glomar Explorer* at the time of the salvage effort.

- Alexandr M. Antonov, senior designer, Malachite submarine design bureau
- Vance Bolding, Global Marine Development Inc., mechanical systems engineer Glomar Explorer
- Tom Bringloe, Larry Glosten Inc., design engineer for the HMB-1
- Charles Cannon Jr., Global Marine Development Inc., naval architect Glomar Explorer
- Guy Cantrell, director of corporate communications, TRANSOCEAN
- Christopher Drew, *The New York Times* and coauthor of *Blind Man's Bluff*
- Dr. Roger C. Dunham, former reactor control operator aboard the USS *Halibut*
- Rear Adm. Viktor Dygalo, Soviet Navy (Ret), former Commander, 29th Submarine Division*
- Raymond Feldman, Lockheed Oceans Systems senior staff engineer (H.G.E.)*
- John Gresham, author and one-time student of ocean engineering
- Master Chief Radioman Pete E. Haddad, USN (Ret), radioman on board at the time of the *Swordfish* periscope incident
- Glenn Helm, librarian of Department of the Navy
- Heinrich Hoffmann, FAG Bearings USA, gimbal engineer *Glomar Explorer*
- John Hollett, Hollett International Development LCC, managing director for international maritime and logistics ventures
- Quartermaster 1st Class Edward E. Hunnicutt, USN (Ret), in the control room at the time of the *Swordfish* periscope incident
- Charlie Johnson, Global Marine Development Inc., heavy lift engineer (H.G.E.)*
- Steve Kemp, naval architect for Global Marine, worked on the *Glomar Explorer*
- Lt. Comdr. Jerry A. Koebel, USN (Ret), quartermaster of the watch at the time of the *Swordfish* periscope incident
- Capt. Richard N. Lee, USN (Ret), engineering officer and officer of the deck at the time of the *Swordfish* periscope incident
- Jim McNary, Global Marine Development Inc., heavy lift officer (H.G.E.)*
- Eugene Miasnikov, PhD, senior research scientist, Center for Arms Control, Energy, and Environmental Studies, Moscow Institute of Physics and Technology

- Capt. Edward Moore, USN (Ret), former commanding officer of the USS *Halibut*
- Kenneth J. Moore, submarine technologist and coauthor of *Cold War Submarines*
- Lt. Comdr. Beauford E. Myers, USN (Ret), former executive officer and acting officer-in-charge of the *Trieste II* support ship *White Sands*
- Capt. John O'Connell, USN (Ret), former assistant chief of staff for operations, plans, and intelligence for Commander, Submarine Force Pacific Fleet
- David S. Robarge, PhD, head of the CIA History Staff
- Eugene Schorsch, Vice President, Sun Shipbuilding and Dry Dock Company
- Rear Adm. Edward O. Sheafer, Jr., USN (Ret). former Director of Naval Intelligence
- Larry Small, Lockheed electrical engineer who worked on HMB-1
- Sherman Wetmore, Global Marine Development Inc. heavy lift operations manager (H.G.E.)[*]
- Thomas Wildenberg, naval historian and editor

And, especially, Markus Cermak of Michael White Films, who created the graphics used in this book and was CGI supervisor for the film "Azorian."

Several persons at the Naval Institute Press have helped to make this book a reality, among them William Miller, Publisher; Richard (Rick) Russell, Director, Naval Institute Press; George Keating, Director of Sales and Marketing; Susan Corrado, Editorial Manager; Chris Gamboa-Onrubia, Director of Design and Production; Judy Heise, head of publicity; and Janis Jorgensen, research librarian. Alison Hope served as copy editor of the book, while Maryam Rostamian performed small miracles in the book's design.

ABBREVIATIONS

AEC	Atomic Energy Commission
AFTAC	Air Force Technical Applications Center
AG	miscellaneous auxiliary*
AGB	icebreaker*
AGER	environmental research ship*
AGI	intelligence collection ship*
AGOR	oceanographic research ship*
AGTR	technical research ship*
ARC	cable-repairing ship*
ARD	auxiliary repair dock*
ASR	submarine rescue ship*
ATF	fleet ocean tug*
CIA	Central Intelligence Agency
CinC	Commander-in-Chief
CL	light cruiser*
CNO	Chief of Naval Operations
CV	Capture Vehicle
DD	destroyer*
DSSP	Deep Submergence Systems Project
DSV	deep submergence vehicle*
ExComm	Executive Committee
FBI	Federal Bureau of Investigation
GMDI	Global Marine Development Inc.

HMB-1	Hughes Mining Barge No. 1
ICBM	Intercontinental Ballistic Missile
IX	miscellaneous unclassified (ship)*
KGB	Komitet gosudarstvennoy bezopasnosti (Committee for State Security)
LOSS	Large Object Salvage System
MEBA	Marine Engineers Benevolent Association
NATO	North Atlantic Treaty Organization
NavFac	Naval Facility (SOSUS)
NAVSTIC	Naval Scientific and Technical Intelligence Center
NRO	National Reconnaissance Office
NSA	National Security Agency
NSF	National Science Foundation
NURO	National Underwater Reconnaissance Office
OpNav	Office of the Chief of Naval Operations
SALT	Strategic Arms Limitation Talks
SIGINT	Signals Intelligence
SOSUS	Sound Surveillance System
SS	submarine*
SSB	ballistic missile submarine
SSBN	ballistic missile submarine (nuclear)*
SSG	guided (cruise) missile submarine*
SSGN	guided (cruise) missile submarine (nuclear)*
SSN	attack submarine (nuclear)*
SSQ	communications relay submarine*
SSR	radar picket submarine
T-	prefix for U.S. Navy ship assigned to the Military Sea Transportation Service (civilian crew)
TO	Target Object (submarine *K-129*)
UFO	Unidentified Flying Object
USIB	U.S. Intelligence Board
USS	United States Ship
VP	patrol squadron (aviation)

---

* U.S. Navy ship classification.

PROJECT
AZORIAN

ONE

THE BUBBLE

T he bubble burst on Friday morning, February 7, 1975, with a front-page story in the *Los Angeles Times* revealing that the Central Intelligence Agency (CIA) had salvaged a sunken Soviet missile submarine. Although the story contained numerous errors, such as locating the salvage effort in the Atlantic and not the mid-Pacific, and reporting that the target of the clandestine lift operation was a nuclear-propelled submarine (accompanied by a photo of a Project 627/North Atlantic Treaty Organization November-class submarine), the story was out.[1] The Howard Hughes–sponsored ocean mining effort was a cover for the most ambitious ocean recovery effort ever attempted.

The following Monday morning some two dozen students in the Ocean Engineering 101 class at the California State University at Long Beach entered their classroom on Seventh Street. They displayed frustration, confusion, and even anger. The instructor was "mad as hell," one student recalled. Frustrated, the instructor almost screamed that they "had taken the department for a ride."[2]

Ocean Engineering 101 was one of scores of classes established in colleges and universities across the United States to teach the principles of ocean engineering and seafloor mining. While the earth was still rich with mineral resources as well as vital petroleum and natural gas, it was obvious that such reservoirs were not inexhaustible. The promise of seafloor resources seemed unlimited when one considered that 70 percent of the planet's surface is covered by water.

Indeed, by the 1970s man was already reaping the harvest of petroleum from offshore oil rigs implanted on continental shelves around the world. But the large "bubble"—the promise of a harvest of resources to be obtained through ocean engineering—began to form when the U.S. Congress passed the Marine Resources and Engineering Development Act of 1966 that sought to advance ocean research, resources development, and meteorological prediction.[3]

Based on that legislation, President Richard M. Nixon appointed a commission to prepare a plan for national action to "increase investment of a broad array of maritime problems ranging from the preservation of our coastal shores and estuaries to the more effective use of the vast resources that lie within and below the sea."[4] Most significant, the commission's report declared,

> Ocean minerals have been hailed by some as a nearly inexhaustible treasure trove. To others, the inaccessibility of most marine minerals and the expensive technology required for their recovery place them on the far horizon of the future in comparison with minerals from more conventional sources.[5]

While the commission found that the truth lay somewhere between these extremes, one man appeared on the scene who believed that the "far horizon" was very, very close. At least, that's what Hughes told the world in 1972 when he revealed that he was building a giant ocean-mining ship to reap a harvest of seafloor nodules containing primarily manganese, but also contained significant amounts of cobalt, copper, and nickel that could be harvested from the ocean floor.

The "agent" for the seafloor mining ship—to be named *Hughes Glomar Explorer*—was the Summa Corporation, formed by Hughes in 1972 as the "umbrella" for his various holdings, replacing the ancestral Hughes Tool Company.[6] The ship would be built, manned, and operated by Global Marine, Inc., a world leader in the development and operation of offshore oil drilling and seafloor coring ships.

And, soon appearing on the building ways at the Sun shipyard in Chester, Pennsylvania, was the giant, 618-foot, 63,300-ton *Glomar Explorer*. The odd-looking ship, almost the size of a battleship, was impressive in physical scale; upon completion it would be conspicuous by the massive lattice tower atop the ship, resembling a huge oil derrick. Within the hull was a cavernous "moon pool" that was presumed to house the top-secret "vacuum cleaner" that would sweep the manganese nodules from the ocean floor.

At the launching of the ship, Paul G. Reeve, manager of the Hughes Ocean Mining Division, observed that it was unlikely that the problems involved in deep-sea mineral acquisition would be solved quickly. He named a number of factors that had to be addressed before commercial operations could be established: "Questions must be answered concerning the sale of raw material, refined metals or intermediate products, transport systems, processing sites and legal factors. All are germane to the final system approach."[7]

The credibility of Global Marine, the scale and complexity of the *Glomar Explorer*, and the Hughes investment—press reports stated that the ship cost some $300 million, at that time more than the cost of a nuclear-propelled missile cruiser—gave credibility to the effort. As details of the venture became known, other firms began considering how to enter into this potentially lucrative field, while various educational institutions began initiating ocean engineering classes, such as the bachelor of ocean engineering program established in 1974 at the California State University at Long Beach. These educational programs would help provide the men and women who would discover, exploit, and transport the resources of the ocean floor.

That "bubble" burst with the story on page one in the *Los Angeles Times* of February 7, 1975. The next day, *The New York Times* carried a similar story. More stories followed in major American and foreign newspapers, with journalist Jack Anderson the first to provide reasonably accurate details of the effort to salvage a sunken submarine on his national radio show of March 18. It was revealed that the "target object" of the massive, bizarre, complex, and clandestine operation was a Soviet ballistic missile submarine—later identified as the *K-129*.

SAILING ON COMBAT DUTY

Moments after midnight on the night of February 24–25, 1968, the submarine *K-129* got under way from her moorings on the western side of Avacha Bay on Kamchatka Peninsula.[1] In that remote, Far Eastern part of Siberia, the bay, with the city of Petropavlovsk on its eastern side, was the second-most-important—if not the most important—Soviet naval complex in the Pacific region. Only the naval complexes in and surrounding the port of Vladivostok were larger.

The Kamchatka base—usually referred to simply as "Petro" by Western intelligence—was isolated from the Siberian mainland, accessible only by sea and air, with highly sensitive communications going through seafloor cables. The importance of the Petro complex—including the submarine facility at Rybachiy—could be seen by the almost 40 submarines based in Avacha Bay in February 1968—possibly more than any other submarine base complex of any navy. The *K-129* was one of these submarines (see Appendix A). Completed in 1960, the *K-129* was a first-line submarine.

The submarine was a Project 629A craft, the Soviet designation for the submarine design. In the West, the submarine class was called "Golf II." The *K-129* carried three liquid-propellant R-21 ballistic missiles (NATO SS-N-5 Serb) with a range of up to 755 nautical miles, twice that of the submarine's earlier R-13 missiles. The R-21 could be launched from keel depths down to 165 feet, providing enhanced survivability for the submarine, with the craft traveling up to four knots at the time of launch. The warhead had an explosive force of one megaton—about 65 times that of the explosive power of the atomic bombs used against Japan in August 1945.

The morning before sailing, the *K-129* had slipped her moorings to the barge that formed part of the "floating base" at Rybachiy and proceeded to the nearby missile facility to load three R-21 missiles and two Type 53-58 torpedoes with nuclear warheads.[2] With the submarine loaded with stores and weapons for a 70-day patrol, at 11 PM the division commander, Rear Admiral Viktor Dygalo, boarded the *K-129*, made a final inspection of the submarine, wished the officers luck on the mission, and departed.[3]

Shortly afterwards, with the pulsating beat of her diesel engines, the *K-129* headed toward the entrance to Avacha Bay, passing the guard boat from which Dygalo waved a last farewell. At about 1:30 AM the submarine passed the Three Brothers Rocks. As the *K-129* entered the waters of the North Pacific, Captain 1st Rank Vladimir Ivanovich Kobzar ordered the submarine to dive. He was the last man to leave the bridge, according to Soviet Navy custom. The lookout position at Zarosshaya confirmed that the submarine had submerged. That was the last direct contact that the *K-129* would ever have with the shore.

The *K-129* went to sea with 98 officers, warrant officers, and enlisted men under Kobzar's command. The submarine's normal complement was 83 men—13 officers and 70 petty officers and sailors. The complement now included 16 enlisted men who were new to the craft, having replaced sailors who were released from active duty after the submarine's last mission. Also on board the *K-129* were 10 sailors assigned for training. Admiral Dygalo later recalled, "Right up to that moment [of departure] we got some newcomers with special training, but who had never been to sea before . . . for instance mechanics, electricians, engine workers who all had to gain some experience. . . . [I]t was usual on all ships in the fleet to take such young sailors on board in order to let them gain experience."[4]

Finally, the submarine embarked a Signals Intelligence (SIGINT) team of a senior lieutenant and three or four enlisted specialists. The SIGINT team was to monitor U.S. radio and radar transmissions that the submarine might intercept while on patrol.[5] The submarine thus carried a total of 14 officers, 3 warrant officers, and 81 enlisted men (see Appendix B).

Absent from the *K-129*'s complement was a senior staff officer. After taking command of a ship, a Soviet naval officer underwent a lengthy process to qualify for "independent command." During that process the division com-

A Golf II missile submarine on the surface. Her elongated sail structure houses three R-21 ballistic missiles. The lower "windows" on the sail are sonar arrays; the upper windows (deadlights) are for her enclosed bridge. The submarine's 35-foot high-frequency antenna is raised, on the starboard side of the sail. It folds down onto the deck when lowered. (Royal Navy/Crown Copyright)

mander or a "staff specialist" with previous command experience would usually ride the ship to observe the newly appointed commander. The "rider" could countermand or modify orders, as he deemed appropriate. A new commander would thus be taken through exercises and training, and sometimes undertook operational deployments with a staff specialist on board before he was fully certified for command at sea. Kobzar was considered qualified for independent command.

An outstanding officer, the 37-year-old captain had served in the Soviet Navy for almost two decades. A Ukrainian, Kobzar, was a graduate of the Sevastopol Higher Naval Engineering School, and had undergone submarine training in Leningrad. He had commanded the *K-129* since 1964 and had recently been promoted to captain 1st rank, the equivalent of a navy captain or a full colonel in Western military services. The commanders of the other Golf-type submarines in Dygalo's 29th Submarine Division all were captains 2nd rank.

The *K-129* had not been scheduled to go to sea on "combat duty"—the Soviet euphemism for a submarine patrol—in February 1968. The submarine had her first post–Golf II conversion patrol, reported to be at least a 60-day operation, from about October 1 to November 30, 1967. Details of where she had operated are not available, but the 60-day voyage was too short a period for operations off the U.S. West Coast, a deployment apparently carried out by other types of submarines. The Petro-based missile submarines would normally deploy on combat duty once or twice per year, sailing on patrol for about 70 days with the interim periods used for replenishment, maintenance, and local area training.

Beginning on December 3 one of the 29th Division's two so-called "blue crews" relieved Kobzar's men aboard the *K-129* and carried out the maintenance and resupply tasks needed after the 60 days at sea. Most of the submarine's crew were sent to the nearby Paratounka Sanatorium for rest and recreation, while several of the officers and warrant officers went on leave on the mainland.

Captain 1st Rank Vladimir A. Kobzar.

Kobzar, his wife Arida, their daughter, age 14, and son, age 5, lived in the town of Rybachiy, as did some of his other officers. However, several had their homes in Vladivostok and traveled there for leave. Many of the *K-129*'s crew were still on leave on February 9 when the decision was made to deploy the submarine to the Hawaii Station. According to Dygalo, "If we had sent another submarine instead of the one according to the schedule, it would have ruined the whole schedule. After some hesitation, it was decided to send the *K-129*."[6]

The unplanned departure of the *K-129* was caused by a problem with the missile system of a Project 675 (NATO Echo II) submarine from the 26th Submarine Division at Konyushkovo Bay near Vladivostok. These large, nuclear-propelled submarines each carried eight surface-launch cruise (guided) missiles that could be armed with nuclear or conventional warheads. They were being replaced on strategic missions by ballistic missile submarines like the Golf series. The need for the Echo II to surface to launch weapons, and the P5D Pyatyorka missiles (NATO SS-N-3 Shaddock) being air-breathing, i.e., turbojet propelled, contributed to their vulnerability to U.S. anti-submarine and air-defense forces, respectively.

The troubled nuclear-propelled Echo II had been ordered to deploy on combat duty in a patrol area northwest of Oahu, the principal island of Hawaii, to replace the ballistic missile submarine *B-62*, a diesel-electric Project AV611/Zulu V type that had been on combat duty north of Hawaii in February 1968. The potential targets for the submarine's two R-11FM (NATO SS-1B Scud A) missiles were the military installations on the island of Oahu —the massive naval base at Pearl Harbor, the adjacent Hickam Air Force Base, and the nearby headquarters for the U.S. Pacific Command at Camp H. M. Smith.

Although the 26th Submarine Division contained several Echo II SSGNs, none was available to cover the Hawaii Station. These craft also were employed in tracking U.S. aircraft carriers in the Vietnam theater as that conflict raged, and were probably kept in position to strike U.S. military installations on the island of Guam—the Polaris submarine support facilities and the B-52 strategic bombers based there. Other Echo II SSGNs were in the Sea of Japan, tracking the U.S. naval forces that had deployed in that area in response to the North Korean capture of the U.S. Navy spy ship *Pueblo* (AGER 2) on January 23, 1968. Consequently, when the Echo II scheduled for the Oahu deployment developed technical problems, the *K-129* was designated as her replacement.

The schedule for strategic submarine deployments was developed by naval headquarters in Moscow and "validated" by the Commander Pacific Fleet, Admiral Nikolai N. Amel'ko, at Vladivostok. Thus, a submarine sailed on combat duty under an order personally signed by the Commander-in-Chief of the Navy. The orders directed that the Kamchatka flotilla would now provide a Golf SSB to cover the Oahu targets. Dygalo, the Golf II's division commander, when told to send the *K-129* in place of the troubled Echo II, immediately protested to the commander of the 15th Submarine Squadron, his immediate superior, that the *K-129*, although an outstanding unit, should not be deployed so soon after her last mission. His appeal received a bureaucratic rejection.

Dygalo then took his concerns to the commander of the Kamchatka flotilla. Again Dygalo's entreaty was rejected—this time with more civility. The schedule for deploying missile submarines was made at naval headquarters; such decisions could not be changed or effectively petitioned by subordinate commanders.

The *K-129*'s crew was recalled for the unexpected sailing, with the submarine being officially turned over from the blue crew to Kobzar's men on February 13. This gave the "main" crewmen 11 days to prepare for their deployment, although some officers did not report on board until 5 days before sailing. During those days the submarine went to sea almost every day for intensive training procedures with division commander Dygalo; in addition, other staff officers were on board on some of the days. On most nights the *K-129* remained at sea, anchoring in nearby bays.

That period was considered sufficient for preparing the submarine for combat duty. Dygalo noted that only if 30 percent or more of the crew had been replaced would it have been necessary to "start combat training from the beginning."[7]

The *K-129* departed her base a few minutes after midnight on the night of February 24–25, stood clear of Avacha Bay, and submerged about an hour and a half later. Kobzar turned his submarine south, probably carrying out several drills and attempting to evade any U.S. surveillance submarine watching the Petropavlovsk base complex, in this case the USS *Barb* (SSN 596). The *K-129* would remain submerged throughout the planned 70-day patrol except periodically—on a set schedule—to surface or at least broach the main deck to place the craft's high-frequency antenna insulator on the starboard side clear of the water when the 35-foot antenna was rotated into the upright position. Once above the water, electromagnetic energy could be fed to the antenna. If the insulator was not clear of the water, the transmission could possibly cause the antenna coupler to short out and possibly to explode.

A reasonable estimate was that the *K-129* would maintain an average speed of 4 to 5 knots while sailing submerged on snorkel—using her diesel engines for propulsion and battery charging—for at least 20 hours in every 24. This procedure was dictated by Moscow headquarters. Operating on snorkel in heavy seas could cause physical discomfort if not major problems for the crew, particularly when the snorkel intake periodically shut down to avoid

TAR'YA BAY, SEP
KH - 4B MISSION 1

967

Tar'ya Bay at the southwest end of the Petropavlovsk complex was a major Soviet submarine base, photographed five months before the *K-129*'s departure on her final "combat duty" by a U.S. KH-4B spy satellite. The three piers farthest to the right were used by the 29th Submarine Division's Zulu and Golf missile submarines. The division's headquarters barge *Neva* was at the second pier, and a submarine tender was at the third pier. (U.S. Coast and Geodetic Survey Center for Earth Resources Observations and Science; annotated by Michael Gray) flooding and the diesel engines sucked air from within the submarine. Crew fatigue and illness would follow such sustained operations in heavy seas.

The primary concern for submarine commanders was not speed, but avoiding detection by U.S. aircraft and surface ships, and maintaining the maximum charge on batteries so the submarine could remain fully submerged and on electric (quiet) propulsion for a sustained period if U.S. forces were encountered. Snorkeling was found to provide the maximum opportunity to remain undetected by aircraft radar and visual searches. When the submarine was snorkeling, the SIGINT team could use its radar intercept equipment for the early detection of U.S. surface ship or aircraft radars to provide ample time for the submarine to cease snorkeling and fully submerge.

Thus, en route to her patrol area the submarine would sail fully submerged on electric motors at about three knots for only a few hours each day. This submerged period was useful for training and to "clear baffles," the term used for submarine maneuvers to determine if another undersea craft was trailing it, "hiding" in the blind area behind a submarine where self-machinery noises could mask the sounds of another submarine.[8]

This procedure could provide an average speed of advance of about four knots, which would place *K-129* at her patrol area after a 15- to 20-day transit.

A submarine departing Petropavlovsk was immediately in the open sea. This was in sharp contrast to Soviet submarines leaving their bases on the Black Sea, the Baltic, or even the Kola Peninsula in the Arctic. Reportedly, submarines from the other Soviets fleets would say of those sailing from Avacha Bay,

> How lucky you are! Once Avacha Bay is behind there is only free space and the ocean around you. No islands, no straits, no narrow places. Distances are counted in thousands of kilometers, depths in kilometers. No anti-submarine barriers and no mines. One can sail as far as one wishes!

Exiting Avacha Bay and submerging, the *K-129* turned south, sailing along longitude 162°E. At sea, Captain Kobzar opened his sealed orders. These orders detailed his patrol procedures, required communication checks, proscribed course and speed requirements, and other sensitive information. At his discretion he could share the orders with his senior officers. Significantly, a copy of the Moscow-originated orders were held by the Kamchatka command headquarters, but could not be opened without specific permission from Moscow. As in the U.S. Navy, orders and patrol areas related to strategic missile submarines were among the most tightly held secrets.

A commanding officer had to follow the route proscribed in his orders with "pinpoint accuracy . . . he was not allowed to judge where it could be better or worse to deviate . . . the submarine followed the route from submersion point to the combat duty area like a circus tightrope walker," according to Admiral Dygalo. And, he continued, "Only in the combat duty area the captain was allowed to maneuver on his own . . . at will . . . underwater . . . surfacing or under snorkel conditions . . . all depending on the tactical situation and weather conditions in the area."[9]

While there were no physical barriers to the submarine's transit toward Hawaii, there were several U.S. anti-submarine "barriers" to a submarine escaping undetected into the depths of the broad Pacific. By 1968 the U.S. Navy was operating nuclear-propelled submarines as "gatekeepers" off major Soviet submarine bases in the Arctic and Western Pacific. Keeping in international waters, the submarine off Petropavlovsk in February 1968 was the USS *Barb*. But she apparently was out of position and did not detect the departure of the *K-129*.

Next was SOSUS—the U.S. Navy's Sound Surveillance System. It was developed to detect Soviet submarines at long ranges when they operated at speeds at which their propellers produced strong, low-frequency cavitation. (Cavitation is the formation and collapse of bubbles produced in seawater by high-velocity propellers.) The prototype full-size SOSUS installation—a 1,000-foot-long line array of 40 hydrophone elements moored in 1,440 feet of water—was deployed off Eleuthera in the Bahamas by a British cable layer in January 1952. After a series of successful detection trials with a U.S. submarine, the Navy decided by midyear to install similar arrays along the entire U.S. East Coast; the first array became operational in September 1954 at Ramey Air Force Base, Puerto Rico. Subsequently, the decision was made to extend the system to the U.S. West Coast and to Hawaii. The first Pacific area SOSUS array had been installed off the southern California coast in 1957; by 1968 the U.S. Navy had deployed at least eight SOSUS arrays in the Pacific area.

These early SOSUS line arrays were positioned on the sea floor at locations that accessed the deep sound channel and were oriented at right angles to the expected threat axis. Their individual hydrophone outputs were transmitted to shore processing stations called "naval facilities"—or NavFacs—via multiconductor, armored cables. At the NavFacs the acoustic signals were processed to create a fan of horizontal "beams," each of which represented the composite sound signal from a small angular sector—on the order of two to five degrees wide—oriented in a particular azimuthal direction.

Narrow-band, time-frequency analysis in the spectral region from 5 to 150 Hz was performed on these multiple beam outputs. The ability of narrow-band frequency analysis not only to discriminate against broadband ocean noises, but also to identify characteristic frequencies associated with rotating machinery was the key to detecting and classifying targets. While the detection ranges of SOSUS are rarely discussed, there is credible evidence that in 1966 a nuclear submarine was detected at a range in excess of 3,000 nautical miles.

When cued by SOSUS, the U.S. Navy would send out P-3 Orion patrol aircraft from Adak in the Aleutian Islands, Iwakuni, Japan, or Barber's Point, Oahu, or—if available—would dispatch a nuclear-propelled submarine to attempt to trail the Soviet submarine. Such trailing efforts sought to understand Soviet submarine tactics and procedures, and to record their individual sounds for subsequent identification. In times of crises the U.S. forces would be ready to attack their opponents.

The U.S. Navy was also monitoring Soviet radio communications with a network of ground intercept stations around the Pacific rim, the so-called Boresight/Bullseye system. Beginning in 1959 the Navy and Air Force constructed a series of high-frequency intercept stations at various locations around the world. Based on the German Wullenweber system of World War II, the U.S. Bullseye intercept arrays could "capture" even second-long "burst" communications from Soviet submarines. Simultaneously, an electronics recording and control system—code-named Boresight—could obtain a line of bearing on a burst transmission for direction finding to locate the source of the transmission.

All of these anti-submarine "aces" were carefully coordinated by the U.S. Navy's intelligence centers, although the "sources" themselves were carefully separated or, in intelligence lingo, "compartmented."

The Soviet Navy had some knowledge of these capabilities, enough to realize that the SOSUS array connected by seafloor cable to the NavFac at Adak, Alaska, could detect a Petro-based submarine traveling eastward.[10] Accordingly, the *K-129* sailed south along 162°N to the 40th parallel and then turned eastward about March 3–4, toward her "holding" position some 1,000 nautical miles northwest of Oahu. The 40th parallel was significant because the U.S. Navy had established a "no-fly zone" between latitudes 39°N and 41°N, i.e., a distance of about 120 nautical miles. This zone was to avoid interference between P-3 Orion ASW/patrol aircraft flying out of Adak and Barber's Point. The regular use of the 40th parallel for the east-west movement of Soviet diesel-electric submarines indicated that Soviet planners were aware of this restriction on U.S. airborne surveillance.

On February 26, while transiting south, the *K-129* did transmit a "burst" radio message at midnight (261200Z)—to acknowledge that the submarine was at sea. The message was compressed into a burst transmission so the duration may have been less than a second; it consisted of the submarine's call sign and a two-letter code.[11] That message was received by Soviet military radio stations in the Far East and immediately relayed to naval headquarters in Moscow.

This transmission also was intercepted by U.S. listening stations in the Western Pacific area. A Naval Security Group intercept station identified the submarine as the *K-129*, actually using her "side" number—722—that earlier had been painted on her sail when training in the Kamchatka area.[12] The ability to identify the specific submarine was probably accomplished by "fingerprinting" the submarine's radio transmitter on earlier operations that were connected to visual sightings by a U.S. submarine or a maritime patrol aircraft that could visually see her side number.[13]

The burst transmission of February 26 was simply a check that the submarine was at sea and en route to her patrol area. Apparently, an erroneous U.S. attempt to decode the brief signal stated "Golf 722 reported patrol finished and returning home."[14] That mistake probably occurred because U.S. naval intelligence had earlier detected the *K-129* at sea on her previous mis-

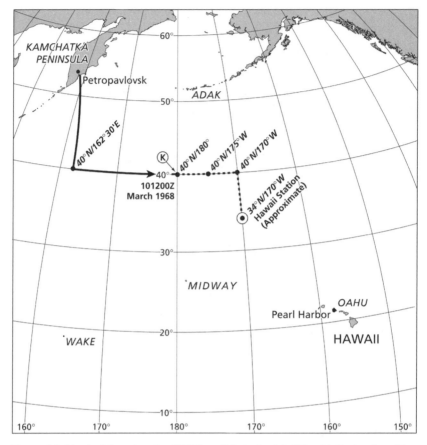

The predicted track of the submarine *K-129* from Petropavlovsk to "K" point, the location of her demise, and her probable planned track to the Hawaii Station.

sion and apparently concluded that the submarine was returning from that earlier patrol. That error was compounded when the U.S. nuclear submarine *Barb*, operating off Petropavlovsk as a "gatekeeper," was not in place when the *K-129* departed Petro early on February 25.

There is a possibility that when Captain Kobzar turned his submarine eastward along the 40° parallel he was scheduled to make another "burst" transmission, but there is no evidence that such a message was sent. Another message was expected to be transmitted from the *K-129* at midnight on March 7–8 (071200Z). Admiral Dygalo said that the submarine had been directed to send a message when she was at approximately mid-point in transit to her station.[15] This missed communication of March 7–8 "rang alarm bells throughout [Soviet] Pacific commands," according to former U.S. naval intelligence officer Lee Mathers.[16] Soviet sources stated that naval communication centers in the Far East reviewed their records in an effort to find an off-schedule transmission from the *K-129*—without success. Nearly constant messages requiring the *K-129* to immediately establish communications were transmitted over the next 48 hours by the Pacific Fleet and Kamchatka commands, again without success.

The *K-129* was "quiet." On March 8 the Kamchatka commander apparently asked permission from Moscow to initiate a search for the submarine. At Moscow naval headquarters there was a higher hurdle to cross than a missed burst transmission before a search effort would be approved. The higher threshold at Moscow headquarters was no doubt an appreciation that missing a burst transmission lasting only a fraction of a second could be caused by atmospheric interference, the submarine's transmitter being off-frequency, or other "normal" communication problems.

Again, according to Dygalo, Moscow headquarters authorized the Kamchatka and Pacific Fleet commands to plan a search operation, but no approval was given to implement such an effort. For two more days there were efforts to elicit a transmission from the *K-129*, with radio calls being sent out for the submarine to immediately establish radio contact.

But there was no transmission from the *K-129* . . . nor would there ever be another one.

THREE

TWO SUBMARINES

T he story of Project Azorian is in large part the story of two submarines: the Soviet *K-129* and her tragic demise, and the USS *Halibut* and her remarkable success in locating the remains of the stricken Soviet submarine.

In the immediate post–World War II era, both the Soviet Union and the United States adopted German missile technologies for their future weapons. Their paradigms were the V-1 guided or cruise missile and the V-2 ballistic missile. The Germans employed these weapons in large numbers in 1944–1945, initially against Britain and then against ports being used by the Allies in northwestern Europe.

A cruise missile uses continuous propulsion and aerodynamic lift (from wings or fins), and can easily maneuver to reach its target. A ballistic missile is launched in a specific direction on a ballistic trajectory; it is powered for only the first few minutes of flight. Both types of missiles are "guided" in the sense that they can be aimed at a target.

With the beginning of the Cold War both countries moved rapidly to provide their fleets—both surface ships and submarines—with missiles capable of attacking the enemy's homeland.[1] The Soviet Navy was the first to take ballistic missiles to sea, on board submarines. After World War II the Soviets, like the Americans, test launched German V-2s and then set about to essentially copy the missile. Fueled with liquid oxygen and alcohol, the V-2 had a range of some 200 miles during a flight that took only three or four minutes. The German V-2 carried a one-ton warhead, but as the Soviets sought to produce and improve the weapon, it would eventually be fitted to deliver a nuclear warhead. This missile was designated R-1.

In 1949 a preliminary design for a missile submarine to strike enemy land targets was drawn up. The diesel-electric submarine was to have a surface displacement of almost 5,400 tons and carry 12 R-1 ballistic missiles as well as the Lastochka (swallow) cruise missile. But the designers were unable to solve the myriad problems in development of such a complex ship, and the concept was not pursued.

The first ballistic missile that offered practical potential for submarine use was the R-11, developed under the direction of the brilliant Sergei P. Korolev, who would design most of the Soviet Union's ballistic missiles as well as most of their space boosters. The R-11 entered Red Army service in 1956. Its liquid-propellant rocket could deliver a one-ton, nuclear warhead to targets at a distance of 80 nautical miles.

In 1953–1954 Korolev proposed a naval variant missile that would be fueled by kerosene and nitric acid in place of the R-11's alcohol and liquid oxygen, the latter being less suitable for long-term storage. Test launches of this R-11FM were conducted at Kapustin Yar in 1954–1955.[2] Three launches from a fixed launch stand were followed by additional launches from a test stand that moved to simulate a ship's motion. For the shipboard launch scheme, the R-11FM missile would be housed in a vertical storage canister, then the submarine would surface and the missile would be elevated up and out of the canister for launching. The Soviet Navy had specified a submerge-launch capability for the missile, but Korolev opposed it, believing that his scheme for employing the R-11FM could provide a missile capability in less time. Beyond the missile, a multitude of problems confronted the program, including establishing the exact location of the submarine, and the bearing to the target, ensuring secure communications to receive the order to launch, and so on. All these problems had to be solved.

The world's first submarine fitted to launch ballistic missiles was the *B-67*, a Project 611 (NATO Zulu) torpedo-attack submarine. She was modified at the No. 402 Molotovsk (now Severodvinsk) shipyard with two R11-FM missile tubes being fitted in the after end of an enlarged sail structure and related control equipment installed.[3] The missile tubes extended vertically through the fourth compartment, replacing one group of electric batteries and the warrant officers' space. Their accommodations were moved to the bow compartment, from which reload torpedoes were removed. The submarine's deck guns also were deleted. The modification was designated Project V611 (NATO Zulu IV$\frac{1}{2}$).

In anticipation of submarine launches, a special test stand was built at the Kapustin Yar test center to simulate the effects on a missile tube in a ship encountering rough seas. Sea trials were conducted hurriedly, and on September 16, 1955, in the White Sea, the submarine *B-67* launched the first ballistic missile to be fired from a submarine. The missile streaked 135 nautical miles to impact in the remote Novaya Zemlya test range. (Later, in the fall of 1957, the *B-67* was employed in an unusual, unmanned underwater test to determine the vulnerability of missile-carrying submarines to depth charge attack. After the tests, divers connected air hoses to the submarine to blow ballast tanks to surface the submarine.)

Late in 1955 work began on the design for a production ballistic missile submarine (SSB) based on the Zulu—Project AV611, armed with two R11-FM missiles. Four of these diesel–electric submarines, each with a surface displacement of 1,890 tons, were built in 1957 at Severodvinsk. In addition, in 1958 the Zulu-class submarine *B-67* was modified to the SSB configuration at shipyard No. 202 in Vladivostok (also designated Project AV611). Thus the Soviet Navy had five ballistic missile submarines with the R-11FM missile becoming operational in 1959.

These were the world's first ballistic missile submarines. Soviet leader Nikita Khrushchev observed an R-11FM launch by the *B-67* commanded by Viktor Dygalo, on October 6, 1959, from on board a destroyer. However, the range of the missiles limited the effectiveness of the submarines to a tactical or theater role. Also, the clandestine operation of the submarines was compromised by their need to periodically surface or snorkel to use their diesel engines to recharge their batteries.

Meanwhile, in 1955 Korolev's design bureau transferred all submarine ballistic missile projects to a special design bureau under Viktor P. Makeyev. This shift enabled Korolev to concentrate on longer-range strategic missiles and space programs. Makeyev, who was 31 years of age when he became head of the bureau in June 1955, immediately pursued the D-2 missile system, which would include the new R-13 missile (NATO SS-N-4 Sark) launched from a new series of submarines.[4] The missile, with a storable-liquid propellant, was also surface launched and had a range of up to 350 nautical miles.

The submarine to carry this new missile would be Project 629 (NATO Golf), employing the same diesel-electric machinery and other components of the contemporary torpedo submarine of Project 641 (NATO Foxtrot). The Golf had a surface displacement of 2,850 tons and could carry three R-13 missiles. The missile tubes penetrated the top and bottom of the pressure hull, extending up into the sail. The missiles were raised up and out of the sail for launching. The R-11FM missile was fitted in the first five Project 629 submarines, which were later rearmed with the R-13 missile.

The lead Project 629/Golf submarine was the *B-41* (later *K-79*), built at Severodvinsk on the White Sea, and delivered in 1959. From 1959 to 1962, 23 Golf-class submarines were completed—16 at Severodvinsk and 7 at the No. 199 shipyard at Komsomol'sk-on-Amur in the Far East. The *K-129* was one of the latter, completed in 1960. The last Severodinsk submarine was an updated design, Project 629B. Additional sections and components for two Golf submarines were fabricated at Komsomol'sk and transferred to China, with one assembled at Darien in the mid-1960s (designated Type 035); the second submarine was never assembled.

Even though part of the prelaunch preparation of R-11FM and R-13 missiles was conducted underwater, the submarine had to surface to launch missiles. According to Captain 2nd Rank V. L. Berezovskiy, "The preparation to launch a missile took a great deal of time. Surfacing, observation of position, the steadying of compasses—somewhere around an hour and twenty or thirty minutes. This is a monstrously long time. . . . The submarine could be accurately detected even before surfacing [to launch]."[5]

The world's first launch of a submarine-launched ballistic missile armed with a thermonuclear warhead occurred on 20 October 1961, when a Project 629 submarine launched an R-13 missile carrying a one-megaton warhead that detonated on the Novaya Zemlya (Arctic) test range in test "Rainbow." (The first U.S. test launch of a Polaris missile with a nuclear warhead occurred a half year later when an A-1 weapon with a warhead of just over one megaton was fired from the submarine *Ethan Allen* [SSBN 608], on May 6, 1962.) Subsequently, R-13 missiles with nuclear warheads were provided to submarines.

In 1955 Makeyev had begun experimental work on underwater launching of ballistic missiles from a submerging test stand. Following launches from the submerging test stand, launch tests of dummy missiles were conducted

An R-13 (NATO SS-N-4 Sark) ballistic missile elevated and being prepared for firing from a Golf I missile submarine. The (light-colored) holding "legs" will fold outward for launching the missile. The *K-129* was the first Pacific Fleet submarine fitted to carry the submerge-launch R-21/SS-N-5 Serb ballistic missile.

in 1957 from the Project 613D4/Whiskey submarine *S-229*. The submarine had been modified at shipyard No. 444 at Nikolayev on the Black Sea with two missile tubes fitted amidships. The dummy missiles had solid-propellant engines to launch them out of the tubes and a liquid-fuel second stage.

Subsequently, the Project V611/Zulu submarine *B-67*, used earlier for the R-11FM tests, was again modified at Severodvinsk for submerged missile tests (changed to PV611). The first launch attempt from the *B-67* occurred in August 1959, but was unsuccessful. On September 10, 1960, an S4-7 (modified R-11FM) missile was launched successfully from the submarine while she was submerged and under way. (Less than two months earlier, the U.S. nuclear-submarine *George Washington* [SSBN 598] carried out the first submerged launch of a Polaris A-1 missile.)

In 1958—just prior to completion of the first Golf SSB—work began at Makeyev's bureau on the liquid-propellant R-21 ballistic missile (NATO SS-N-5 Serb) with a range up to 755 nautical miles, twice that of the R-13 missile. The R-21 could be launched from keel depths of 130 to 165 feet, providing enhanced survivability for the submarine, with the submarine traveling up to four knots at the time of launch.

Initial underwater launches of the R-21 dummy missiles took place in 1961 from the *S-229;* that submarine was fitted with a single missile launch tube aft of the conning tower. A year later two R-21 launch tubes were installed in the *K-142*, the last Golf submarine built at Severodvinsk (designated Project 629B). Completed in 1961, that submarine made the first underwater launch of an R-21 missile on February 24, 1962. Thirteen additional submarines of Project 629/Golf submarines were converted to carry three underwater-launch R-21 missiles and were redesignated Project 629A. The *K-129* was the first Pacific Fleet Golf to be converted to this Golf II configuration. The work was carried out at the No. 202 Dalzavod shipyard in Vladivostok in 1966–1967.

Following the Project 629/Golf SSB program, the Soviet Union initiated a nuclear ballistic missile submarine program, Project 658 (NATO Hotel). Similar in concept to the Golf class, these SSBNs each carried three ballistic missiles—the R-13. (Subsequently, seven of these SSBNs were refitted with the R-21.) But this program was truncated after only eight submarines were built at Severodvinsk, completed from 1960 to 1962. These submarines suffered major engineering problems with their early-design reactor plants.

Only eight units were built—more were planned—because, according to the semi-official history of Soviet shipbuilding, "the characteristics of the Soviet oceanic missile installations and submarines, the carriers of the first generation [missiles], were significantly behind the American submarines and missile installations. Therefore, during the beginning of the 1960s work began on constructing a more modern system for the next generation."[6] But in 1958, under Khrushchev's direction, there was a major restructuring of

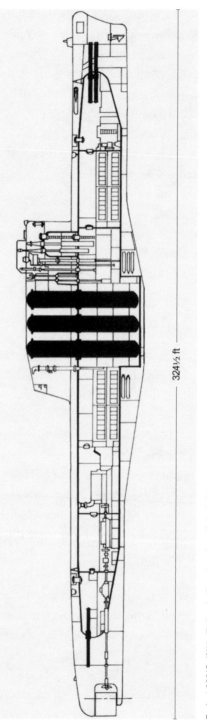

Project 629/Golf II ballistic missile submarine. (© A. D. Baker III, from *Cold War Submarines*)

324½ ft

Soviet strategic forces. The Hotel SSBN and possibly Golf SSB construction programs were terminated, the Strategic Rocket Forces was ordered established in December 1960 as a separate military service, and large-scale Intercontinental Ballistic Missile (ICBM) production was initiated. And, the design of the Project 667A/Yankee SSBN, similar in several respects to the 16-missile U.S. Polaris submarines, was put on hold.

The next-generation Soviet SSBN would not appear until the late 1960s, when the effects of the Cuban missile crisis of 1962 led to a further acceleration of Soviet nuclear strike forces.

The first Project 667A/Yankee was completed in 1967 with large-scale production following. The older, far-less-capable Golf SSB and Hotel SSBN missile submarines continued to have a role. As Yankee SSBNs became available, the older missile submarines were employed as theater nuclear strike platforms and some were employed as missile test platforms, or were converted to communication relay ships.

However, the Golf-class submarines had important political-military roles. Following the Cuban missile crisis in the fall of 1962 that brought the United States and Soviet Union closer to nuclear conflict than at any other time during the Cold War, the Soviet government agreed not to introduce nuclear weapons into Cuba. On May 2, 1972—a little less than a decade after the crisis—a U.S. Defense Department spokesman stated that a Soviet Golf missile submarine had entered the port of Bahía de Nipe on Cuba's northern coast. A Golf II also visited Havana, the capital of Cuba, in 1974.[7] (No nuclear-propelled ballistic missile submarines entered Cuban ports, although nuclear-propelled torpedo and cruise missile submarines did so.)

And Golf-class submarines became an issue in the Soviet–U.S. Strategic Arms Limitation Talks (SALT) that began in 1972. Over the next few years efforts were made to restrict the growth of the strategic (nuclear) attack forces of the two superpowers. With respect to submarines, an agreement was reached that the United States could have up to 44 missile submarines with 704 missiles and the Soviet Union up to 62 "modern ballistic missile submarines" with 950 missiles.

During subsequent debates and discussions in Congress and in the press, Ambassador Paul H. Nitze, a key member of the SALT negotiations, pointed out that the agreement's language could be construed as missile launchers on "modern submarines," and to the 22 Golf-class craft, which could add almost 70 missiles to the Soviet total.[8] Later, when a reporter asked if the Soviets could be allowed the increase in force levels because the Golf class was not nuclear propelled, and their missiles were pre-1965, Secretary of State Henry Kissinger called such arguments "a sort of legalism that would be totally rejected by the United States."[9] Furthermore, he instructed U.S. officials who were to testify before Congress that the Golf-class submarines could not be modernized without counting against the 950-missile ceiling. In the event, the slow retirement of the Golf SSBs as newer missile submarines entered the Soviet fleet, and the trade-off of certain land-based missiles, led to an eventual end of the Golf SSB controversy. Little was said in these discussions and debates about the eight Hotel-class SSBNs with their 24 missiles.

Thus the Golf-class submarines—including the ill-fated *K-129*—would have political as well as military and intelligence importance. The last Golf submarine was retired from the Soviet Navy on October 1, 1990—at the end of the Cold War and more than 30 years of service since the first Golf SSB was completed.

The Soviet Navy also emphasized the development of cruise missile submarines, both nuclear and diesel-electric, for the strategic (nuclear) attack role. This development lagged slightly behind Soviet ballistic missile submarine programs. Subsequently, as modern, Yankee-class SSBNs became available, the cruise missile submarines were modified for the anti-ship role, carrying both nuclear and conventional missiles.

In the U.S. Navy the development of cruise missile submarines significantly preceded ballistic missile submarines. Navy leaders felt that their kerosene-like fuels and aircraft structures could be more easily handled on board ships than could ballistic missiles, with their stability and volatile fuel problems.[10] Beginning in early 1947 the U.S. Navy began launching American duplicates of the V-1 missile—designated Loon—from surfaced submarines. Development continued at a rapid pace and a new, highly innovative cruise missile was developed for shipboard use—the Chance Vought Regulus I.

The Regulus I was a subsonic (Mach 0.9) missile that was surface launched with a range of 500 nautical miles; it was the first Navy missile to carry a nuclear warhead.[11] It could be launched from ramps on surfaced subma-

Although soon succeeded by more-capable, nuclear-propelled missile submarines, the Golf-class submarines continued to have significant military and political importance in the 1960s and beyond. They served as theater strike platforms in the Baltic and Far East and—from a political perspective—were important in Soviet-American politics related to Cuba and arms limitation talks. These three Golfs are at a base on the Kola Peninsula. (Malachite Design Bureau)

rines or surface warships, and by catapults from aircraft carriers. Regulus was guided by intermittent beacons on ships or surfaced submarines and, later, by preset guidance to a geographic point. The missile became operational in October 1959, and was fitted in several cruisers and aircraft carriers as well as in five submarines—two converted World War II diesel boats (two missiles in each), two purpose-built diesel submarines (four each), and one nuclear-propelled submarine (five). The nuclear submarine was the USS *Halibut* (SSGN 587), commissioned in 1960. By that time the follow-on Regulus II program had been cancelled.

The success of the Regulus had led to initiation of an improved, supersonic (Mach 2) missile with a range of 1,200 miles at lesser speeds. Designated Regulus II, the missile carried a nuclear warhead and had inertial guidance. It, too, was intended for launch from surface ships as well as from surfaced submarines. Plans were developed to arm 12 cruisers and 12 nuclear-propelled submarines with the Regulus II, in addition to the two diesel-electric submarines and the *Halibut*. The new nuclear submarines would carry four missiles each, and the *Halibut* and the two newer diesel boats could each accommodate two of the larger missiles.

The first Regulus II test flight was conducted on May 29, 1956. Two and a half years later the entire Regulus program was cancelled. Despite a highly successful development and test program, on December 12, 1958, Secretary of the Navy Thomas S. Gates ordered the termination of the Regulus II program because of the decision to accelerate development and deployment of the Polaris submarine-launched ballistic missile—and to help pay for the Polaris program.[12]

From October 1959 to July 1964, submarines armed with Regulus I missiles were continuously on patrol in the North Pacific area with their missiles targeted against Soviet Siberia. At any given time one or two submarines were "on station" carrying a total of four or five missiles. Forty-one missile patrols were conducted by the five Regulus I submarines, seven of them by the *Halibut* during her brief career as an SSGN. The patrols for the diesel-electric submarines lasted up to 82 days toward the end of the program; the *Halibut*, over the winter of 1961–1962, made one patrol of 102 days. As one observer commented,

> Regulus patrols were *Hard Labor* considering the submarines, the sea conditions, facing Cold War conditions . . . and the reality of a single crew often making 3 patrols in a year, and many [sailors] having to endure hot bunking, too little water for showers and the monotony of the operations.[13] (Emphasis in original)

The conditions on board the *K-129* and other Soviet submarines making strategic missile patrols were similar.

The Regulus always was considered to have some capability for use against surface ships, and could be fitted with conventional or nuclear warheads, much as the Soviet Navy employed their cruise missile submarines as they were removed from the strategic attack role. But this was not considered a viable role for the U.S. cruise missile submarines because of their high operating costs and the massive attack capabilities of contemporary U.S. aircraft carriers.

The retirement of the Regulus I cruise missile in July 1964 occurred five months before the beginning of the first patrol by a Polaris SSBN in the Western Pacific when the USS *Daniel Boone* (SSBN 629) departed the island

The USS *Halibut* (SSGN 587) as a cruise missile submarine launching a Regulus I surface-to-surface missile. The improved Regulus II was cancelled in December 1958, making the *Halibut* available for later conversion to a special mission submarine. She deployed from 1961 to 1964 carrying five nuclear-armed Regulus I missiles. (U.S. Navy)

of Guam on December 25, 1964. The submarine carried 16 Polaris A-3 missiles to cover targets in Soviet Siberia—including the Petropavlovsk naval complex.

Of the five Regulus submarines, the diesel-electric *Barbero* was decommissioned and sunk as a target. The *Tunny* was converted to a transport submarine for swimmers and commandos and served in the Vietnam War. The newer *Grayback* also was converted to a transport submarine for special forces with her twin missile hangars forward being ideal for stowing large rubber rafts. The newer *Growler* was to undergo a similar conversion, but funding shortages during the Vietnam War and shipyard workloads led to her conversion being cancelled. She ended up as a museum ship in New York City.

A major question was the future of the *Halibut*, the U.S. Navy's only nuclear-propelled cruise missile submarine and a relatively new ship, having been completed in 1960. A journalist who was on board the *Halibut* while she was still a missile submarine later labeled her a "white elephant."[14] Two other journalists, Sherry Sontag and Christopher Drew, in *Blind Man's Bluff*, their best-selling account of submarine espionage, wrote of the *Halibut*,

> She was a marine oddball, one of the least hydrodynamic of the nuclear fleet and one of the most ridiculous-looking creations ever born in a dry dock. Unlike the flat fish she was named for, *Halibut* wore a huge hump that might have been appropriate on a gargantuan desert creature except for the fact that it opened up into a large shark's-mouth hatch, part of the original missile hangar. Perhaps in another time, *Halibut* would have been quietly scrapped. After all, this boat was not only odd, she suffered from what was a near-fatal malady for a submarine: hydromechanical cacophony. *Halibut* was loud. Submariners heard the din, saw only potential flooding when they gazed upon the hatch, and shuddered when they examined her cumbersome ballast tanks, gaping caverns originally designed to allow her to surface fast, shoot a missile, and submerge even faster.[15]

But there was a future role for the *Halibut*.

A SERIES OF EVENTS

On the evening of March 8, 1968, Rear Admiral Viktor Dygalo, commander of the 29th Submarine Division at Petropavlovsk, joined other officers and their wives at the home of the Rybachiy base commander to celebrate International Women's Day, an official holiday in the Soviet Union. About 10 PM, Dygalo later recalled, "suddenly the telephone rang . . . [and] it was for me. . . . I took the receiver and was told that the squadron commander requests my presence urgently."[1]

A short time later, in the office of Rear Admiral Yakov I. Krivorochenko, the commander of the 15th Submarine Squadron, Dygalo was told that the *K-129* from his division had not responded to radio calls to immediately establish radio contact. "Of course . . . this provoked a shock especially for me as division commander," continued Dygalo.

The *K-129* should have been at about 172° 30' E and 40° N at midnight on the night of March 7–8 (071200Z). At that time she should have sent a burst radio transmission. While neither Dygalo nor the squadron commander knew the contents of the Moscow-generated communication orders given to the *K-129*, they now realized that a communication checks had been missed: the ballistic missile submarine *K-129* had failed to transmit her communications checks scheduled about March 7–8.

Subsequent attempts to elicit communications from the submarine were unsuccessful. Thus, by 10 PM on March 8, according to Dygalo, the Soviet Pacific Fleet commands had "hit the panic button." The Kamchatka submarine commander had expressed his concern over the missed radio checks

Rear Admiral Viktor A. Dygalo.

to naval headquarters in Moscow and was advised to begin preparations for a search for the submarine, but not to initiate any action.

After meeting with Admiral Krivorochenko, Dygalo called together his senior staff officers and available submarine commanders for a late-night meeting to discuss what could have prevented the *K-129* from making her radio checks. At about 11 PM Dygalo met with his deputy division commander, several staff specialists, and several submarine officers. They put forth their speculation on what could have caused the failure of the *K-129* to communicate.

On the morning of March 9 the Kamchatka flotilla commander, the senior commander of the Kamchatka complex, Rear Admiral Boris Ye. Yamkovoy, arrived at Dygalo's 29th Division headquarters and listened to a discussion of possible reasons for the missing communication checks. Dygalo later recalled that the opinions expressed at the meeting centered on

- internal waves in the ocean or crossing a frontal zone where the water was warmer or less salty (less dense) led the submarine to become "heavier" and lost depth control and exceeded its collapse depth (the Golf II-class submarine *K-126* had suffered a sudden loss of buoyancy during her pre-operational workup in January 1968).
- an explosion of one of the submarine's electric storage batteries.
- collision of the submarine with a surface ship while the submarine was operating near the surface using her snorkel; in such conditions the submarine's passive sonar is "blinded" by the noise of her diesel engines, and the submarine's search radar would not be used in order to maintain stealth.

- an underwater collision with a U.S. submarine that was trailing the *K-129*.

Significantly, based on Dygalo's recollection of these discussions, the participants appear to have accepted that the submarine had sunk. These views did not address the possibility that the submarine suffered communications or electrical problems that would have prevented the prescribed transmissions.

While Dygalo later said that he was absolutely certain that the *K-129* was lost due to a collision with the U.S. nuclear-propelled submarine *Swordfish* (SSN 579), there is a question about how seriously that possibility was addressed at the time of these early discussions. U.S. nuclear-propelled submarines were in fact beginning to trail Soviet strategic missile submarines to determine their operational procedures and to record their individual sound signatures, although the Soviet Navy had yet to appreciate the extent and frequency of U.S. submarine trailing operations.

The accidental explosion of one of the submarine's three R-21 missiles was discussed, according to Dygalo, "but this was rejected as the R-21 missile had not given us any [reason] to conclude it could provoke such a catastrophe." The R-21 had earlier suffered problems following its introduction into the fleet in 1963, but it was believed that those troubles had been corrected.

Still, at the meeting the staff specialist for missile systems stated that the propellant and oxidizer tanks for one of the liquid-propellant R-21 missiles might have developed leaks. Such leaks could lead to a fire or explosion and could destroy communications as the submarine's large, high-frequency antenna folded down onto the deck adjacent to the missile tubes, on the starboard side of the submarine. Again, those discussions on March 9, according to Dygalo, addressed the probable loss of the *K-129* and not whether the submarine could still be afloat but without communications.

On March 10, naval headquarters in Moscow approved the search for the submarine to commence. The surface ships and submarines dispatched on the search would steam at predetermined distances between one another, with radar and sonar searching for the lost submarine, with radios being tuned to the submarine's transmitter frequencies. Four diesel-electric submarines, including the Golf II-class *K-126* from Dygalo's division, and one nuclear torpedo-attack submarine were dispatched over the next few days.[2] Dygalo sailed on board the nuclear boat. The number of surface ships that sailed from Far Eastern ports totaled 36 warships and naval- and civilian-manned auxiliaries. Also, naval reconnaissance aircraft—Tu-95RT Bear-D and Tu-16R Badger types—joined the search. They would fly 286 missions from Yelizovo airfield, immediately north of Petropavlovsk, and Burevestnik airfield in the Kurile Islands during the search effort. These flights of Bear aircraft would provide U.S. intelligence agencies with confirming indications that something was amiss in the area.

Dygalo's principal deputy, Captain 1st Rank Valentin Bets, sailed in a large, ocean-going tug on March 10 to coordinate information from the surface search forces. An analytical team with Bets attempted to determine the effect of weather and other factors on the probable track of the *K-129* to assist the search forces. While Dygalo repeated on many occasions that this was the assignment of his deputy, in later statements he revealed that Bets was in charge of the "tow group" for the problem-plagued missile submarine *B-62*. In retrospect it appears likely that his group—comprising the icebreaker *Vyuga*, the submarine rescue ship *SS-23*, two oceanographic research ships, and an ocean-going tug—was initially sent to assist the *B-62*, and then was sent to join the *K-129* search. (The *B-62* had suffered major problems with her diesel engines beginning in late February.)

Rear Admiral Valery Aleksin, a submariner, later recalled,

> On arriving in the area, four submarines were lined up at 10 [nautical mile] intervals and we ironed the ocean that way for almost a month in the surface condition. The sea state was from 4 to 8, and it was impossible to make anything out and find anything in the seething water under such conditions. When the wind died down, American shore-based Orion ASW aircraft appeared above us. If we had the very same kind of aircraft at that time it would have been possible to discover traces of the tragedy on the surface without difficulty.[3]

His term "ironed" referred to the submarines' tracking back and forth across the possible route of the *K-129*, using radar and sonar in an attempt to detect the submarine. The P-3B Orion patrol aircraft were from U.S. Navy

A Project AV611/Zulu V ballistic missile submarine, similar to the problem-plagued submarine *B-62*. Radio transmissions to and from the *B-62* confused U.S. intelligence officials. Apparently, the submarine intended to replace the *B-62* encountered technical problems, causing the unexpected deployment of the *K-129* to provide missile coverage of the Hawaiian Station. (U.S. Navy)

Details of the sail structure of a Zulu V missile submarine showing the covers for the two ballistic missile tubes. The tubes penetrated through the sail and pressure hull, and into a section beneath the hull. The submarine's periscopes and masts are located between the bridge (forward) and missile tubes. (U.S. Navy)

Patrol Squadron (VP) 9. Flying from Adak, Alaska, the planes sighted the Soviet submarines several times from March 18 to April 2. The VP-9 official history noted,

- (S[ecret]) 18 Mar–2 Apr: "Kennel Door" operations involved the continuous surveillance of a number of Soviet naval surface vessels and submarines.
- March: The "Kennel Door" operation comprised most of the squadron's operational efforts in March.
- Acoustic intelligence was obtained on three classes of Soviet submarines.[4]

In addition to the four diesel-electric submarines, a nuclear-propelled Project 627/November-class attack submarine participated in the search. Admiral Dygalo was embarked in the "nuke," with side number 715, that was also detected by the Orions. The postdeployment intelligence report of Patrol Squadron 9 showed almost continuous surveillance of these submarines from March 18 through April 2 (see Table 4-1).[5] The "detections" are those that were able to identify specific Soviet submarines; some of these submarines were detected on additional occasions but were not conclusively identified.

TABLE 4-1 Detection of Submarine Search Effort

CONTACT	SUBMARINE	TYPE	SIDE NO.	FIRST LOCATION	DETECTIONS
S-4	SS	Foxtrot	812	42° 10' N 166° 20' E	10
S-5	SS	Zulu	828	45° N 165° 50' E	15
S-6	SSB	Golf II	720	42° 30' N 164° 30' E	8
R-3	SS	Zulu	830	39° 45' N 164° 18' E	8
S-7	SSN	November	715	41° N 164° 30' E	2

During the period of Operation Kennel Door, the nine P-3B Orions of VP-9 also sighted numerous surface ships participating in the search for the *K-129*, including destroyers, frigates, minesweepers, and naval auxiliaries, including a submarine tender. The aircraft flew 184 flights from Adak for a total of 1,268 flight hours.

This effort earned the squadron the Navy's Meritorious Unit Commendation, awarded

For meritorious service from 1 December 1967 to 31 May 1968 . . . while deployed to Adak, Alaska. Despite operational commitments requiring a virtually continuous maximum effort, the officers and men of Patrol Squadron NINE, while completing every assigned task in an outstanding manner, maintained a measure of anti-submarine-warfare and intelligence-collection effectiveness unparalleled in recent Navy experience.[6]

The exodus of Soviet ships and submarines from Petropavlovsk was observed by the U.S. nuclear-propelled submarine *Barb*. The authors of *Blind Man's Bluff* related that the *Barb*'s commanding officer, Bernard M. (Bud) Kauderer,

> had never seen anything like it. Four or five Soviet submarines rushed out to sea and began beating the ocean with active sonar. The submarines would dive, come back to periscope depth, then dive again.
>
> The Soviets made no effort to avoid detection, no effort to hide. Their cries filled the airwaves, shattering the air . . . with unencoded desperation.
>
> As Barb and other U.S. surveillance craft listened, it was clear that the Soviets had no idea where to find their submarine.[7]

Indeed, the Soviet search forces were looking within about 350 nautical miles of the entrance to Avacha Bay in the event that the *K-129* had sunk shortly after her first and only radio transmission. The searching submarines subsequently sailed southward to longitude 40°N, and then turned eastward to cover the expected track of the *K-129* up to her mid-transit checkpoint position.

Beyond the *Barb*, which had been on station to observe the submarine and surface ship activities off Petro, the U.S. Navy was monitoring Soviet radio communications with a network of ground intercept stations around the Pacific rim and SIGINT aircraft—EC-121 Super Constellations—of Navy reconnaissance squadron VQ-1 flying from Atsugi, Japan. (One of these EC-121 aircraft would be shot down by North Korea fighters over the open sea on April 15, 1969; all 31 U.S. military personnel on board were killed.)

The Project 629A/Golf II–class submarine *K-126* in the North Pacific in 1968 while searching for her sister submarine *K-129*. The ill-fated *K-129* was the first Golf SSB in the Pacific to be converted to launch the R-21/SS-N-5 Serb missile; the *K-126* was the second submarine to be converted. (U.S. Navy)

The U.S. Navy's monitoring of the massive Soviet search effort for the *K-129* detected a series of radio messages from the Zulu V ballistic missile submarine *B-62*. She had departed Petropavlovsk about January 26 and had arrived on station some 500 to 600 nautical miles northwest of Hawaii about February 21. She had made the required burst radio transmissions en route to the Hawaii Station, revealing her progress to U.S. Navy intercept stations as well as to Soviet naval headquarters. Possibly before arriving on station, the *B-62* suffered a breakdown of one of her three diesel engines. Within a week she had lost a second diesel engine; after an exchange of messages with naval headquarters, apparently permission was given for the *B-62* to commence a return transit to Petro about March 8. Probably two days later she lost her third diesel engine, leaving her with only electric-battery power. She thus had no effective propulsion and was left immobile on the surface, awaiting assistance.

The group of five Soviet auxiliary ships commanded by Captain 1st Rank Bets, Dygalo's deputy, reached the *B-62* by March 16. Technicians from these ships and spare parts that they—especially the submarine rescue ship *SS-23*—carried, could have been key to carrying out repairs on the submarine's 37D Kolomna diesel engines and purging the submarine's fuel tanks of possible saltwater contamination. The *B-62*, having been assisted by Bets's ships and with some propulsion restored, was held on the Hawaii Station for almost 30 days, apparently to provide missile coverage of Oahu. The tow home was begun on April 14 and the icebreaker *Vyuga* with the *B-62* in tow reached Petropavlovsk on the 23rd. Bets's other ships apparently remained at sea, participating in the search of the *K-129*.

There is, however, some question about the actual cause of the emergency situation commencing on March 8. Some contemporaneous U.S. intelligence sources indicate that the unusual deployments of Soviet aircraft and ships into the North Pacific from March 10 to 14 were actually in response to the *B-62* crisis. These sources identify those additional deployments that began about March 14–15 as responding specifically to the *K-129* search, to which the previous *B-62*-related deployments were also assigned. Still, as soon as it became obvious that the *K-129* was missing, the massive search for that submarine was undertaken.

The Soviet Navy's frustration and lack of knowledge about the *K-129* was obvious as ships, aircraft, and submarines freely communicated. In particular, the five submarines carried out the "position checks" with burst transmissions, revealing the standard track followed to reach the Hawaiian Station and marking the progress of the submarine searches.

Two groups of Soviet surface ships searched along the predicted outbound track of the *K-129* and also the area 34° 46' N and 168° 57' W, more than 1,000 nautical miles northwest of Oahu. The total area encompassed some 854,000 square miles, one-quarter the size of the entire United States. The weather in the search area was stormy during most of the search period with wave heights up to about 25 feet.

In time these search areas were expanded, and included the Great Circle route from Petropavlovsk to the Hawaii Station. Although there had been reports of oil slicks in the area, the Soviet ships, submarines, and aircraft found absolutely no evidence of what had happened to the *K-129*. The diesel-electric submarines returned to Kamchatka after four weeks of searching. The other ships remained at sea until, after 72 days of searching, the operation was called off on May 5—the day that the *K-129* had been scheduled to return to Kamchatka.

The Soviet ships and aircraft found no trace of the missing submarine. The large, civilian-manned research ships *Akademik Sergei Vavilov* and *Petr Lebedev*, remained in the search area for a while longer.

After Admiral Dygalo learned of the failure of the *K-129* to make the required communication checks, and returning from the search effort on board a nuclear-propelled submarine, there are reports that he flew to Madras, India, to inform the Pacific Fleet commander, Admiral Nikolay Amel'ko, of the details of the *K-129* situation. Amel'ko was conducting the first visit of a Soviet squadron to India. Dygalo boarded the flagship, the cruiser *Dmitry Pozharsky*, and made his report. Captain Peter A. Huchthausen, later the U.S. naval attaché in Moscow, related an account told to him by a Soviet naval officer on Amel'ko's staff

> It was a day I'll never forget. Amel'ko appeared sad and already resigned that the lost communications with one of his Pacific Fleet submarines was not only the end of his career but possibly a harbinger of something worse—an encounter with the American navy that might portend a heightening of tensions.[8]

Then Huchthausen related a strange account of the missing submarine, again quoting Captain 1st Rank Lev Vtorygin of Amel'ko's staff. After listening to Dygalo's report, Amel'ko was said to have asked him,

> "What was her mission prior to her scheduled report?" the admiral asked. "Reconnaissance of the departure channel of Pearl Harbor, Comrade Admiral," Dygalo replied. "Why are we using a strategic unit for that mission?" Amel'ko asked.
>
> "I'll never forget the response," said Vtorygin sadly. "Admiral Dygalo shifted uneasily and then responded that it was impossible to use any other submarine because of the high probability of counterdetection by U.S. submarines guarding the area. Dygalo continued, saying that their few nuclear-powered units with the Pacific Fleet were too easily detected because of their noisy engineering plants to conduct close surveillance of the U.S. submarine departure zone off Pearl Harbor."[9]

Dygalo continued, according to Vtorygin, saying he suspected the *K-129* was being trailed by an American submarine. He explained that there had been a radio message from an expendable communications buoy saying that the *K-129* was being pursued by American anti-submarine forces. And, according to Vtorygin, Dygalo also explained that the *K-129* operation was the last close surveillance mission in the Pacific area by a diesel-electric submarine.[10]

But Captain Huchthausen's account was a complete fabrication. In response to inquiries by the authors of this book, Dygalo responded,

> First, Admiral Amel'ko . . . knew what submarine would be assigned to what mission before I did. He could never have asked me such a stupid question. Assignments were developed in the Soviet Naval Staff and then sent to the fleets to decide what sub would go where.
>
> Second, I could have never given him such an idiotic answer as that.
>
> Third, I have never been to India.[11]

The Soviet high command concluded the obvious—the *K-129* had been lost with all hands at an unknown location. Although scores of submarines of several nations had been lost in peacetime since the beginning of the twentieth century, the loss of the *K-129* was highly significant: she was the first strategic missile submarine to be lost. Later, as Britain, France, the Soviet Union, and the United States placed a major portion of their nuclear strike forces at sea in submarines, the unexplained loss of one of those submarines could have frightening implications.

Furthermore, there had been survivors from most previous peacetime submarine losses. From those survivors or by other means the location of each submarine's wreckage was known almost immediately. The Soviet search, along the expected track of the *K-129*, revealed that the Soviet naval high command did not know the location of the wreckage.

Finally, more submariners died in the *K-129* than in any other Soviet submarine loss to that time. The 98 men who died in the *K-129* compared to 99 lost in the Royal Navy's worst submarine sinking, HMS *Thetis* on June 1, 1939, and the deadliest American submarine disaster, the USS *Thresher* (SSN 593), which sank on April 10, 1963, with 129 men on board.[12]

Sunday, May 5 was a day of mourning at Rybachiy. It was openly stated at a ceremony, held at the monument to the submarine *L-16* sunk in World War II, that the *K-129* had been lost with all on board.[13] That pronouncement, however, was restricted to the local, relatively isolated community. The information was withheld from the rest of the world while the Soviet Navy and government pondered the loss of a nuclear-armed submarine.

The *K-126*, having returned from participating in the search for her sister ship, entered the No. 202 Dalzavod yard at Vladivostok where she and the *K-129* had been converted to the Golf II configuration. There, during May–June 1968, technicians and specialists inspected the submarine in an attempt to determine what could have gone wrong with the missing undersea craft. At every level of the Soviet Navy, submarine designers, commanders, and specialists sought answers.

In August a commission was established by the Soviet government, chaired by Leonid Smirnov, the Deputy Chairman for the Defense Industry in the Council of Ministers, to provide a top-level review of the *K-129* disaster. (The Council served as the executive branch of the Soviet government, and was made up of the senior ministers, chairmen of state committees, and other leading government officials. It was by decrees of the Council that the five-year economic plans became law; the Council coordinated their implementation, thus managing virtually all economic and military activity of that country.)[14]

A second investigation was led by Admiral Sergi Gorshkov, the imposing Commander-in-Chief (CinC) of the Soviet Navy, and his First Deputy CinC, Admiral Vladimir Kasatonov, considered one of the most brilliant naval officers of the time. Their writ was to examine the preparation of the *K-129* and her crew—had they been ready for combat duty?

The Smirnov commission's findings remain classified. It was obvious, however, that the panel members could find no specific reason for the submarine's loss, and could find no culpability. Furthermore, at that time there was no "conclusion"—as was put forth later with great certainty—that a collision with the U.S. nuclear submarine *Swordfish* had sunk the *K-129*. Indeed, Admiral Aleksin, who had participated in the search, stated that the government commission "at that time . . . named the most probable cause of the [submarine's] loss to be her possible falling beyond maximum diving depth as a result of water entering the hull through an allegedly unserviceable float valve while snorkeling."[15]

The Gorshkov-Kuznetsov panel found that the submarine had been fully prepared for combat duty, and that the crew had been properly trained.

A key witness in their inquiry was Admiral Dygalo, who had high praise for Captain 1st Rank Kobzar, the commanding officer of the *K-129*. Dygalo had been to sea on board the *K-129* on three occasions during the submarine's preparations for missions. The admiral later stated, "Captain Kobzar was one of the best [commanders] in the Pacific Fleet. He was especially talented and had an enormous experience [and] that's why I had a special trust in him."[16] And Kobzar was the most senior of the eight commanding officers of Golf-type submarines in Dygalo's division, and his submarine had been the first to undergo the Golf II conversion.

In fact, after completing the Hawaii Station deployment, Kobzar had been scheduled for a senior staff position. His second in command, Captain 2nd Rank Aleksandr Zhuravin, who had served in the *K-129* since the summer of 1967, was scheduled to become the commanding officer. Zhuravin was also highly regarded; he was to have become one of the few Jewish officers to hold important commands in the Soviet Navy.

Now all were gone. Their loss was not publicly announced by the Soviet government until November 13, 1993, when the military newspaper *Krasnaya Zvezda* (Red Star) published the list of the crew of the *K-129* that had gone down in the Pacific Ocean more than 25 years earlier.

No trace of the *K-129* was found by the Soviet search forces, nor was there any indication of the submarine's fate detected by the Soviet acoustic detection system with planar arrays in the Pacific. This system, called Cluster Lance by NATO, included arrays placed near the entrance to Petropavlovsk.

But the death sounds of the *K-129* in fact had been detected. The U.S. Navy cable ship *Albert J. Myer* (T-ARC 6), manned by a civilian crew, was operating in the Eastern Pacific at latitude 29° 32' N and longitude 147° 06' W on March 11. The *Myer* was carrying out acoustic surveys for a planned SOSUS array site and had deployed a hydrophone to the seafloor, 4,000 feet down. The hydrophone recorded a series of major acoustic events. The first signal appeared to have been produced at about midnight with the second following exactly six minutes after the first. Later in March, the U.S. Navy began looking into the meaning of the massive Soviet search effort and the *Myer*'s acoustic detections as well as other possible sources of information on the March 11 "incident," as the U.S. Navy labeled it. The principal players

The Navy cable ship *Albert J. Myer* (T-ARC 6) detected acoustic signals produced by the loss of the submarine *K-129*. The ship had a single hydrophone lowered in conjunction with determining deep-sound channels related to installing SOSUS arrays. At the time, the *Myer* was operating in the east central Pacific area, 1,730 nautical miles from the *K-129*. (U.S. Navy)

in the U.S. Navy underwater enterprise were Dr. John Craven and Captain James (Jim) Bradley.

Craven was the chief scientist of the Navy's Polaris–Poseidon submarine missile program (Special Projects) and also the head of the newly established Deep Submergence Systems Project (DSSP). DSSP was organized following the loss of the nuclear submarine *Thresher* in 1963 and a realization of the Navy's limitations for operations in the deep-ocean environment.[17] The new agency, initially a part of the Naval Ship Systems Command, was intended to develop capabilities for (1) recovering of surviving personnel from disabled submarines, (2) investigating the ocean floor and recovering small objects (e.g., satellite payloads and reentry vehicles), (3) recovering large objects (e.g., missiles and submarines), and (4) enabling man to work and live on the ocean floor (at a depth of 1,000 feet by 1970).

As chief scientist for Special Projects, Craven also directed the deep submergence effort from when it was established in June 1965. DSSP was made a separate Navy office in February 1966, with Craven serving as both chief scientist of Special Projects and also DSSP project manager, with many of his senior people in Special Projects also being "double-hatted" in DSSP. The new agency would manage both "white" (publicly known) and "black" (highly classified) projects.

Bradley was assistant for undersea warfare in the Office of Naval Intelligence in the Pentagon. A veteran of amphibious operations in the Pacific at the end of World War II and a submariner, Bradley was considered highly intelligent and innovative.

Craven and Bradley now sought out Captain Joseph P. (Joe) Kelly, the "father of SOSUS" and one of the Navy's leading acoustics experts. At Kelly's direction, the paper records of the extensive Navy SOSUS arrays in the Pacific were examined, but a check of those records failed to reveal any acoustic disturbance related to a missing submarine being recorded during the period March 1–15, 1968.[18]

There was, however, another U.S. acoustic source in the Pacific area—a series of hydrophones operated by the U.S. Air Force Technical Applications Center (AFTAC) to detect Soviet nuclear detonations. In 1947, because of concern over Soviet nuclear weapons development, then–Army Chief of Staff Dwight D. Eisenhower directed the Army Air Forces (soon to become the U.S. Air Force) to establish the capability to detect atomic explosions anywhere in the world. The new organization was formally activated on April 1, 1948, eventually evolving into the AFTAC agency.[19]

Starting with aircraft configured to detect the fallout from nuclear explosions, the Air Force deployed devices to identify such detonations on the surface, underground, in the atmosphere, in space, and underwater. This requirement led to the Air Force installing seafloor monitors that terminated at the islands of Eniwetok, Midway, Oahu, and Wake. AFTAC also received an acoustic feed from a single hydrophone in the Navy SOSUS array that terminated at Adak, Alaska. These Air Force sensors detected the sounds emanating from the *K-129* at distances from about 700 nautical miles (Midway) to 1,930 nautical miles (Eniwetok).

On May 14 Navy acoustic and intelligence specialists met in Washington, D.C., with AFTAC officials and asked them to search their data records for explosions or implosions, or evidence of radioactive debris or other activity that might indicate a submarine in extremis. Thereby U.S. naval intelligence learned of the AFTAC detection of two acoustic signals some six minutes apart. The AFTAC data on the arrival times of the two signals at the various stations were:[20]

STATION	1ST EVENT	2ND EVENT
Midway	12:14:30	12:20:28
Adak	12:18:56	12:24:55
Wake	12:30:12	12:36:10
Hawaii	12:33:22	12:39:20
Eniwetok	12:40:30	———

By comparing the detection times of these acoustic events recorded at the four AFTAC sites and the Adak SOSUS array, Air Force technicians in the Washington suburb of Alexandria, Virginia, determined that the *K-129* was lost *within two nautical miles* of 40° 06' N and 179° 57' E, and—as will prove suggestive—the initial event occurred within *one second* of 1200Z on March 11—precisely midnight on board the *K-129*. The event occurred at a distance of 1,590 nautical miles northwest of Pearl Harbor (Oahu) on a bearing of 320 degrees.

Navy officials in Washington asked AFTAC for the tapes to review the two principal signals.[21] The AFTAC tapes were delivered to Craven, and a very cursory review by the Navy of the AFTAC detections led to the (erroneous) conclusion that the submarine had broken apart in the two major events that had been detected, separated by about six minutes. The first sound, it was subsequently estimated, could be the implosion of the *K-129* pressure hull at approximately 1,000 feet, and the second the collapse of such components as 6,000-pounds-per-square-inch air flasks, which could occur at depths greater than 12,000 feet.[22]

In order to better calibrate the AFTAC sensors to refine the estimated position of the *K-129* wreckage, the decision was made to detonate a series of four-pound explosive charges in the North Pacific basin; these charges were planted by a U.S. submarine using inertial navigation for precise positioning. (Those explosives were detonated on June 9 and permitted a refined estimate of the submarine's location; to avoid compromising U.S. knowledge of that position, they were not detonated near the *K-129* site.)

On May 20, AFTAC specialists briefed Navy personnel. Records list the following persons attending that meeting, held at Building 52 of NAVSTIC, then located at the Naval Observatory in northwest Washington:[23]

From Air Force Technical Applications Center
> Captain John C. Birkholz, USAF
> Mr. William Brooks
> Mr. Bob Drake
> Mr. Doyle Northrup
> Dr. Carl Romney

From Office of the Chief of Naval Operations
> Naval Scientific and Technical Intelligence Center (NAVSTIC)
> Mr. Bill Patterson

From Naval Electronic Systems Command
> Captain Joe Kelly, USN

From Naval Ship Systems Command (Special Projects)
> Dr. John P. Craven

Doyle Northrup was one of the most senior people at AFTAC, having been involved with the 1949 detection of the first Soviet atomic bomb test by a modified B-29 Superfortress.

Because the single Adak SOSUS hydrophone tapped by AFTAC detected the sounds believed to be associated with the loss of the *K-129*, there were expectations that other components of the Adak array should have detected those sounds. It was also probable that SOSUS arrays located in other areas of the Pacific detected those sounds, especially those near the U.S. West Coast, because there is an unobstructed deep-water acoustic transmission path from the *K-129* site to those arrays. But a search of SOSUS records disclosed no submarine "breaking up" sounds, as had been recorded by many of the Atlantic area SOSUS stations when the *Thresher* had imploded as she sank in 1963.

The collective failure of the SOSUS network to recognize and report the *K-129* sounds is attributed to their brief duration—not more than several seconds for the strongest signals. The SOSUS system operators normally sought extended-duration signals, such as the machinery sounds generated by snorkeling submarines, not relatively brief, "transient" sounds. Based on

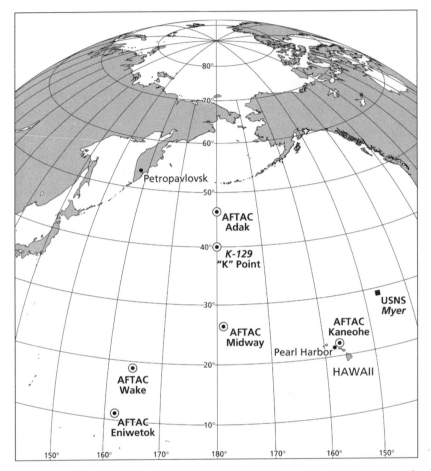

The locations of the U.S. Air Force Technical Application Center's sensors that detected the acoustic events of the *K-129*. "K" point—the location of her sinking—and the location of the Navy cable ship *Albert J. Myer* (T-ARC 6) are indicated.

the AFTAC detections, the best-estimated position for the remains of the *K-129* were placed about 600 nautical miles northwest of the location where the Soviet naval auxiliary ships under Captain 1st Rank Bets had "shepherded" the *B-62* for almost a month, i.e., the Hawaii Station. Several methods were proposed at the May 20 meeting for refining the precise location of the wreckage. How could the submarine's wreckage be pinpointed and its condition ascertained?

FINDING THE TARGET OBJECT

The wreckage of the *K-129* was estimated to be resting at a depth of some 16,800 feet. The U.S. Navy had several systems that could be used to search for the remains at that depth. Most notable was the *Trieste II*, a bathyscaph (Greek for "deep boat"). The *Trieste* was essentially a 6½-foot-diameter steel sphere, which carried up to three personnel and instruments, attached to a large gasoline float. The gasoline, which is lighter than water, would bring the craft back to the surface after the release of up to nine tons of steel pellets that served as ballast. Acquired by the U.S. Navy in 1958, the *Trieste* dove to the deepest location in the oceans, the Marianas Trench, reaching a depth of 35,840 feet in 1960.[1] Subsequently, the *Trieste* was extensively modified and became known as the *Trieste II*. She had located the remains of the USS *Thresher* at a depth of 8,400 feet during dives off the U.S. East Coast in 1963 and 1964. But the *Trieste II* had two major limitations: First, she had very limited horizontal mobility—she was best described as a "deep-sea elevator." Second, the craft was surface-based, transported to a dive area in a towed dock and openly placed in the water in preparation for a dive. Thus, she was readily visible to all in the area.

Another U.S. Navy capability for deep-ocean search was the use of cameras and sonar devices towed at great depths by the civilian-manned research ship *Mizar* (T-AGOR 11). That ship could tow search devices to a depth of 16,800 feet, but, again, her purpose was well known to the Soviets and fully observable to nearby ships and aircraft.[2]

In 1968 another deep-ocean search capability became available to the Navy: the USS *Halibut*. The *Halibut* had been the first—and as events evolved—the only nuclear-propelled Regulus missile submarine. When the Regulus cruise missile was retired in 1964, the one-of-a-kind *Halibut* became available for other roles.

In early 1965, Dr. John Craven, the chief scientist of the Polaris–Poseidon submarine missile program and head of the Deep Submergence Systems Project (DSSP), was called to the Pentagon to discuss the Sand Dollar program. This was a highly classified or "black" Air Force–Navy program that sought to identify and—when possible—recover objects from the ocean floor. These were objects that the Soviets had "dropped" into the sea—such as missile reentry vehicles, satellite packages, weapons—as well as some objects similarly dropped by the United States. During the Cold War the recovery of such objects by the opposing side could provide valuable technical and even operational intelligence about the enemy. (Despite a lack of "stealth," the bathyscaph *Trieste II* did recover several small items from the ocean floor, some of Soviet "origin." On April 25, 1972, she lifted an item of several hundred pounds from a depth of 16,400 feet.)

While there were means available to possibly locate objects on the ocean floor, such as the *Trieste II* and the *Mizar*, as noted above, these were *surface*-operated vessels; what was required was a platform that could operate clandestinely, underwater, to search for lost objects and to possibly recover them. By this time, Craven, as the head of DSSP, had initiated the development of several systems to provide such capabilities. In the "white" world of DSSP was a program to construct two deep-submergence search/recovery vehicles that could operate to 20,000 feet to locate and recover small objects. They would be carried into the target area clandestinely on board a nuclear-propelled submarine, which could launch, recover, and replenish the 50-foot vehicles. And, in a collaborative effort between DSSP and Admiral H. G. Rickover's nuclear power directorate, the Navy was building a nuclear-propelled search and recovery vehicle, the *NR-1*. This 146-foot, 393-ton submersible could be towed underwater by a submarine but was primarily surface supported. (In the event, the 20,000-foot search vehicles were not built; the *NR-1*, with a 3,000-foot operating depth, was in service from 1969 to 2008.)

Craven, fascinated by the Sand Dollar list of targets on the ocean floor, and supported by the director of the Defense Intelligence Agency and his scientific advisory board, initiated a black seafloor search and recovery program. He later outlined the three capabilities that had to be developed:

> The most immediate was a means of conducting a clandestine search in the deep ocean. We had a particular interest in finding and recovering Soviet missile reentry bodies and guidance systems. . . . The second immediate requirement was to develop a capability for manned inspection and recovery of small and intermediate-sized objects from the deep ocean floor. The third was the capability to clandestinely place divers on the seafloor for the recovery of objects that required some form of handling.[3]

These efforts obviously would require an underwater "platform" to carry out such missions, one that could not be easily detected by Soviet surveillance activities. This meant a submarine, and the USS *Halibut* was the obvious solution. The 350-foot, 4,775-ton submarine was available following the retirement of the Regulus missile. Although relatively new, completed in 1960, the *Halibut* was considered too large, too slow, and too noisy and lacked advanced sonar to be effectively employed as a torpedo-attack submarine.

With Craven secretly funding the work, and being careful to make minimum changes to the external appearance of the *Halibut*, the submarine was modified at the Pearl Harbor naval shipyard during a $70 million "overhaul" that lasted from February to September 1965; additional modifications were made at the Mare Island (California) shipyard and the Keyport (Washington) naval base. Her new features included:

- darkroom photographic facility
- facilities to enable the submarine to stow, release, tow, and recover "Fish"—towed sensor devices—with winch and cable
- sail structure increased in height to house additional surveillance antennas

A thruster device was installed atop the *Halibut*'s hangar to improve maneuverability, but it was not used. It was found to be too noisy and was not needed. The Fish was a towed "body" about 12 feet long weighing two tons that contained cameras, strobe lights, and sonar for detecting seafloor objects. A tunnel-like chute installed in the bottom of the *Halibut*'s large bow

The USS *Halibut* (SSN 587) as a special-mission submarine. Her first major operation in that role was locating and photographing the remains of the *K-129*. The "hump" forward of her sail structure is over the "bat cave"—the former Regulus missile compartment converted to house computers and other special equipment, and to house and launch towed sensor vehicles. (U.S. Navy)

hanger—labeled the Bat Cave—permitted the launching and retrieval of the Fish. The development of such devices that could successfully operate *and survive* at depths to 20,000 feet was exceedingly difficult. Developing lights, cameras, and sonar to operate at great depths was difficult and very expensive. These costs as well as those for other black programs were "hidden" by Craven in the Polaris–Poseidon and DSSP white programs.

The Fish was designed to be towed for about six days, and then be winched back up into the submarine—cruising at a depth of about 200 feet—a process that took several hours. For the *K-129* mission the tow cable would be about 25,000 feet long.[4] The Fish depth could be easily and accurately controlled by reeling cable in or out, and with slight changes in the *Halibut*'s speed. Once the Fish was back in the Bat Cave the camera film would be extracted from the Fish for on-board developing and its batteries would be recharged. The *Halibut* would normally carry two of the Fish.

The hangar itself—originally designed to house two large Regulus II missiles—was almost 30 feet wide, 50 feet long, and 30 feet high. The crew said that when she was still a missile submarine if the racks for torpedoes and missiles were removed they "would have a great basketball court."[5] The rebuilt hangar had three levels and now contained bunkrooms for the technicians embarked for special missions, a computer area, photographic darkroom, and stowage and handling gear for the two Fish. (The *Halibut* retained her four forward and two stern 21-inch torpedo tubes, with torpedoes being carried.)

The reconfigured *Halibut* first tested the Fish system off Hawaii, searching for a prepositioned target on the ocean floor. One of the cable strands broke and created a snarl that prevented normal recovery. As the crew and specialists sought to correct the situation, the Fish was lost, probably snagged on the ocean floor and torn away. Next came the *Halibut*'s first operational mission: to locate and examine the reentry body from a Soviet missile test in the Pacific in February 1968. Unfortunately, as the *Halibut* launched the Fish during an evaluation prior to the operation, the $5 million device slid out of the chute . . . and was lost; the wire cable had not been properly attached to the device![6] Another *Halibut* Fish had been inadvertently shipped to South Vietnam. It was finally recovered in time for the mission, but the mission failed to locate the reentry body. When the *Halibut* left the target area—without Soviet support ships detecting her presence—there were problems with winching in the tow cable; the submarine had to surface and put men on deck to help with the problem. One man went overboard at night at which point a "rogue wave" swept over the submarine. (The sailor was recovered. The maneuvers to rescue the sailor required the *Halibut* to "back down— emergency," which probably put the Fish on the bottom even though it was being reeled in as fast as possible. The vital Fish was not lost.)[7] According to Captain Edward Moore, commanding officer of the *Halibut* from February 1967, "during these early missions we had become quite good at controlling both ship and Fish depth, and in searching for targets, but we had not yet learned how to accurately position the Fish for photographs."[8]

Subsequently, the *Halibut* was dispatched to locate the remains of the sunken submarine *K-129*. Commanded by Moore, the *Halibut* carried 13 officers, 123 enlisted men, and 6 technical specialists as she departed Pearl Harbor. The *Halibut* sought to locate the "target object"—as the *K-129* wreckage would be called in official documents—from late April to late May 1968. The code name used by some Navy offices for the search was Velvet Fist.

The nuclear "spy sub" reached the search area some 1,600 nautical miles northwest of Oahu and, using satellite navigation, planted a series of acoustic transponders. Launched through the submarine's bow torpedo tubes, these devices came to rest on the ocean floor where they would each transmit a "ping" when interrogated by the *Halibut*. Each "ping" was coded so that an acoustic grid could be mapped on board the *Halibut* to determine the area being photographed by the Fish. The accuracy of the grid was about 500 yards at the depth of three miles, with transponder responses being received by both the *Halibut* and the Fish. Within 36 hours the acoustic grid was established on the ocean floor.

Then began the tedious task of launching and towing the Fish. Sonar images transmitted through the Fish tow cable were carefully studied in the Bat Cave as technicians sought to identify potential targets on the ocean floor. *Halibut* sailor Roger Dunham recalled the monotonous operation of towing the Fish—using the fictitious name "*Viperfish*" for the submarine:

> Because it was essential for the Fish to remain a specific distance above the bottom of the ocean, in order to prevent its destruction by contact with terrain irregularities, precise submarine depth control

was mandatory. Alternatively, if the *Viperfish* pulled the Fish too high above the bottom, its ability to "see" anything below it would be compromised. . . .

The speed of the vessel also dramatically affected by the altitude of the Fish above the ocean floor; if the *Viperfish* inadvertently slowed for a few seconds, the Fish could easily sink and be destroyed against rocks or ridges. Cable length had a nearly immediate effect on the Fish's altitude and careful control of the spool rotation was top priority. Reactor power and turbogenerator power were essential to operation of the Special Project's computer system that analyzed information from the Fish. Finally, the *Viperfish*'s buoyancy, depth, and direction, which were controlled by the ballast control operator, the planesman, and helmsman required close communication and teamwork.[9]

This complex operation was astutely orchestrated by Moore as day after day the *Halibut* trawled in the area where the "event" had been recorded. Dunham later wrote, "As time passed, we all became increasingly frustrated. We experimented with different methods of moving the boat, and we varied circular patterns and Fish elevations. Each new trial consumed days at a time and resulted in nothing."[10]

The *Halibut*'s search phase employed the Fish-mounted sonar to identify several seafloor objects of potential interest within the area. Preparations were made to begin using the Fish-mounted camera when there was a failure in the cable slip-ring assembly in the sail structure. The *Halibut* sailors, always innovative, jury-rigged a solution that enabled the search to resume. The photographic phase of the search continued with the Fish periodically reeled back into the submarine to recover the camera film. Sometime later, as the film was being developed, a photographer came running into the captain's stateroom saying, "I think we have found our target." The remains of the Soviet submarine had been located.

After a period of intensive photographic coverage during which more than 20,000 photos were taken, the Fish was retrieved for the last time and stowed, and the *Halibut* headed back to Pearl Harbor. It was none too soon: her nuclear fuel was all but exhausted. After a stopover at Pearl, and transfer of the photos that showed the *K-129* wreckage to personnel who would transport them to Washington, the *Halibut* went on to Mare Island, arriving in

These images show the remains of the *K-129* as seen from the capture vehicle's video cameras. The 130-foot section was sought for the possible R-21 missile warhead that was believed to remain in the damaged tube in the sail structure, as well as cryptographic material. The submarine's after section, housing the submarine's engineering spaces and stern torpedo tubes, lay about 100 yards away.

August for refueling and additional modifications. Her Sand Dollar mission had begun about mid-July and ended in early September.

In Washington submarine and intelligence analysts pored over the trove of photographs showing the wreckage of the *K-129*. The *Halibut* had justified the faith shown by Craven, Moore, and several members of the intelligence community in pursuing the submarine's second career. And she would go on to further accomplishments as a "spy sub." For the success in seeking the remains of the *K-129*, Commander Moore was presented the Distinguished Service Medal in Washington, D.C., on September 19, 1968. The *Halibut* and her crew were awarded the Presidential Unit Citation, the highest award given to a naval ship in peacetime, on September 27, 1968. The carefully crafted citation read, in part,

> For exceptional meritorious service in support of National Research and Development efforts while serving as a unit in the Submarine Force, U.S. Pacific Fleet. Conducting highly technical submarine operations, over an extended period of time, USS HALIBUT (SSN 587) successfully concluded several missions of significant scientific value to the Government of the United States. The professional, military, and technical competence, and inspiring devotion to duty of HALIBUT's officers and men, reflect great credit upon themselves and the United States Naval Service.

Several sources reported that President Nixon had secretly flown to Oahu at that time and personally presented the award to the *Halibut* and her crew.[11] But the date of the actual presentation was September 27, 1968, when Lyndon Johnson was still president. (Nixon may have presented the second Presidential Unit Citation award to the *Halibut* in 1972 for "special missions.") Rather, the 1968 award was presented by Admiral John Hyland, the Commander-in-Chief U.S. Pacific Fleet.[12]

The *Halibut*'s next series of special missions—beyond the scope of this book—would earn the remarkable "white whale" a second Presidential Unit Citation. These were part of the Ivy Bells program in which, using especially equipped (saturation) divers, the *Halibut* would tap into Soviet offshore communication cables, including those from Petropavlovsk to the Siberian mainland. The *Halibut*'s subsequent operations, however, were in reality controlled by the National Underwater Reconnaissance Office (NURO). This activity was established in 1970 as a counterpart to the National Reconnaissance Office (NRO), the joint CIA–Air Force, super-secret agency that had been created in 1960, to coordinate U.S. "overhead" reconnaissance by U-2 spyplanes and satellites. The NURO was a joint CIA–Navy activity. In time, the CIA would gain sufficient influence in the "underwater business" to take absolute control of Project Azorian.

The photographs taken by the *Halibut* brought ecstatic response in Washington from Craven; Rear Admiral F. J. (Fritz) Harlfinger, the new head of naval intelligence and a veteran submariner; and Captain James Bradley, the assistant for undersea warfare in the Office of Naval Intelligence in the Pentagon.[13] There were some 9,000 useable *Halibut* photos showing wreckage of the submarine. As Sherman Wetmore, who would serve on board the *Hughes Glomar Explorer*, would remark, "Each frame . . . was like looking at an elephant from three inches away and you couldn't tell what you were looking at until somebody put it together in a collage that did make some sense."[14]

What the *Halibut* photos showed was the wreckage of the *K-129* lying on her starboard side. The submarine had broken into two sections, probably when she struck the ocean floor. The *K-129* had fallen to the ocean floor—a distance of some three miles—at a sink rate of about 12 knots. This estimate is based on actual data from the sinking of the U.S. target submarine *Sterlet* (SS 391) in 1969, which had been fitted with appropriate instrumentation, and analytical modeling.

But beginning in 1998 with publication of the book *Blind Man's Bluff*, there have been statements that the *K-129* reached a velocity of 200 knots as she fell three miles to the ocean floor. A velocity of 200 knots, however, would have carried away a submarine's sail structure, diving planes, and rudder, and possibly the "light" outer hull of the double-hull *K-129*. The *K-129* was relatively intact except for the massive damage to the after section of the sail, and the breaking of the hull into two sections, the latter most likely occurring when she struck the ocean floor. Still, several subsequent published accounts credit the *K-129* with having descended at some 200 knots.[15]

The forward section included the missile compartment. The after section, about 100 yards away, contained the engineering compartments and stern torpedo tubes. The first few feet of the submarine's bow—ahead of the pressure hull—had also broken off. The photography revealed that the submarine's snorkel intake mast, a periscope, and antenna were in the raised position, indicating that the *K-129* was at periscope/snorkel depth when the "incident" occurred.

Significantly, the after portion of the sail structure was torn away. The missing portion of the sail contained the two aftermost R-21 missile tubes; the tubes and their missiles were gone. The forward missile tube remained; while damage was visible, the cap to the No. 1 missile tube appeared intact, indicating that the missile could have survived the mishap and sinking. The forward section—which would be the target of Project Azorian—was 136 feet long.

Other details were clearly visible in the *Halibut* photos. Raymond Feldman, an engineer who later worked on the recovery project, later recalled, "I remember seeing one of the photographs . . . a sailor . . . lying on the bottom . . . just a skeleton . . . no clothes . . . no foul weather gear . . . just a skeleton . . . with boots on."[16] (Later press accounts told of the skeleton wearing foul weather gear, "proving" that the submarine was on the surface at the time of the fatal event.)

As they looked at the mass of *Halibut* photographs, excitement seemed to pulse though Craven, Harlfinger, Bradley, and others. The images of the *K-129* showed that, although severely damaged, the forward section of the submarine's hull appeared to still contain a relatively intact missile tube and, quite possibly, an R-21 missile. And, now the U.S. Navy knew its location and condition—and the Soviet Navy did not.

THE PLAN

Historically, all submarine salvage operations were undertaken with the use of cables or chains passed under the stricken submarine. This procedure required the use of large pontoons or specialized lift ships rigged for handling cables. Divers were required for these operations, limiting submarine salvage to depths of a few hundred feet at most. Before 1974 the deepest submarine salvage effort had been the raising of the USS *Squalus* (SS 192) from a depth of 245 feet off Portsmouth, New Hampshire, in 1939. The U.S. Navy in 1968 was developing the Large Object Salvage System (LOSS) to recover a submarine—with the use of divers—from a depth of about 1,000 feet.

Even if divers were not required, such salvage procedures would be difficult if not impossible in the heavy seas of the northern Pacific, even in summer, and such operations could not be clandestine. The Soviets would certainly keep watch on such activities by communication intercepts, by long-range aircraft, and even by surface ships.

Thus, a totally innovative approach to raising the *K-129* was required, one that could lift a submarine from a depth beyond all existing or even proposed salvage systems. And the effort would have to be totally denied to Soviet surveillance. Such an endeavor was far beyond the capabilities and investment resources of the Navy although, it was thought, the Navy could benefit greatly from the access to such a submarine, its weapons, cryptographic equipment, and possibly even its important publications.

Accordingly, discussions of the feasibility of recovering "components" from the *K-129* took place between technical representatives of the CIA, the Office of the Secretary of Defense, and the Navy in late 1968 and early 1969.[1] Based on these exchanges, on April 1, 1969, Deputy Secretary of Defense David Packard asked the Director of Central Intelligence, Richard Helms, to undertake a study of the feasibility of recovering significant "components" of the submarine during the "next few years."[2]

While the Navy and intelligence agencies of the Department of Defense had great interest in the recovery of submarine-related equipment and related analysis of the *K-129*, the Defense Department and, subsequently, then–National Security Advisor Henry Kissinger were primarily interested in the one-megaton warhead of the submarine's remaining R-21 missile and related guidance system. CIA officials never have acknowledged publicly that the missile warhead and guidance were the principal object of the Azorian effort. However, in 1994 Army Lieutenant General Daniel O. Graham, who served as CIA deputy director from 1973 to 1974 and as director of the Defense Intelligence Agency from 1974 to 1975, stated that retrieval of the R-21 warhead "would have given us better data points on their nuclear technology," and "That was a worthwhile endeavor, as far as I was concerned."[3] This primary objective of the effort being recovery of an R-21 missile's nuclear warhead was confirmed to one of the authors of this book as recently as 2009 by a retired U.S. Navy captain who had been in the Department of Defense involved with nuclear issues in the early 1970s.[4]

But how could a nuclear-armed missile and, if possible, the entire forward section of the *K-129* be recovered—and clandestinely—from a depth of more than 16,000 feet?

By July 1969 the CIA had initiated a program to develop the means to recover the *K-129* missile and possibly other equipment. The CIA task force for Project Azorian was established on July 1, with John Parangosky as head of the team. He had held key roles in the agency's development of the U-2 and A-12 spyplanes and reconnaissance satellites. His deputy was Navy Captain Ernest J. (Zeke) Zellmer, a senior CIA officer who had served in submarines during World War II.

On August 8 the CIA team outlined a preliminary plan to an Executive Committee (ExComm) consisting of Helms, Packard, and presidential science advisor Dr. Lee DuBridge. The ExComm approved the plan, including its organization and the allocation of resources and personnel to the recovery

The mystery man of Project Azorian was CIA official John Parangosky. He was head of the Azorian team at CIA headquarters and, in many respects, was the driving force behind the project. This rare photograph of the man is believed to have been taken in Iran; a U.S. Air Force C-117 Skytrain/Dakota is in the background. (Courtesy Chris Pocock)

effort. It was decided to inform Nixon of the plan; this was done in a memorandum from Dr. Kissinger, which the president approved.

Within the CIA a new security compartment—code-named Jennifer—was established to further separate the actual Azorian effort from other classified programs. The name "Jennifer" had originated within the Navy when Captain Bradley asked his colleague, Commander Brad Mooney, for suggestions of a code name to help further hide the *K-129* salvage effort. Mooney, a *Trieste* pilot and submariner, suggested Jennifer—his daughter's name. The CIA history noted,

From the beginning, extraordinary security was imposed and clearances severely limited to those with an absolute need-to-know. It was clear at all stages of the AZORIAN Project that it had to be leak-proof to enable the mission to be conducted without diplomatic or physical interference from the Soviets.[5]

Parangosky and his team immediately began to examine possible methods for raising the remains of the *K-129*. At least four basic lift concepts were considered: (1) "brute force"—using massive winches on surface craft and wire ropes, (2) a "drill-string"—a three-mile "string" of connected pipes from the surface with a "claw" at the end, (3) "trade ballast/buoyancy"—buoyant material that would be carried down to the submarine using excess ballast that would be released after the buoyancy material was attached to the submarine, and (4) "gas generation"—creating the necessary buoyancy "at depth" to lift the submarine. Ironically, the drill-string was discarded early in the discussions for two reasons: because it was too difficult to envision how the massive length of interconnected pipes could be employed, and because the weight of the pipe itself would be too great for a salvage lift of the stricken submarine.

By July 1970—after a year of pondering methods to lift the *K-129*'s remains—"brute force" was clearly the favored system. At an ExComm meeting on October 30, 1970, the concept of lifting the estimated 1,750-ton "target object" from 16,500 feet was described, to be accomplished by mounting heavy-lift winches on a surface ship 565 feet long with a beam of 106 feet. About this time the probability of success of the operation was estimated at about ten percent. The estimate would continue to rise, as would costs, but the promise of recovering a Soviet nuclear-tipped missile and possibly its guidance technology continued to justify the program.

Meanwhile, another approach to the salvage was being developed, employing the drill-string or pipe-string technique. On November 3, 1969, CIA officials met with Curtis Crooke, vice president of engineering of Global Marine of Los Angeles. Crooke later recalled that two CIA officials showed up at his office: "They walked in my door and closed it, and my office door was never shut. They wanted to know if my company could build something to lift something of so many tons and in about 15 to 20,000 feet of water."[6]

The CIA had approached Global Marine because by 1969 the firm was operating several deep-sea drill ships, primarily in support of the oil industry. The firm had pioneered the concept when it took delivery of the pioneer drill ship *Cuss I,* the converted 260-foot Navy barge *YFN 730.*[7] The *Cuss I* was innovative because it could drill into the ocean floor without anchoring the vessel by the use of thrusters for dynamic positioning. She was able to keep a precise location based on sonar bearings to moored buoys. Such a positioning system would be required if the ship were to maintain position in very deep water, beyond the depths in which anchoring was possible. The *Cuss I*—like other drill ships—was distinguished by the tall pipe-assembly tower, resembling an oil-drilling derrick, and the stacks of 60-foot "double-length" pipes on her deck. During March–April 1961—in National Science Foundation–sponsored Project Mohole—the *Cuss I* drilled into the earth's crust off the coast of Guadalupe, Mexico. The ship successfully drilled 600 feet into the crust in water 11,680 feet deep.

Three other deep-sea drill ships were converted by Global Marine, and in 1967 construction was begun on the 393½-foot *Glomar Challenger.*[8] Completed in August 1968, she would operate under a long-term contract from the National Science Foundation. This ship was built with thrusters for dynamic positioning that could enable her to maintain a precise location for several days while drilling seafloor core samples. Over the next 15 years, the *Glomar Challenger* would drill cores around the world, the deepest water being 20,483 feet. In 1970, in a remarkable example of station keeping and deep-sea drilling, the *Glomar Challenger* drilled a hole in the ocean floor at a depth of 10,000 feet off New York City, withdrew the drill bit, and maintained position precise enough to enable a new bit to be placed in the same drill hole. Significantly, the technique did not rely on holding the ship in a precise location, but in knowing where the bottom of the free-swinging drill-string (the drill bit) was located in relation to the hole. A sonar transponder lowered through the drill pipe was able to locate a 16-foot-diameter cone that had been drilled into the seabed.

The firm's success in seafloor drilling provided the obvious path to deep-sea salvage. After the initial CIA discussion with Curtis Crooke, additional members of the firm were brought into the "fold," including the firm's chief engineer and principal naval architect, John R. Graham. Described as a "very motivated or driven person, obvious workaholic, and very demand-ing, . . . [h]e demanded results and he demanded [them] of himself just as much as he did [of] anyone else . . . [and] he was the hardest working individual there."[9] Graham became the principal in the design of the *Glomar Explorer* and the related systems.

Global Marine subsequently served as prime contractor for the project with Global Marine Development Inc. (GMDI) established to actually handle the salvage program, and with Curtis Crooke as its president as well as vice president of Global Marine Inc. Thus, the bureaucratic labyrinth was being created to retain tight control over the various aspects of the salvage effort while hiding both the purpose and the ownership of the effort. The major subcontractors included Lockheed Ocean Systems Division for the actual lift device and the Hughes Tool Company to develop and produce the pipe-string. Scores of people were hired by GMDI and its subcontractors—engineers, naval architects, draftsmen, and specialists of every sort; some were "read into" the real Azorian project, and others were hired on a com-pletely unclassified basis.

Ray Feldman was taken on by Lockheed. He was contacted because some years earlier he had worked on the top-secret Corona satellite program. Parangosky and his CIA colleagues were reaching out to former colleagues. Feldman later recalled,

> They contacted me and said they needed someone who was really knowledgeable on digital systems and said they were involved in a proj-ect that would be mining minerals on the ocean floor . . . and would I be interested.
>
> I said I was very interested . . . and so they arranged an interview with the supervisor on the program.
>
> After some negotiating back and forth I was told that they'd love to have me on board the program . . . and after I was briefed on what was actually happening, what the mission was actually about . . . I was a bit shocked.
>
> Well first I thought . . . oh God another black program . . . and then after speaking about it more I wondered could this be possible . . . could we actually achieve something like this.[10]

At this time the CIA required more information about the site where the *K-129* rested—the soil properties of the seabed where the target object was partially buried—to enable development of the lift devices. The submarine's hulk had slid down a gentle slope, and had dug into the bottom silt. On May 15, 1970, the go-ahead was given to Global Marine to use the small drill ship *Glomar II* for a survey *near* the submarine's location. She was provided with thrusters for position keeping, and she was fitted with cameras, coring devices, and grab buckets. The *Glomar II* undertook two search missions to refine the information about the ocean floor near the wreckage. These missions were of limited value; indeed, one ended with a drill-pipe failure and lost search and recovery devices. Subsequently, another ship, the research ship *Seascope*, an ex-Navy minesweeper, was chartered and outfitted with a winch, several miles of wire, and a bucket device. She, too, sailed to a nearby area in early 1972 and used the bucket to scoop up manganese nodules—part of the cover story—and some soil samples.

These 1970–1972 operations of Global Marine ships did not go unnoticed. The Soviet Pacific Fleet headquarters, upon learning of the *Glomar II*'s appearance in the North Pacific, dispatched the large intelligence collection ship *Gidrograf* to observe the U.S. ship; a short time later she was joined by the submarine rescue ship *SS-23* employed in the shadowing role.[11] Soviet sensitivity to the *Glomar II* operation was due to a note that had been passed to the Soviet Embassy in Washington—believed to have been addressed to the naval attaché. Reportedly, the anonymous letter was dated October 22, 1970, and stated,

> In March 1968 a Soviet submarine sank in the Pacific. The U.S. Central Intelligence Agency is using the minesweeping [*sic*] vessel Glomar to hunt for the submarine; she departed Honolulu 17 October and will be at the point latitude 40° North, longitude 180° East in early November. A Well-Wisher.[12]

A possible source for the note has been considered by many in the U.S. intelligence community to have been John A. Walker, a U.S. Navy warrant officer, who began spying for the Soviets in 1967 or 1968. At the time the *K-129* was lost he was a watch officer and message center officer at the headquarters of the Submarine Force, U.S. Atlantic Fleet, and would certainly have had

The diminutive drill ship *Glomar II*, shown here when named *Cuss II*, made early probes of the ocean floor at the site of the *K-129*. Soviet naval intelligence took an immediate interest in U.S. commercial surface ship activities in the area, but saw no indications of any military or intelligence activities.

access to the most secret U.S. Navy communications on the subject. However, Walker was spying for money and it was unlikely he would have sent anonymous information to the Soviets, and by that time he had a message delivery system well established with the KGB.[13]

Rear Admiral Dygalo later said, "I know this issue came up in the General Headquarters and was brought to the attention of the Commander-in-Chief [Admiral Sergei Gorshkov]. But because of the depth . . . the doubt about the technical feasibility prevailed."[14]

While the CIA sought information on the character of the ocean floor where the *K-129*'s remains rested, the decision had been made to proceed with the pipe-string lift concept. Two factors became manifest from the start of the effort: First, this would be a unique recovery system, unparalleled in size and complexity, and the first ever to operate at these depths and loads. Second, the system design was based on a one-time operation, not a series of repetitive test and development actions such as would occur with a new aircraft.[15]

By March 1971, Global Marine and the Sun Shipbuilding and Dry Dock Company in Chester, Pennsylvania, had completed design of a specialized lift ship. The Sun shipyard, which had been building merchant-type ships since 1917, was highly innovative, having constructed some of the first roll-on/roll-off vehicle cargo ships and supertankers constructed in the United States. The yard also built the advanced gas-turbine vehicle ship *Admiral W. M. Callaghan* for the U.S. Navy and converted the large tanker *Manhattan* for her two pioneering ice-breaking voyages through the Northwest Passage. Crooke later observed, "I must say Sun did a tremendous job and they had a terrific engineering group going . . . which took all of Global's engineering work and reduced it to the construction drawings."[16] The ship's design was centered on the massive internal, fully enclosed docking well or "moon pool." This feature prevented the ship from having a traditional keel—the main center-line structural member of a ship's hull, running fore and aft along the bottom of the ship.

Derived from seafloor oil-drilling technology, the basic concept was developed by Crooke and his colleagues John R. Graham and James F. McNary. Their design was subsequently summarized as

> a deep ocean mining ship in which heavy mining equipment can be raised between the vessel and the ocean floor. The ship includes a large well in the center thereof which passes through and is enclosed by the hull. This well is closable across the bottom by moveable gates. The vessel also includes a pipe handling system for moving mining pipe sections between a storage position and the drill string extending from the vessel to the mining machine and to support the mining machine.
>
> Two vertically movable, tiltable legs, one located at the forward end and one located at the aft end of a large open well internal to the hulls of a vessel for deep ocean mining operations for docking and undocking a subsurface mining vehicle and for raising and lowering the mining vehicle into or out of the well. Each leg includes a panel at the lower end thereof for engaging pins on the mining vehicle.[17]

John Graham.

The Sun shipyard began construction of the lift ship in May 1971 as the yard's hull No. 661. In the same period contracts were awarded for the several major systems.

In Washington, the Ex-Comm meeting of August 4, 1971, was the first of a number of recurring occasions on which Project Azorian almost foundered because of increasing costs and estimates of the operational risks. At that first meeting, Deputy Secretary of Defense Packard stated that he considered it necessary to terminate Azorian for those reasons. According to the CIA history, "Each time, however, consideration of the intelligence potential carried the day."[18]

In some respects as important as the lift capability itself was the development of a cover story to hide the CIA effort—from friendly as well as unfriendly eyes. This aspect of Project Azorian was especially difficult because the Soviet Navy would certainly be conducting surveillance of the general area. At the same time, an unusual surface ship of any configuration would draw press attention in the United States.

It is not clear who—within the CIA or elsewhere—came up with the idea of having Howard Hughes "sponsor" the salvage effort under the "cover" of a seafloor-mining venture. CIA officials knew that there was a group within Lockheed developing the concept of seafloor mining for mineral nodules. The cover story was a stroke of genius. The CIA contacted Hughes and the billionaire recluse immediately offered his assistance. The Hughes empire was the perfect "front" for the endeavor: it was a collection of privately owned corporations, not responsible to stockholders or to the Securities Exchange Commission. And Hughes was known for undertaking unusual projects. As Curtis Crooke observed, he had a very general mystique to him and he had been involved in all sorts of things and so he was an ideal person to lay this off to and nobody would really question that you are gonna go in the deep sea mining business.

Crooke continued:

And we liked the deep sea mining as a cover because, one, we knew a little something about it and really we had done a little bit of work in the mining business for Kennecott Copper and Collier Carbon . . . it was a logical story and you could design a mining ship because who knew what a mining ship looks like?

Then Crooke explained—to the extent that it could be explained by anyone—how the finances were handed between Global Marine, Hughes, and the CIA:

[W]e did have to figure out how to make money move back and forth . . . it was very easy. We [Global Marine] had a commercial contract—a white open commercial contract—with the Hughes Tool Company. And [we] also had a black contract with him. . . . We did eventually have a black contract with the federal government so that there was no question as to who owned what and where the money was coming from. And Hughes then did provide the pipeline for moving the money back and forth. We used to bill Hughes and in the white and unclassified or unsecured accounting department they didn't know any difference. They thought they were billing Hughes . . . at the same time out of another office [they] were billing the federal government.

Hughes then would move the money to Global Marine and it juggled around. I never really understood exactly how it worked.[19]

Indeed, few people anywhere in the Byzantine empire of the Azorian project fully understood the convoluted methods of accounting—or the title and legal ownership of the lift ship.

At the July 28, 1972, ExComm meeting the ever-increasing cost of the project was discussed, although the CIA has continued to classify the costs of the effort.[20] These increasing costs were caused by modifications to the ship, including the provision of a sewerage system to meet new maritime ecological standards, and a second, more-expensive subcontractor being brought into the pipe-string production to meet the tight delivery schedule. Operational deployment was planned for the summer of 1974.

It was agreed at the July 28 meeting that the president's Forty Committee should be asked for an early evaluation of the *political feasibility* of conducting the mission in mid-1974 in light of increasing concern that by that time the political climate might prohibit mission approval. The Forty Committee, chaired by then–National Security Advisor Henry Kissinger, was the president's mechanism for approving covert activities by the CIA. The "Forty" approved almost 40 CIA actions between 1972 and 1974.[21]

But there were significant questions being raised about Project Azorian. On August 15, Kenneth Rush, the Deputy Secretary of Defense, sent to CIA director Helms copies of three memorandums from Admiral Elmo R. Zumwalt, the Chief of Naval Operations; Dr. Albert Hall, the Assistant Secretary of Defense (Intelligence); and Vice Admiral Vincent de Poix, the director of the Defense Intelligence Agency. All three documents expressed concern that the value of the intelligence to be gained was less than the ExComm estimated and argued either termination of Azorian or (Zumwalt) that the cost-benefits be further studied. Subsequently, Admiral Thomas Moorer, Chairman of the Joint Chiefs of Staff, sent a memo to the Forty Committee on August 28 stating that he could not support Azorian, primarily because of the decreased intelligence value of the *K-129* with the passage of time since her loss, the escalating costs, and the possibility of strong reaction from the Soviet Union if the mission were detected.

Helms countered on September 14 with a memo to Kissinger that argued for the continuation of Azorian. The head of the CIA believed that the intelligence value of the submarine was significant.

> He further believed the technical risks were acceptable in view of the expected intelligence value, and that a political judgment as to whether to conduct the mission could be made satisfactorily only at mission time. He also believed the risk of further significant cost increase was low, and that in any case the costs recoverable if the program were terminated would be small.[22]

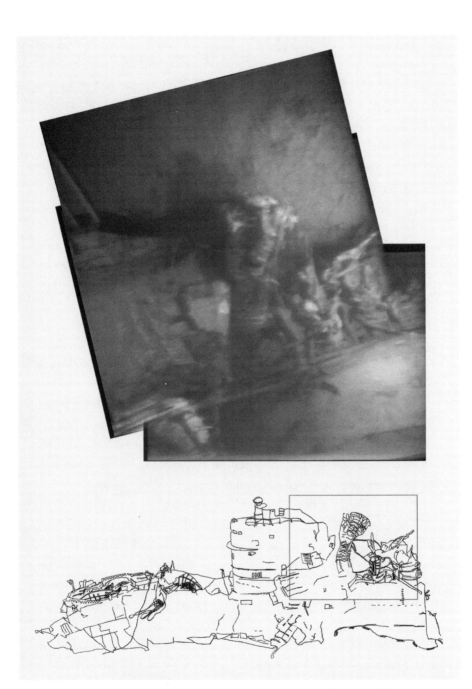

Project Azorian's primary goal was to recover the nuclear warhead on the R-21 missile believed to have survived in this damaged tube of the *K-129*. The light-colored tube cap implied that the missile was still in the tube. The raised periscopes and masts of the submarine, visible at far left in these video images, indicate that she was most likely at periscope depth when catastrophic events occurred.

Arguing against the salvage plan, Rush, the No. 2 man in the Defense Department, declared that because of the ongoing, favorable political relationship and negotiations with the Soviet Union it was "undesirable" to execute Azorian as planned. The Soviets, he believed, would "react strongly with physical force" if they learned of the mission while the project was under way, and U.S.–Soviet relationships would be "seriously damaged" if they learned of it afterwards. At the time, the estimated chances of technical success were put at 20 to 30 percent based on the existing program schedule and budget. However, Rush did share Helms's concern about the effects of termination on contractor relationships because the major contractors had committed themselves to a large, highly publicized ocean mining endeavor. "Helms felt that a termination now would appear capricious to contractors and jeopardize future cooperative efforts with the intelligence community when contractor support would be needed."[23]

One former intelligence officer has asked why Helms would override the concerns of the Secretary of Defense, Chief of Naval Operations, Chairman of the Joint Chiefs of Staff, and director of the Defense Intelligence Agency. This officer suggests that it was "Only because another player was very keen on continuing the mission. While AEC [Atomic Energy Commission] is a possible voice lobbying for continuation—the most logical heavyweight would be NSA [National Security Agency]."[24] Would the NSA, the nation's largest intelligence organization, covet the cryptologic material enough to warrant overriding the views of the other members of the intelligence community as well as the nation's senior military officials?

Subsequently, Rush established a review panel under Hall to again look into technical risks and costs of the program. The panel reported back to Rush on December 11 that program management had been "highly effective with the result that all key phases of the program were on schedule."[25] The report—still heavily censored by the CIA as of this writing—concluded,

1. The saving to the government, if AZORIAN were terminated, would range between [censored] depending upon the effectiveness of the cover operation and availability of a competitive market.
2. Should the program be continued, the estimated cost growth could range from [censored] assuming that the mission was accomplished on the planned date.

3. Current schedule and program office planning should allow the mission to be performed on the target date [summer 1974].

4. There was no way to test the full system in advance of the actual lift operation, and engineering unknowns at the time provided the greatest uncertainty in the program.

The Azorian debate ended on December 11 when, "After the most intensive, detailed, and broad-based examination to date of all facets of the program, the final decision, made by the President [Nixon], was to continue the AZORIAN project."[26]

The purpose of the *Glomar Explorer* "required a design incorporating unique solutions which were well beyond the state-of-the art in numerous engineering and scientific disciplines, particularly mechanical engineering."[27] Much of the specialized design features and the equipment of the ship were derived from the offshore oil–drilling industry, a field pioneered by Global Marine.

Beyond the lowering of a "capture vehicle" or "claw" at the end of a pipe-string and then recovering the submarine, the system would have to raise the capture vehicle, submarine hulk, and pipe-string up through an open well. There would be strong dynamic forces at work in the North Pacific even in summer, and it would be necessary to hold the ship in an exact position over the three-mile pipe-string. As the *K-129* was raised it would be necessary to ensure perfect alignment with the opening of the docking well or moon pool. And, of course, the recovery had to be unobservable by outsiders. The specific engineering features in the ship that were considered unique and representative of major advances in mechanical engineering design were:

*   A massive gimbaled platform to isolate the suspended load from the ship's dynamic pitch and roll; thus, regardless of the ship's motion, the platform—on which the pipe-lowering system was mounted—would remain stable.
*   Hydraulic/pneumatic heave compensation system to prevent the ship's heave (vertical) motion from dynamically affecting the suspended load (i.e., pipe-string).
*   Hydraulic hoisting system to lower and raise massive loads via the pipe-string.

The massive moon pool of the *Hughes Glomar Explorer* was a driving factor in the ship's design, the size of which was dictated by the dimensions of the capture vehicle and the hoped-for prize of a 130-foot section of the submarine *K-129*. The mechanism at the far end of the moon pool was for raising and lowering the docking leg. Note the man standing at the end of the moon pool.

The complexity of the *Hughes Glomar Explorer*'s heavy lift system is evident in this photo of her derrick-like tower structure. The pipe-string had to be raised and lowered more than 16,000 feet with the entire pipe-handling system fully stabilized against ship motion. The ship and lift system comprised the most capable ocean engineering facility ever developed.

- Pipe-handling gear to convey pipe sections to the hydraulic heavy-lift system.
- Massive enclosed center well—moon pool—capable of being flooded and pumped dry, with sliding bottom doors or "gates."
- Docking system to permit a massive, 2,000-ton capture recovery vehicle —with or without target object—to be mated with the ship in a dynamic seaway.

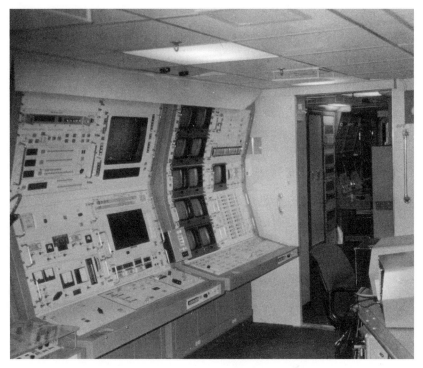

This view of one of the ship's control vans shows the complexity of the control and monitoring systems for Project Azorian. These vans—for a variety of purposes related to the salvage operation—turned the *Hughes Glomar Explorer* from a "white" ship into a highly secret "black" ship.

- Dynamic positioning system using bow- and stern-fitted thrusters to enable the ship to maintain station in a seaway.

These features that had previously been incorporated in drill ships were provided on a substantially larger scale in the *Glomar Explorer*. For example, the gimbaled platform's outer ring was 40 by 40 feet, with four gimbal bearings that were unique in size and design, each with a capacity of 5,000 tons, i.e., able to support up to 20,000 tons—the lift system pipe-string, capture vehicle, and submarine. Similarly, the heave compensation system—essentially a giant spring—used two massive, hydraulic rams to mitigate the vertical motion of the ship while the pipe-string was suspended.

The hydraulic/pneumatic hoisting system had an 8,000-ton capacity, the expected weight of a 17,000-foot pipe-string, the capture vehicle, and the target object. The system was designed for a constant lifting/lowering speed of 18 feet of pipe per minute, although actual operations would be conducted at a slower rate. The ship had deck stowage for 17,000 feet of pipe, assembled in 60-foot lengths, weighing in total about 4,250 tons. The handling system enabled the pipe to be easily and continuously moved to the hoisting system day or night, under most weather conditions.

The docking system for the capture vehicle was another highly innovative feature. It had to stabilize a 4,000-ton load suspended from a single point (i.e., the pipe-string) in a dynamic seaway and to hoist it into the narrow confines of the ship's center well. The system had two semirigid structural arms or "docking legs" that could be lowered beneath the hull, at either end of the docking well, to engage massive "pins" at both ends of the capture vehicle and guide it up and into the center well. During docking and undocking the 200-foot docking legs could tilt up to seven degrees fore and aft, facilitating recovery in a seaway. When not in use these docking legs were retracted vertically and protruded upward, through the main deck, fore and aft of the pipe-hoisting system.

The *Glomar Explorer* was a huge ship: 618 feet, 8 inches long with a beam of 115 feet, 8½ inches. Originally, the ship was to have had a beam of just under 106 feet to allow passage through the Panama Canal's 110-foot locks when the ship sailed to the Pacific. Charles Cannon, a naval architect at Global Marine, later recalled that the ten-foot increase in beam, "was all driven by lack of stability, and a fear that we still didn't have a good handle on topside weights like the heave compensator gimbaled platform, pipe-handling equipment, A frame, hydraulic hoses, etc."[28] Thus, stability was enhanced by increasing the beam, but at the cost of requiring the ship to travel to the Pacific around Cape Horn, about a 50-day voyage.

The ship's size, especially the moon pool, was dictated in large part to incorporate the various special features needed to recover the sunken *K-129*. Sized to accommodate both the 2,000-ton capture vehicle and a submarine hull segment weighing up to 2,000 tons and approximately 136 feet long, the moon pool was 199 feet long and 74 feet wide with a minimum vertical clearance of 65 feet.[29] Two massive doors or "gates" closed the bottom of the moon pool. These gates were each 9-feet thick, 80-feet wide, and 98-feet long. They were motor driven and slid along tracks to close the bottom of the moon pool. Air was pumped into the gates, compressing a hard rubber seal, to force them upward to help seal the bottom of the moon pool so that it could be pumped dry.

Internally the ship incorporated all features found in a modern merchant ship—plus. There were accommodations for 178 people: single staterooms for the ship's senior officers and senior CIA officers, two-man staterooms for most of the ship's crew, and four-man staterooms for the technical staff and "others." Modern kitchen and dining facilities were fitted, with an excellent galley staff provided that would provide highly palatable food, and plenty of it.

The lift ship was launched at the Sun shipyard on November 4, 1972, and was christened with champagne by Mrs. James R. Lesch, wife of the senior vice president of Hughes Tool Company. She named the "deep ocean mining vessel" the *Hughes Glomar Explorer*—after some debate. Global Marine executives had wanted the ship named the *Glomar Hughes Explorer*, in the fashion of the firm's other ships. The CIA—for unknown reasons—wanted the ship named *Hughes Glomar Explorer* and so she was. The usual speeches followed, telling of the great opportunities ahead of the ship for exploiting a new ocean industry.

The launching was a festival with shipyard employees, their families, and numerous guests attending the launching of a "secret project." The Navy destroyer *Lowry* (DD 770) was at the yard, open to public visiting, and there were exhibits of employee arts and crafts, a band concert, refreshments, and plenty of balloons for the children.

The *Glomar Explorer* went to sea on builder's trials on April 12, 1973. She easily passed under the Delaware Memorial Bridge as she sailed down the Delaware River to the open ocean because the upper, 28-foot section of the "derrick," which would rise to a height of 263 feet, had not yet been installed. There were 203 people on board from the shipyard, Global Marine, the American Bureau of Shipping, the Coast Guard, and, of course, the CIA's special project. All of the tests were successful as Sun shipbuilding personnel operated the ship, and only minor discrepancies were noted. The ship's pipe-handling system and other special features were not tested. Crooke later recalled, "I think up until a few days before the end [the shipyard workers] had no idea that it was anything but a commercial contract."[30] The ship returned to the shipyard early on April 15.

More work was undertaken to complete the ship, and on July 24 the *Glomar Explorer* again went to sea to test several special features, with Curtis Crooke as the overall test director. This time, once past the bridge, the 28-foot

A view of the *Hughes Glomar Explorer* showing the twin docking legs for the capture vehicle partially lowered. The ship had her bridge forward with accommodations and working spaces in the after superstructure. A small helicopter platform was fitted above the fantail.

upper section of the derrick was lifted from the deck by a floating crane and secured to the top of the pipe-handling structure.

After shallow-water tests off Delaware Bay, the ship proceeded south to deep water some 80 nautical miles northwest of Bermuda. There the automated station-keeping system was tested, as was the pipe-handling system, although the three miles of pipe for the salvage operation would not be loaded aboard until the ship reached Long Beach. The ship then proceeded to Bermuda for crew change and preparations for the transit around South America to her home port of Long Beach. All systems were "go" and the ship was ready in virtually all respects for her outfitting with "special" equipment.

At this stage, the *Glomar Explorer* was a white ship. There was no classified equipment or material on board; visitors saw only the unique and unusual features of the world's first large, seafloor mining ship. The stated purpose of the massive moon pool was to house the giant "vacuum cleaner" that would sweep up manganese nodules from the ocean floor.

The *Glomar Explorer* remained at Bermuda from August 9 to August 11 while a crew change was undertaken and all preparations were made for the 12,700-mile voyage around South America, planned to require just over 50 days at an average speed of 10.5 knots. The transit crew initially numbered 96: 47 crew members and 49 Global Marine engineers and technicians. The captain, Louis Kingma, was in charge of all ship's operations and maneuvering. However, from this time onward there would be a senior U.S. government representative on board who would be responsible for security and mission activities, although at this stage she was still a white ship. It is not clear from available CIA material whether, at this time, the CIA official was listed as ship's crew or, more likely, a Global Marine employee.

The ship got under way from Bermuda in the afternoon of August 11. The on-board naval architect from GMDI, Chuck Cannon, had a list of some 80 jobs that the crew and on-board engineers was to accomplish during the voyage. The ship rode well in good weather and even when 50- to 60-knot winds and 15- to 20-foot seas were encountered. On September 5 the ship anchored in Possession Bay on the island of South Georgia; two Chilean pilots embarked to guide the ship through the Strait of Magellan. The ship encountered a cold front and strong winds, but entered the Pacific Ocean without difficulty at about 3 PM on September 6. She was now in the same ocean as her target—the wreckage of the *K-129*. Heavy weather immediately encountered in the Pacific caused the ship to heave to for a brief period.

As the ship entered the port of Valparaiso late on September 12, a Chilean naval launch came alongside and told the *Glomar Explorer*'s officers of the military coup in the country that had begun early the day before, and the curfew that was then in effect. The launch took off the two Chilean pilots.

Immediately prior to the coup, a team of Global Marine personnel had flown from Los Angeles to Santiago with 28 boxes of parts and supplies for the ship and a bag of personal mail. Seven technicians were to board the ship at Valparaiso. After checking into their hotel, early on September 11 the Global Marine personnel were awakened by the sounds of the revolution in the streets. The Global Marine team was able to get permission to board the ship with all of their baggage, and the ship weighed anchor in the afternoon of the September 13.

The CIA history observed,

> The presence of a covert U.S. intelligence ship in a Chilean port during the military coup was a bizarre coincidence quite unrelated to the rumors that "the CIA had 200 agents in Chile for the sole purpose of ousting [President] Allende." There were no unfavorable incidents involving the ship, crew members, or the Global Marine representative.[31]

Without further incident, the *Global Explorer* steamed northward, arriving at Long Beach on September 30, 1973. She had traveled 12,745 nautical miles in 50 days, 7 hours, 30 minutes, at an average speed of 10.8 knots. Now she was ready for conversion from a "white" ship to a "black" ship.

SEVEN

GET READY, GET SET . . .

The *Hughes Glomar Explorer* arrived at her home port of Long Beach, California, on September 30, 1973, and was soon berthed at Pier E. The pier was a few hundred feet from the massive hangar on Terminal Island that housed the famed Spruce Goose flying boat. Built by Howard Hughes during World War II, the seaplane—the largest aircraft in the world—flew for less than a minute in 1947. While Hughes maintained the aircraft in prime condition, it was looked on by many as a gigantic hoax; several members of Congress called it a fraud visited on the U.S. government and the American people. Hughes, in collaboration with industrialist Henry Kaiser, had built the "Spruce Goose" as a prototype for a fleet of wooden aircraft that could fly troops and cargo across the Atlantic Ocean during World War II and that would be immune to U-boat attacks. This prototype was far behind schedule and far over budget.

But the *Glomar Explorer* was looked on by almost all who voiced an opinion as the harbinger of the future exploitation of the ocean's resources for the betterment of mankind. Again, the ocean mining cover story was reinforced, this time by the proximity of the Hughes aircraft and his ocean mining ship.

Before the ship undertook her mission there was much to be done with respect to the ship and, especially, the various subsystems. Time was a critical factor because weather in the North Pacific would permit lift operations only from July through mid-September. For planning purposes, 14 to 21 days were expected to be required for the actual positioning of the ship and conducting the salvage lift.

It would be more than a month before the *Glomar Explorer* went back to sea, and more than eight months before she departed Long Beach to recover the remains of the *K-129*. During this period the ship was converted from "white" to "black," being fitted with all of the equipment and machinery necessary to undertake history's most ambitious ocean recovery effort. And all preparations had to be conducted in the "open" because Soviet merchant ships continuously docked some 400 yards across the channel at Berth 10 and, of course the association with recluse Howard Hughes would continually garner press attention. The CIA report noted, "Even though the Soviet ships were close to the [ship] and had the opportunity for close inspection, there has been no evidence that the Soviets gained prior knowledge of its true mission, a tribute to the security precautions and mining cover lived by the ship's crew during West Coast mobilization."[1]

Among the first additions made to the ship was the installation of 24 mission vans. These were prefabricated, standard-size, 8 x 8 x 20–foot containers fitted with specialized gear, including two mission control vans and other vans equipped for communications; the ultrasonic cleaning and preservation of items recovered from the submarine; processing for the great volume of manuals, documents, and other papers expected to be recovered; drying spaces for handling documents and other items that would require special care; a darkroom for processing the photos that would be taken of all interesting material; waste handling to safeguard contaminated or radioactive material; decontamination for personnel who might be exposed to radioactivity from the submarine's nuclear weapons; dressing spaces for people requiring cleanup after possible contamination; and for wrapping and crating recovered items for shipment back to the United States. Work continued on board ship on many systems and equipment.

On January 11, 1974, the ship was moved from her berth to an outer anchorage in Long Beach Harbor. The principal reason for the move was the sagging morale of the trials crew after more than three months of working alongside the pier. Also affecting morale was Global Marine's confrontation with the local labor organization, the Marine Engineers Benevolent Association (MEBA). The MEBA had set up picket lines in an attempt to boycott the *Glomar Explorer*. This situation escalated on November 12 with mass picketing by about 100 persons, including what the CIA called "strong-arm types," after some of the marine crew decided that they wanted union representation.

The merchant sailors often felt that they were treated as second-class citizens compared to the lifting-system crews and other specialists and engineers on board the ship.[2] The resulting tense situation continued for about ten days, during which time the ship's crew and shipboard workers were harassed and delivery trucks were stopped. One secretary had her Volkswagen "bug" lifted off the ground by pickets when she tried to drive up to the gate, while others approaching the ship were cursed and threatened. Special security measures had to be put into effect to keep unwanted visitors off the ship. The union problem, added to technical problems, wreaked havoc with the ship's schedule. With the Christmas–New Year holidays approaching, departure for sea trials was delayed until mid-January 1974. The primary purpose of the trials was to test the pipe-handling and heavy-lift systems.

The *Glomar Explorer* pulled away from Pier E at 12:30 PM on January 11 and, with two union picket boats present, moved to an outer harbor anchorage. There the mining crew ran a practice double pipe—60 feet in length—through the system two or three times; the moon pool was flooded and the pipe-handling system tested, and the docking legs were lowered beneath the hull. Myriad problems were discovered and the system demonstrated limited reliability during the five days at the anchorage.

Still, it was decided to continue with trials because of the tight schedule if a lift effort was to be attempted during the summer of 1974. The *Glomar Explorer* subsequently sailed to a position about 160 nautical miles southwest of Long Beach. The trials also would include checks of the ship's station-keeping, control, and navigation systems. The ship arrived at the site late on January 19. The water depth in the trials area was some 12,500 feet.

The ship immediately dropped seafloor transponders as well as a wave-riding buoy, all intended to assist position-keeping over the submarine. On January 21 and 22 high seas and winds delayed further tests, including flooding the moon pool and opening the bottom doors or gates. On January 23 the weather abated, enabling the moon pool to be flooded, but as the bottom gates were being opened the operating machinery was damaged. The casualty occurred during heavy wave surges in the moon pool. The damage was severe and the gates had to be hauled to the closed position using rigging cables and winches. It was impossible to continue the trials and the *Glomar Explorer* arrived back in Long Beach Harbor on January 24, anchoring rather than coming alongside the pier, which she did later.

The well gates were examined, from within the moon pool and from under the ship by divers. Although the sea states encountered on the trials appear to have been within the upper limits of the specifications for opening and closing the bottom gates, the heavy seas stressed the system and caused the failure. After a thorough evaluation, engineers estimated about two weeks would be needed to accomplish repairs. With this work added to the lengthy list of work required, it was calculated that the ship could be ready to continue sea trials by mid-February.

The repairs to the moon pool gates and some of the other required work were difficult because there was no time to move the *Glomar Explorer* into a dry dock, with none that could accommodate the big ship being readily available. Thus, inspection and some of the work was undertaken by divers. One small but persistent leak was never corrected and the seepage of a few gallons of water into the moon pool per hour was accepted. The *Glomar Explorer*'s crew thus lived with a small puddle in the massive moon pool.

Major efforts were undertaken to ensure that the pipe-string handling system worked perfectly. Any problem with this system would immediately spell doom for the project: some three miles of pipe—lowering the capture vehicle or claw of some 2,000 tons and raising up to 4,000 tons—had to function flawlessly. The pipe-string consisted of 570 sections, each 30 feet long, a total weight of some 4,000 tons. Accordingly, the recovery system would have to be able to handle almost 8,000 tons.

Because of the high loads on the pipe, there was the need to "share" the load among all of the threads as the sections were connected. The "male" pipe ends were extremely tapered so there was no contact with the "female" threads until the pipe was about 80 percent embedded; then it would take only three turns of the pipe to bring it to full engagement, thus spreading the load among all the threads. By the time the pipe-string—with capture vehicle attached—reached the ocean floor it would have stretched about 40 feet.

The pipe material and the manufacturing process were derived from military specifications for producing large-bore gun barrels. To minimize the weight of the pipe-string yet meet the strength requirements, six different outer-pipe diameters were used, ranging from 15½ inches to 12¾ inches, with all pipes having a constant, 6-inch inner diameter. Although each pipe was 30 feet in length, each was premated into 60-foot sections before being stowed aboard the *Glomar Explorer* to speed handling. The pipes were color-coded to facilitate forming the pipe-string.

There was sufficient pipe to reach 17,000 feet with several spares. The pipe-string sections are listed in Table 7-1.

TABLE 7-1 Pipe-String Sections

COLOR	NUMBER	LENGTH	DIAMETER	TOTAL	NOTES
Red	49	60 ft	15½ in	2,940 ft	—
White	44	60 ft	15 in	2,640 ft	—
Blue	51	60 ft	14 in	3,060 ft	—
Yellow	51	60 ft	13¼ in	3,060 ft	—
Green	51	60 ft	13¼ in	3,060 ft	—
White	45	60 ft	12¾ in	2,700 ft	—
Red	1	30 ft	15½ in	—	Dutchman
Red-white	1	60 ft	—	—	Reducer
Blue-yellow	1	60 ft	—	—	Reducer
Green-white	1	60 ft	—	—	Reducer

The first (bottom) pipe in the string was known as the "Dutchman" and configured for attachment of the capture vehicle or claw. The three "reducers" would serve as connecting pipes as the diameter changed in the pipe-string. Seawater under pressure would be pumped from the *Glomar Explorer* down through the pipe-string to provide hydraulic power for various functions of the capture vehicle. Two cables for electrical power, video, and data transmission cables would be run down the outside of the pipe-string, attached to the pipes, but be sufficiently flexible to withstand the estimated 40-foot expansion of the pipes as the weight on the pipe-string increased.

At this time, the massive claw or capture vehicle was being assembled in the floating hangar known as HMB-1—the Hughes Mining Barge No. 1. Constructed by Lockheed in Redwood City, California, the capture vehicle that would grasp the remains of the *K-129* was designed specifically to match the forward section of the submarine, a length of some 136 feet, weighing up to 2,000 tons. The "grabbers" of the capture vehicle had to be designed to align perfectly with the hull, with three points on the submarine designated as alignment points. This alignment scheme was based on the *Halibut* photographs of the submarine's forward section. The term "grabber" was used

The "pipe farm" covered Pier E in Long Beach as the *Hughes Glomar Explorer* prepared to load the 295 sections of the pipe-string, all 60-feet long except for the 30-foot "Dutchman," the link between the pipe-string and the capture vehicle. The pipe-string and the shipboard pipe-handling system were based on oil-field drilling technology and experience.

to include the eight beams and davits that protruded down from the capture vehicle, all of which were hydraulically operated.

The core of the capture vehicle was a strongback or "spine" that was composed of two massive steel beams, 179 feet long and 31 feet wide. The total weight of the capture vehicle, with all of its components, would be 2,170 tons dry and 1,864 tons in water. Mounted on the beams were a variety of sensors, transducers, thrusters, cameras, and lights, along with the grabbers that would lift the submarine. Water jets were mounted along the sides of the grabbers and davit arms to help evacuate the soil and silt so the davit tips could penetrate deeper into the soil and pass under the submarine, which was embedded in the bottom. It was critical that the grabbers pass beneath and not pierce the submarine's hull and thus cause damage to both the submarine and the lift arms.

There were eight grabbers—five that would be on the port side of the submarine and three that would be on the starboard side. Also on the starboard side were two beams that held and opened a steel containment net that would be deployed to restrain the hoped-for surviving missile should it begin to slide from its severely damaged tube. Mounted on the strongback were 26 lights to illuminate the work area and the wreckage, 12 cameras to provide pictures of the recovery operation to the control vans, sonar, pressure-proof spheres to house the electronics, eight hydraulic thrusters to help align the capture vehicle, and two 15-horsepower electric yaw thrusters to ensure that the capture vehicle did not rotate and "unscrew" from the pipe-string. The two 15-horsepower thrusters were to ensure that if the ship turned to port or just from its own weight there would not be a tendency for the pipe-string sections to begin unscrewing from its own weight and the motion of the capture vehicle!

During near-bottom operations, an acoustic positioning system gave commands to the eight hydraulic thrusters to position the capture vehicle over the submarine irrespective of the position of the ship three miles above. For this part of the operation the *Glomar Explorer*'s positioning system would sense the "bias" in the positioning system of the capture vehicle and commanded the ship's thrusters to maintain the ship directly over the claw and align with it. The fully outfitted capture vehicle was supported by a three-point, hinged bridle that was attached to the end of the pipe-string by the pipe length called the Dutchman.

At each corner of the capture vehicle was an extendable "breakout leg." These were huge cylinders, ten-feet in diameter, with a 40-foot maximum stroke, that could telescope to act like jacks to lift the (captured) submarine out of the silt. At the base of each leg was a "cookie cutter" that would extend to dig into the silt to help firmly anchor the breakout legs. Using pressurized water pumped through the pipe-string, the breakout legs could exert more than 2,000 tons of breakout force. Once the capture vehicle with the *K-129* within its grasp was free of the bottom, the legs would be released and would remain on the ocean floor.

As the capture vehicle was assembled, it was given the nicknames "Crab" and "Clementine," the latter soon becoming synonymous with the device.

The CIA had prohibited use of the term "claw." The capture vehicle was assembled within the HMB-1, which had been built by the National Steel and Shipbuilding Company in San Diego. Raymond Feldman, an engineer on the project, told of his first encounter with the capture vehicle:

> When I got to Redwood City . . . the first time I was confronted by this huge barge [it was] sitting out in front of the plant and it was absolutely immense. I had never seen anything like it before.
>
> And, the first time I went into the barge and could see what we called the capture vehicle . . . the structure and size of it was overwhelming . . . the mass of scale just was so impressive that it was hard to take all these [in] at once.[3]

Like the other key components of Project Azorian, the HMB-1 was a unique endeavor, intended specifically for a single mission: to provide a concealed space to assemble the capture vehicle and then, by submerging the barge, allowing the *Glomar Explorer* to moor above the barge and lift Clementine up into the moon pool without being observed by others.

The HMB-1 was the world's largest submersible barge. Its keel was laid at National Steel on July 1, 1971, and was launched the following January. The HMB-1 was 324 feet long and 106 feet wide; with the assembled capture vehicle on board it displaced 10,875 tons. The barge's hull and "wing walls" were mostly ballast tanks. It was non-self-propelled, unmanned, with controls, air, and power provided from a nearby support ship. On April 20, 1972, the HMB-1 was towed off nearby Coronado, and was submerged in an ocean depth of 55 feet. It remained on the bottom overnight and then was surfaced in a flawless operation. After some additional work, the HMB-1 began the tow on May 10, 1972, to the Lockheed facility at Redwood City for assembly of the capture vehicle.

Like all other aspects of Project Azorian, the HMB-1 concept fit well with the cover story of an ocean mining endeavor. The configuration of what the press referred to as a "vacuum cleaner" to sweep up manganese modules was of a secret design, hence it had to be assembled within the HMB-1 and, eventually, mated with the *Glomar Explorer* in secret.

Repairs to the various *Glomar Explorer* systems continued. The ship again put to sea for trials off the southern California coast and the especially critical pipe-handling system was tested. A total of 40 "doubles" (2,400 feet) were deployed and recovered with minimal problems. After recovering the pipe-string, the ship again got under way on February 26 and arrived some 65 nautical miles southwest of Catalina Island to conduct further trials. A compelling reason to operate farther at sea was that on March 1 all commercial vessels in California coastal waters were subject to a special state tax. Rather than possibly face close examination by California state officials who might uncover the ship's real owner—the U.S. government—the decision was made to be in international waters on the tax deadline. The ship returned to her Pier E berth on the afternoon of March 2.

For the next three weeks the *Glomar Explorer* remained pierside as repairs and outfitting continued, with some teams working around the clock. The ship again departed Long Beach Harbor early on March 28 and sailed to a test site eight miles off Catalina Island. Beginning on March 29 various ship systems were tested with an emphasis on crew training, and the capture vehicle was "mated" with the *Glomar Explorer*. The last occurred within a few hundred yards of a crowded beach, with many small sailing craft in the area, and large merchant ships steaming in the distance.

The HMB-1 with the recovery vehicle hidden inside had earlier been towed to the site and anchored in Isthmus Cove. Power, air, and control umbilicals were connected from the support ship *Ore Quest* to the barge. There was some press interest in the activity, but with the press-labeled "vacuum sweeper" out of sight, there was little public interest in the strange craft. The transfer up into the *Glomar Explorer* would be done at night, to reduce possible visits by interested swimmers or scuba divers. A couple of CIA-manned patrol boats would keep small craft away.

The barge was flooded and submerged without difficulty, the process taking 2½ days. The *Glomar Explorer* maneuvered over the barge. Then, in an intricate operation, the roof of the submerged barge was slid open, and, with the moon pool open, the ship's two docking legs were lowered into the barge, aligning precisely with the capture vehicle. The locking pins were engaged and, for the first time, the capture vehicle was pulled up into the moon pool.

With the moon pool gates pulled shut, the docking well was pumped out, and the *Glomar Explorer* moved out of the cove. Trapped in the moon pool were thousands of dead squid, attracted by the lights during the nighttime transfer operation. Subsequently, the HMB-1 was pumped out and surfaced, to be towed back to Redwood City and to await the triumphant return of the ship and capture vehicle from their mission.

On May 12, 1974, the mission director advised the CIA project head-quarters that all scheduled tests were complete. The *Glomar Explorer* arrived back at Pier E early on May 13 to begin a monthlong period of fitting out and taking on board provisions and other material for the recovery mission.

It was now becoming clear that while further testing of the recovery systems would create additional confidence in their reliability and could provide useful crew training, such testing would increasingly place wear and tear on a system that was intended for a one-time operation.

Meanwhile, during April and May 1974 in Washington, an ad hoc committee of the U.S. Intelligence Board (USIB), at the request of Dr. Kissinger, now Secretary of State, had made one more evaluation of the expected intelligence benefits of Project Azorian. The USIB was responsible for supervising the national intelligence estimates. This evaluation was done in support of the Forty Committee's next discussion, to be conducted in June, regarding final approval for the project. The USIB study was forwarded to Kissinger on May 7 with a covering memorandum that was of special significance. It read,

> The United States Intelligence Board has reviewed and updated its intelligence assessment of Project AZORIAN. On the basis of this review, the Board concludes that there have been no significant developments since the last Board assessment which would detract from the unique intelligence value of this target.
>
> Successful recovery and exploitation [censored] expected to be on board [censored]. Acquisition of the nuclear warheads and SS-N-5 missile system, together with related documents, would provide a much-improved baseline for estimates of the current and future Soviet strategic threat. The Board also expects that recovered documents would provide important insights into Soviet command and control and certain aspects of their strategic attack doctrine.
>
> In its evaluation the Board assumed a successful mission. On this basis the Board continues to believe that recovery of the AZORIAN

A cover that worked: While bathers and pleasure sailors ignored the scene, the barge HMB-1, in which the capture vehicle was assembled, and the *Hughes Glomar Explorer* (visible behind the barge) rendezvoused at Catalina Island off the southern California coast to transfer the capture vehicle to the lift ship. There were CIA security personnel in some of the boats.

submarine would provide information which can be obtained from no other source, on subjects of great importance to the national defense.[4]

The USIB cover memorandum thus indicated that "something" other than the SS-N-5 Serb missile and related fire-control system was the primary object of Project Azorian. The censored passage appears to address cryptologic equipment and documents. If this assumption is correct, was that only the view of the USIB and not of the Director of Central Intelligence, the Secretary of Defense, Dr. Kissinger, and others who had placed top priority on acquiring the submarine's ballistic missile with its nuclear warhead?

Or did all of these individuals, in classified as well as the very few open comments, put forward the missile as a "cover within a cover" for NSA's high priority for obtaining cryptologic material? An open-source confirmation of this theory comes from a *Soviet* source, Rear Admiral Anatolyi Shtyrov, in 1973–1974 the deputy head of intelligence for the Pacific Fleet. He later wrote,

> The principal objective of Project Jennifer was to penetrate the holy of holies of the Soviet Navy—the communication codes, i.e., to "crack," or "hack" as it is in fashion now, the radio-traffic, especially between submarines and their bases. The security of the latter was reputed as particularly "crack-proof." The loss of the Soviet submarine off Hawaii tempted the U.S. with a fast solution to the problem. Hence the idea— to raise the submarine and to remove code tables, documents and coding equipment. "Cracking" those codes would enable the CIA to read the whole radio-communications log of the Naval Forces of the USSR, and the system of development, deployment, and command of its submarine fleet. But foremost—to develop the key to the logical construction of these codes through computer analysis, and to gain control over the whole system of Soviet information encoding of the 1970s was the ultimate goal. What can be achieved by that is not obvious only to accomplished spooks. And of course the Americans were interested in Soviet nuclear [weapon] technologies.[5]

Unfortunately, Shtyrov had only his professional judgment on which to base his arguments. While it is certainly possible that the CIA and the Department of Defense sought to raise the submarine primarily to access the nuclear weapons technology, another player in the operation was certainly the NSA, responsible for making and safeguarding U.S. codes and crypto-logic material, and penetrating foreign communications. As part of Azorian, but unknown to the other sponsors, NSA might have driven the top-level decisions to undertake the salvage effort. If the code machines and related documents were a primary rationale for undertaking Project Azorian, they might also have been among the most perishable in intelligence value. In the six years since the *K-129* was lost there had been significant changes in Soviet naval and strategic codes and possibly equipment. This was especially likely because of the deployments of the more-capable Project 667A/Yankee stra-tegic missile submarines from 1969 onward.

When attempting to undertake an objective analysis of the available information to determine the "why" of the Azorian mission, one finds that the U.S. Navy was apparently "lukewarm" because the Navy's leadership considered such a project too expensive an undertaking, especially in view of the costs of the ongoing Vietnam War, and the service's very limited deep-ocean engineering capabilities. The CIA was "hot" for the program for domes-tic political as well as technical intelligence reasons, and was especially hot to obtain the nuclear warhead of the remaining missile. NSA cared little for the weapons technology: its priority was crypto material, which the agency appears to have believed justified the operation. Based on the heavily cen-sored CIA report on Project Azorian that was released in early 2010—and reading "between the lines"—and based also on other sources that cannot be acknowledged in this book, NSA supported the CIA. That NSA support apparently tipped the scales to obtain final program approval.

Thus, the different government agencies rated their intelligence objec-tives differently. One could therefore conclude that it was *both* the nuclear warhead (and related fire control) technology *and* the crypto material that drove the U.S. government to undertake the politically dangerous, expensive, and technologically risky effort to raise the *K-129*.

One U.S. official, however, took issue with either the cryptologic mate-rial or the missile being the purpose of Project Azorian. Dr. John Craven, who had been a key player in the Navy's search for the remains of the *K-129*, postulated a totally different rationale:

> Its purpose . . . had nothing to do with recovering Soviet code books or weapons technology or missile technology. It had everything to do with whether the submarine was where the explosion [*sic*] occurred, why it was there, what it was up to, and who had authorized its mission.[6]

Craven—among others—came to believe that the *K-129* was in the process of launching a nuclear-tipped missile against Hawaii at the time of the submarine's "explosion" and sinking (see Chapter 11).

The Forty Committee met on June 5 and Dr. Kissinger prepared a memorandum for President Nixon that covered the essential points of the committee's discussion and recommendation to go forward with the project. The president approved the mission on June 7 with the proviso that the actual recovery must not be undertaken before his return from an impending visit to the Soviet Union, scheduled for June 27 to July 3. One cannot but wonder at the analogy with President Dwight D. Eisenhower's direction to the CIA in the spring of 1960 that the next U-2 spyplane flight over the Soviet Union must be carried out prior to May 1 because the president was meeting with the leaders of Britain, France, and the Soviet Union in Paris beginning on May 16, 1960.[7] The U-2 overflight—piloted by Francis Gary Powers—was made on May 1 and shot down, and wrecked the Paris summit meeting.

With all political and technical problems solved, and a tentative lift date set for July 4 or later, preparations for sailing were well under way when another problem arose. This problem threatened to reveal the secret operation to the world. Two weeks before the sailing date the Romaine Street offices of the Summa Corporation in Hollywood were broken into by thieves. They stole money *and files:* shortly after midnight on June 5, four men entered the offices, overpowered and tied up the one guard, and used an acetylene torch to open two safes. During a four-hour rampage, they ransacked desks and files. (A second guard was in a soundproof room monitoring a switchboard.)

According to the newspaper stories, the thieves took $68,000 in cash, some Wedgewood vases, and company papers. There were no follow-up stories and the burglary was soon forgotten—by the public. Not mentioned in the newspapers was the removal of two cases of documents belonging to Howard Hughes. A few weeks later one of the thieves telephoned the Summa offices and offered to return the stolen Hughes documents for $1 million in cash. The offer was summarily refused in the belief that the thieves would simply make copies of the documents, return the originals, and then demand more payments or else reveal the Hughes company "secrets."

Unexpectedly, after the *Glomar Explorer* had sailed on her mission, Summa officials,

> made a dismaying discovery. They learned that a memorandum outlining Project Jennifer was missing from the Romaine center. The Summa officials concluded that the buglers had made off with the Project Jennifer memo and that one of the nation's top intelligence secrets was in the hands of unknown safe-crackers.
>
> In consternation and embarrassment, Summa informed the CIA of this disaster.[8]

The *Glomar Explorer* had moved from Pier E to an anchorage in Long Beach Harbor on June 19. Late on the 20th the ship moved to a prearranged location outside the three-mile limit marking U.S. territorial waters. The following day several Global Marine and Summa Corporation officials, as well as members of Howard Hughes' staff, flew out to the ship by helicopter for the ceremony that marked formal acceptance of the ship by the Summa Corporation from Global Marine. The guests were given a "limited" tour of the ship and shown several of her features; they then posed for photographs and celebrated with cake and champagne in the ward room. The cake, rectangular with chocolate icing, had a rough outline of a ship with "HGE" in its center, and the names or initials of Lockheed, Summa, Honeywell, and Global Marine above the ship, and the date beneath. The event was "staged" for tax purposes and to emphasize the ship's cover story of starting on a seafloor mining expedition. The official party then flew back to Long Beach. Later that same day the ship set course for the Northwest Pacific and the target object.

EIGHT

THE LIFT

The *Hughes Glomar Explorer* got under way from a position off Long Beach on June 21, 1974, sailing northwest from the coast of southern California. There were 178 men on board. The ship's crew, now commanded by Captain Thomas J. Gresham, stood bridge watches, navigated, manned the engine rooms, cooked, baked, served meals, did the laundry, and performed other tasks to keep the ship operating. While this crew performed the daily ship's operations, the recovery team under the CIA mission director prepared for the unprecedented salvage operation.

The recovery team would operate the ship's lift system, man the mission control and other specialized vans, handle the remains of the *K-129*, and perform a multitude of other functions. In addition to the CIA specialists, the mission crew included engineers and technicians from Global Marine, Honeywell, Lockheed Ocean Systems, and the Mechanics Research Institute; the last was a CIA cover company. At least one naval officer was on board: Captain Fred Terrell, the director of operations. There were also ten scuba divers from various agencies on board to assist in undocking and recovering the capture vehicle and, hopefully, the target object.

The CIA and Navy mission personnel almost all had "cover names"— usually their true first name and a pseudonym for the second, but with their actual last initial. Thus, the CIA mission director's cover name on board ship was Dale Nagle. There were a few nicknames such as "Greyjack," the CIA security officer for the operation. He probably earned that name for his beard. Another individual, also from the CIA, had a straggly reddish beard and was called Redjack; his cover name was Jack Steelman. The real names of the CIA personnel aboard the ship remain "classified" although most were known to all on the ship and are signed to photos taken on board.

There were two mission crews for Project Azorian: on board the *Glomar Explorer* for the recovery and initial examination of the remains of the *K-129* was the "A crew," also called the "Judge crew." Later, when the submarine was safely ensconced in the ship's moon pool, the "B crew" or "Jury crew" would be brought on board the ship at a preplanned location to continue exploitation of the remains, package them for transfer to intelligence facilities, and to clean up, disposing of the remaining material and parts of the submarine. The A crew was given some basic lessons in the Cyrillic alphabet so that when the submarine was recovered the technicians could recognize such words as "danger" and "radioactive."

Many of the Global Marine crewmen were "people from a southern background and we got a lot of people from the Nevada test site [who] drilled these big holes for atomic blasts . . . so they'd already been cleared."[1] Obviously, many of the mission crew had previously handled pipe-strings in oil fields. All, of course, had to be cleared by the CIA before they could join the project, as had the technical personnel from the various contractors. The pay for nongovernment personnel was relatively high to avoid personnel wanting to change jobs if they received other offers. The pay levels quickly became obvious as the parking lots adjacent to the pier filled with new or almost new cars, including a couple of Cadillacs.

Once at sea—when not working—the men had many "creature comforts": The ship had three recreation lounges, with games and cards (although gambling for money was strongly discouraged), color television sets with videotape players—there was a library of about 75 films—and a small exercise gym. A daily newspaper was published, based on news reports picked up from various radio broadcasts. The food on board was described by several crew members as "superb." Four meals were served daily—breakfast, lunch, dinner, and midnight, the last called "mid-rats" (midnight rations) by the Navymen on board. Except for brief periods of cleaning, the mess was open continuously with fresh fruit, ice cream, coffee, soft drinks, pastries, and similar items always available. In addition, at about 10 PM platters of cheeses and cold cuts were put out.

Lunch and dinner, the big meals, included a variety of choices, as shown in Table 8-1.

TABLE 8-1 Meals On Board the *Glomar Explorer*

DAY	LUNCH	DINNER
Friday	fried shrimp meat loaf	shrimp creole meat loaf
Saturday	barbecue chicken pork chops	barbecue chicken steak
Sunday	turkey and dressing ham	filet and lobster
Monday	roast beef corned beef and cabbage	roast beef franks and beans
Tuesday	sirloin tips lamb chops	sirloin tips steak
Wednesday	roast beef turkey à la king	roast beef spaghetti and meat balls
Thursday	barbecue beef Swiss steak	steak
Friday	salmon cakes roast pork knockwurst sausages	fried oysters fried shrimp
Saturday	ham veal cutlets	T-bone steak
Sunday	Cornish game hen ground beef patties	Cornish game hen barbecue pork and beef
Monday	lamb chops steak	barbecue spare ribs hamburger steak

While the food was plentiful, so was the exercise: the ship was inundated with ladders. And there were preparations to be made while en route to the salvage site. Engineer Ray Feldman explained,

> While we were going out to the site there was a lot of preparation that had to be done . . . there was a lot of testing to insure . . . that all the equipments were operating.
>
> We had made the connection at Long Beach between the [capture vehicle] and the control vans, but everything had to be tested. There were tests of the acoustic system, tests of the camera system, and then there was ship operations, of course. At some point we had to test the automatic station-keeping equipment so there was a lot of preparation that was going on while we were sailing to the site. It wasn't that we were not busy—we were.[2]

Once on station, there would be plenty of backbreaking work for the mission crew, which would be working 12-hour shifts. The living conditions, the camaraderie of men on a "secret mission," and the knowledge that they were taking part in a historic operation led to excellent morale on board ship. While there were several different teams and groups on board, Sherman Wetmore, who served on board, observed, "As far as any animosity between groups, I never felt any ill will or any jealousy."[3]

During the voyage all spaces were open to the crew except for the two communications vans. These, manned by NSA personnel and possible CIA personnel, handled most of the communications for the ship and, additionally, appear to have had some communications intercept capabilities to detect radio transmissions from other ships in the area. The control van was restricted to personnel directly involved with the recovery operation.

The voyage to the target area was made without incident. On June 27, 28, and 29, several merchant ships on an easterly course passed the *Glomar Explorer*, but none was closer than two miles. On June 30, with the ship well past the halfway point on her voyage, the deputy for exploitation conducted a drill for the control and flow of personnel into and out of the moon pool in the event of nuclear contamination from the submarine's torpedoes or missiles. The deputy for recovery also conducted target acquisition training, and there was an emergency drill for the destruction of classified documents and equipment. There was a model of the forward 136 feet of the *K-129* on board the *Glomar Explorer* as well as the pertinent *Halibut* photographs for use in training sessions for the recovery team.

The classified material destruction drill was considered highly significant because of the Israeli attack on the U.S. spy ship *Liberty* (AGTR 5) in 1967 and the North Korean seizure of the spy ship *Pueblo* in January 1968. There was concern in several quarters for the security of the ship should the Soviets learn of her true mission. Indeed, the *Glomar Explorer* was considered even more vulnerable by virtue of having the guise of a civilian ship, while the *Liberty* and *Pueblo* had been Navy-manned ships. Feldman later recalled,

We were in mind of the incident in 1968 when the *Pueblo* was attacked by North Koreans and the ship and the entire crew was taken into captivity.

So we were aware that such things could happen . . . and suppos-
edly in international waters, too. We didn't have any specific training
about what to do except don't offer any resistance.[4]

There was no "official" U.S. military plan to provide protection for the
Glomar Explorer. However, the Commander-in-Chief Pacific Feet, Admiral
M. F. (Mickey) Weisner, was advised of Project Azorian, and he told several
of his key subordinates of the effort. Subsequently, his submarine force commander, Rear Admiral Frank D. McMullen, and two of the latter's staff developed a contingency plan in the event that the *Glomar Explorer* was attacked
and boarded by Soviet forces. Nothing was committed to paper.[5]

The Commander, Submarine Squadron 1, based at Pearl Harbor, Captain Roy White, was directed to keep one of his nuclear-propelled submarines, the USS *Tautog* (SSN 639), armed and ready for immediate departure.
A second SSN was also designated for the mission if the *Tautog* was unable to
immediately depart. The submarine ready to depart had some of her Mark
37 torpedoes—primarily an anti-submarine weapon—replaced with additional Mark 14 and 16 torpedoes. These weapons, dating to the 1930s, were
more effective for sinking surface ships.

This contingency plan was in many respects one of desperation. It was
obvious that it would be difficult if not impossible for the U.S. government to
prevent Soviet forces from attacking the recovery ship unless there was timely
warning of such a Soviet effort. Rather, the submarine force's plan could only
ensure that the *Glomar Explorer* would never reach a Soviet port. The *Tautog*,
with a top speed of just over 25 knots, would require about 2½ days to travel
the 1,600 nautical miles from Pearl Harbor to the recovery area. Then, the
submarine's only option would be to sink the lift ship. To some observers, it
was a lose-lose situation.

The 178 men on board the *Glomar Explorer* knew nothing of this plan.

On July 4—Independence Day—the lift ship arrived at the recovery site
at 1:01 PM local time. President Nixon had departed Moscow on the previous day. It had been a 13-day voyage at an average speed of eight knots.
There were no other ships on the horizon. The wreck of the *K-129* had been
located within six nautical miles of the intersection of latitude 40° North and
longitude 180°—the international date line. Upon arrival at the location, the

A computer-generated image showing the *Hughes Glomar Explorer* stationary over the barge HMB-1 while the capture vehicle is lifted up into the moon pool. The twin docking legs are extended downward, into the HMB-1, to align with and engage the CV. This event occurred just off Catalina Island, at night, but within sight of tourists and sailing craft.

PROJECT AZORIAN SYSTEM CONCEPT

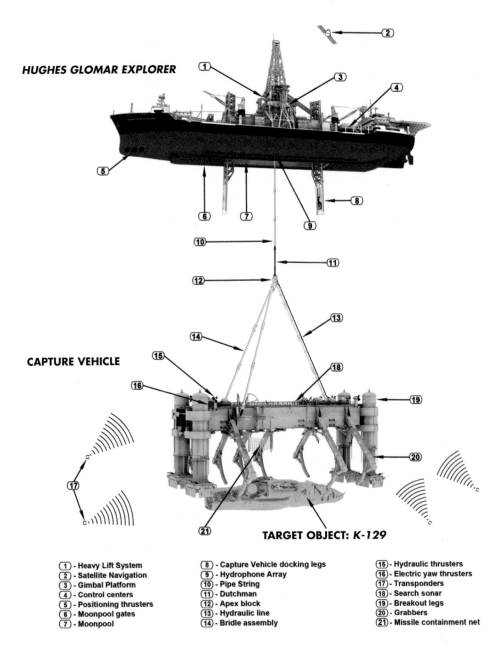

HUGHES GLOMAR EXPLORER

CAPTURE VEHICLE

TARGET OBJECT: *K-129*

① - Heavy Lift System
② - Satellite Navigation
③ - Gimbal Platform
④ - Control centers
⑤ - Positioning thrusters
⑥ - Moonpool gates
⑦ - Moonpool

⑧ - Capture Vehicle docking legs
⑨ - Hydrophone Array
⑩ - Pipe String
⑪ - Dutchman
⑫ - Apex block
⑬ - Hydraulic line
⑭ - Bridle assembly

⑮ - Hydraulic thrusters
⑯ - Electric yaw thrusters
⑰ - Transponders
⑱ - Search sonar
⑲ - Breakout legs
⑳ - Grabbers
㉑ - Missile containment net

The *Hughes Glomar Explorer* sliding down the building ways at Sun Shipbuilding in Chester, Pennsylvania, on November 4, 1972. The openings for the ship's three bow thrusters—part of the precision station-keeping system—are visible; two additional thrusters are fitted in the ship's stern.

The salvage lift ship *Hughes Glomar Explorer* at rest at Long Beach shortly before departing on her historic mission. The massive ship provided the United States with the world's most capable deep-ocean engineering platform. In this view the twin docking legs are in the raised position, forward and aft of the massive derrick that handled the pipe-string. The legs guided the capture vehicle into and out of the moon pool.

HUGHES GLOMAR EXPLORER

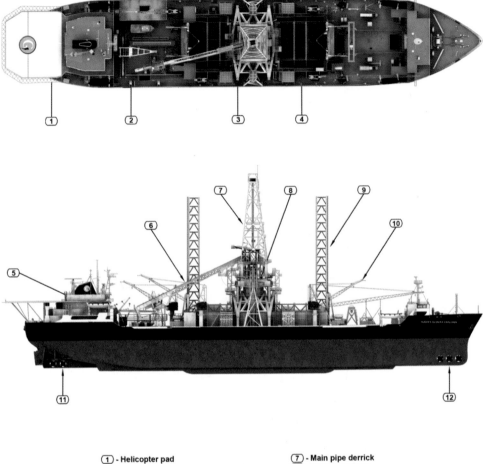

1 - Helicopter pad
2 - Transfer crane
3 - A - Frame
4 - Moonpool area
5 - Command & control vans
6 - Pipe transfer cart

7 - Main pipe derrick
8 - Gimbal platform
9 - Docking legs x2
10 - Crane x4
11 - After thrusters
12 - Forward thrusters

CAPTURE VEHICLE

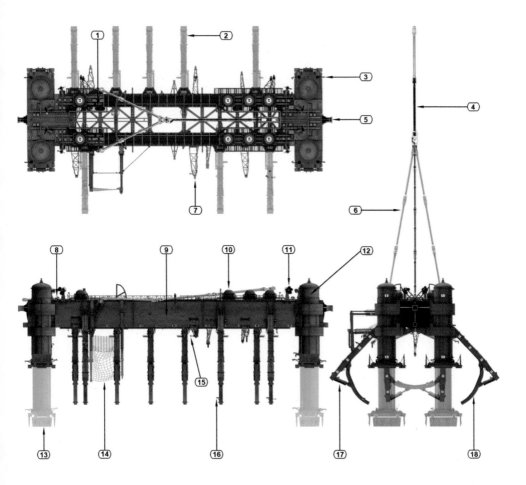

1 - Transponders x4
2 - Grabbers x8
3 - High resolution sonars x16
4 - Dutchman
5 - Docking arm engagement stud x2
6 - Bridle assembly

7 - External arms sonars x15
8 - Electric Yaw Thrusters x2
9 - Strongback
10 - Electronic pressure spheres x8
11 - Hydraulic thrusters x8
12 - Extendable Breakout Legs x4

13 - Cookie cutter pads x4
14 - Missile containment net
15 - Cameras x12
16 - Lights x26
17 - Grabber lower cylinder x8
18 - Davit arms x8

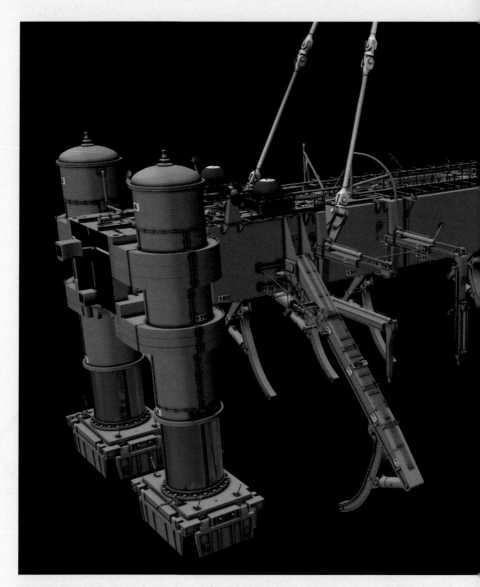

The massive capture vehicle (above) weighed more than 2,000 tons. The four break-out legs at the end of the capture vehicle are shown in the lowered position in this computer-generated image. Following termination of the Azorian and Matador projects, the *Hughes Glomar Explorer* was reconfigured for the commercial seafloor mining of manganese nodules. The tethered mining device (lower right) that was evaluated in the late 1970s is shown here in the ship's moon pool. The ship was not successful in that role. The manganese nodule at far right was recovered from a depth of approximately 16,000 feet in the mid-Pacific.

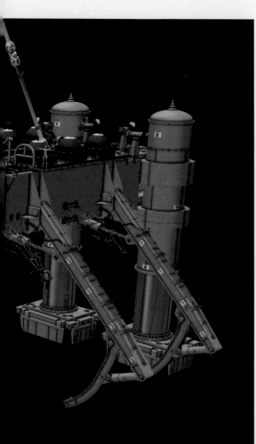

HUGHES MINING BARGE HMB-1

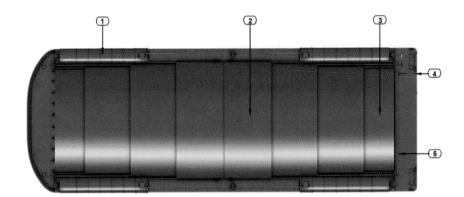

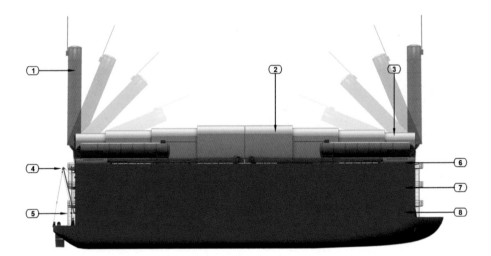

1 - Stabilizing Cylinders
2 - Traveling Roof
3 - Fixed Roof
4 - 5 -Ton Boom

5 - Portable Inclined Ladder
6 - 03 Level
7 - 02 Level
8 - 01 Level

The barge HMB-1 at Catalina Island, being maneuvered into a four-point moor prior to submerging. The *Hughes Glomar Explorer* then moved over the barge and extended its docking legs to retrieve the capture vehicle up into the ship's moon pool. The tug *Windy Foss* is in the foreground and the support/control ship *Ore Quest* is in the background. The computer generated image, at left shows the HMB-1 with its sliding roof partially open. In both views the stabilizing cylinders are in the lowered position.

This computer-generated image depicts the capture vehicle being lowered from the open moon pool of the *Hughes Glomar Explorer*. The twin docking legs are lowered and swung outboard after releasing the CV. One of the many remarkable features of the ship was its ability to hold position over the pipe-string for days, regardless of sea and wind conditions.

Glomar Explorer immediately began deploying transponders on the ocean floor to establish a bottom navigation grid. Several of the transponders had flaws and were rejected before the ship was able to establish a six-transponder grid. Subsequently, the ship's crew deployed two wave-rider buoys and calibrated the automatic station-keeping system.

The moon pool gates were slid open on July 8 and testing of the capture vehicle's main components continued, first the cameras and then the hydraulics, water jets, davits, and other components were checked. But further tests were put on hold because of typhoon Gilda approaching the area. Heavy seas and strong winds plagued the ship until July 13.

That same day, the 13th, the British merchant ship *Bel Hudson*, en route from Yokohama to Los Angeles, hove to near the *Glomar Explorer*. The British ship had earlier radioed a request for emergency medical assistance: a sailor, Les Burke, was complaining of severe chest pains. The *Bel Hudson* had been about 35 nautical miles from the *Glomar Explorer;* the lift ship radioed that she had a doctor on board. Planning for the Azorian lift mission had anticipated such a situation. The American ship had to respond both because of humanitarian considerations and to further substantiate the ship's cover story.

The British ship arrived on the scene just after 11 AM—providing confirmation in her log of the location of the *K-129*'s remains. The *Glomar Explorer*'s surgeon, accompanied by a medical technician and a "security officer," made the precarious trip to the *Bel Hudson* in a British launch. After determining that Burke had not suffered a heart attack as had been suspected, the ill sailor was taken over to the *Glomar Explorer* for X-rays and treatment. He was accompanied by the *Bel Hudson*'s first mate and third engineer. After being diagnosed with inflammation of a rib, and provided with medication, the British sailor was sent back to his ship, with the *Bel Hudson*'s motor launch encountering heavy swells and stiffening winds. The launch returned once again to the *Glomar Explorer*, this time with a cargo of about ten cases of beer and a couple of cases of gin and whisky. In grateful exchange, the American ship sent back about ten cases of steaks.

The event had caused no compromise of the *Glomar Explorer*'s mission. Rather, it had further established her credentials as a commercial, seafloor-mining ship.

By July 14 the rough weather subsided sufficiently to consider beginning to lower the capture vehicle on the following day. But on the evening of the

14th cracks were discovered in the forward and after docking leg structures, a serious problem. Repairs were essential and canvas screens were rigged on deck to protect men from the wind as they worked on the structures, raised above the ship's main deck. The work, which involved extensive welding, took 72 hours to complete. And, the weather began to worsen as tropical storm Harriet approached.

Accordingly, the bottom gates to the moon pool were closed, and it was pumped out amid six-foot waves on July 16. Preparations were made to leave the recovery site if necessary. The weather did not worsen and on July 17 the ship was advised by U.S. surveillance activities that a Soviet missile range instrumentation ship was en route to the site. She was expected to reach the *Glomar Explorer* about 4 AM on July 18.

The *Glomar Explorer*'s arrival at approximately the same site as earlier Glomar-operated ships did not go unnoticed in the headquarters of the Soviet Pacific Fleet at Vladivostok. Then–Captain 1st Rank Anatolyi Shtyrov, the fleet's deputy head of intelligence, had been responsible for dispatching the Soviet ships that had earlier observed the survey ship *Glomar II*. Shtyrov again brought the U.S. ship activity in the North Pacific to the attention of the fleet commander, Admiral Nikolai Amel'ko, who ordered a Soviet ship to undertake visual surveillance of the *Glomar Explorer*'s operations.

On the morning of July 18, "the fog burned off and out of the mist came this . . . what looked to me like a white, beautiful ship [with] very odd radomes on top and some funny looking antenna aft. Our security people were pretty excited at the time."[6] The shadowing ship was the *Chazhma*, a large missile range tracking ship.[7] The Soviet ship had departed Petropavlovsk about June 15 to support a Soyuz/Salyut space event and was en route back to her base from a position near Johnston Island when she was directed to observe the American activities. The ship was fitted with a massive radome, tracking devices, and antennas, and had a helicopter hangar and flight deck aft. With the ship playing the role of intelligence collector, or AGI in NATO parlance, a Kamov Ka-25 (NATO Hormone) helicopter was soon pulled out of the hangar. As a precaution against the helicopter seeking to land on the *Glomar Explorer*, the mission director ordered that a stack of crates be placed on the ship's helicopter deck to preclude that possibility.

The *Chazhma* initially closed to within approximately two miles of the *Glomar Explorer*. At 2:30 PM the Soviet ship further closed the distance to one

The Soviet missile range instrumentation ship *Chazhma* was dispatched to observe the *Hughes Glomar Explorer* when the lift ship arrived at the site of the *K-129* sinking. Although the electronics-laden ship kept careful watch on the American ship, the true mission of the *Glomar Explorer* was never detected by the Soviet "watchers."

mile, and crewmen began taking photographs of the U.S. ship; the helicopter took off. The Ka-25 carried a camera and began circling the ship while a crewman snapped photographs from all angles.

Crates had been intentionally stacked on the *Glomar Explorer*'s small helicopter deck and the mission director now sent crew members to the ship's bow to preclude an attempt by the helicopter to hover and lower men onto the American ship. Although rifles and pistols were on board the ship, none was issued at the time. Undoubtedly the men in the communication vans and others thought about the several steel, weighted, wire baskets, and the slide for the baskets located on the port side, below the bridge. The wire baskets were about 30 x 30 x 18 inches. The plan was that if the ship were boarded all secret papers and code material would be shoved into these weighted baskets and slid overboard. (In the event that Soviet sailors only boarded the ship to search and then departed, a hidden steel box would be used to store the codes needed to reestablish contact with CIA headquarters and others.) At 4:19 PM the helicopter landed back on board the Soviet ship.

At Vladivostok, Captain Shtyrov, still very concerned about the *Glomar Explorer*'s activities—as he had been about the earlier *Glomar II* operations—later related,

At night, when relative calm set in at the Fleet command post [head-quarters] and communications were not loaded down, I went to the communicators and called up the commander of the *Chazhma*. I pumped information from him by bits and pieces. He confirmed that all signs were that the Americans were looking for oil.[8]

The heavily censored CIA history of Project Azorian relates,

These actions by the *Chazhma* caused a measure of concern that the Soviets had become knowledgeable from other sources of the true mission of the HGE. The HGE was vulnerable sitting alone in the vast Pacific Ocean, miles from any friendly supporting forces and very much aware of other unidentified contacts in the vicinity which its communications unit had picked up the preceding few days. Accordingly, [censored] advised the officer in charge [censored] to be prepared to order emergency destruction of sensitive material which could compromise the mission if the Soviets attempted to board the ship. The team was designated to defend the control room long enough to destroy the material [censored] was alerted, but guns were not issued.[9]

At 4:30 PM on July 18 the *Chazhma* started blinking a signal lamp message to the *Glomar Explorer* that was difficult to read because of the lighting conditions. The Soviet ship then passed 500 yards astern of the U.S. ship and signaled that she would communicate further. The *Glomar Explorer* responded by signal lamp, "I am going to communicate with your station by means of international code signals." The *Glomar Explorer*'s "communications" team—monitoring the Soviet ship's communications—detected indications that another launch of the *Chazhma*'s helicopter was imminent.

A few minutes later the *Chazhma* put up a flag hoist signifying, "Understand your signal," then crossed the bow of the *Glomar Explorer* at a distance of 1,000 yards. At 5:11 PM the *Chazhma* transmitted a radio message *in Russian* asking if its transmission was heard. The *Glomar Explorer* did not respond. At about 5:30 the *Chazhma*'s helicopter was again airborne and made several low passes over the U.S. ship, with its crew taking more photographs. After a half hour it returned to the missile tracking ship.

The *Chazhma* carried a Kamov Ka-25 helicopter (NATO Hormone-C). The helicopter made several flights around the American ship, extensively photographing her. A cameraman is visible in the doorway of the Ka-25. The *Hughes Glomar Explorer*'s security team was concerned that the Soviets might try to land aboard the lift ship, either for a "friendly visit" or—if they had detected the ship's real mission—an armed assault.

For several hours the *Glomar Explorer* attempted to respond to the Soviet ship's communications, and at 6:47 PM the *Chazhma* radioed that she was ready for the U.S. ship's message. The *Glomar Explorer* answered, "We have no message. Understand you have a message for us." The Soviet ship replied, "Stand by five minutes." A short time later the *Chazhma* transmitted, "We are on our way home and heard your fog horn. What are you doing here?"

The *Glomar Explorer* answered, "We are conducting mining tests—deep-ocean mining tests." The Soviet ship then asked, "What kind of vessel are you?" to which the *Glomar Explorer* replied, "Deep-ocean mining vessel." When asked how long the American ship would be there, the answer was "We expect to finish testing in two or three weeks." The Soviet ship signed off with "I wish you all the best." The *Chazhma* departed the recovery area about 9 PM on July 18, en route to Vladivostok. She had been relieved of her shadowing assignment because she was low on provisions.

The weather cleared sufficiently on July 19 for the moon pool to be flooded and the bottom gates opened. System checks were carried out, and on July

21 the *Glomar Explorer* began to lower the capture vehicle on the pipe-string at a rapid rate. The ship's Lift Log Book noted, "01:27 UNDOCKED—very smooth. . . . 10:00 STARTED LOWERING CV." Divers checked out the capture vehicle while men in the control vans kept careful watch on dials, pointers, and television screens. The recovery operation had truly begun.

On the morning of July 22 the Soviet naval seagoing tug *SB-10* arrived on the scene to watch the *Glomar Explorer*.[10] She initially maintained a distance of some three to four miles from the lift ship, but subsequently closed to within 200 yards, passing up and down both sides of the *Glomar Explorer*. When the *SB-10* came close aboard at night she was illuminated by a searchlight from the lift ship. The Soviet ship was manned by a crew estimated at 43, including two women. Some of the crew wore fatigue-type outfits, others swim trunks or shorts. On board the *Glomar Explorer* some crewmen believed that the two women traded their dresses every day or so. The Soviet ship—with its mixed-gender crew—received almost as much attention from the Americans as the *Glomar Explorer* did from the Russians. Ray Feldman recalled,

> The Global Marine people [on the *Glomar Explorer*] had lots of fun with them. They would fill plastic trash bags with unclassified computer printouts that had to be disposed of anyway. Well, they would smear aqua lube over these papers—aqua lube is the slipperiest substance known to man—stuff them into the plastic trash bag, tie it up, and throw it overboard. Sometimes they put a little acetylene in to make sure that it was buoyant . . . and it would skip across the waves as the wind took it. . . . Whenever a bag of trash was thrown overboard they would immediately go after it.[11]

On the *SB-10* the crew took photos of the huge U.S. ship and then the tug moved off to keep watch from a distance of several miles. On the July 24 the Greek-registry ship *Pelleas* passed within two miles of the *Glomar Explorer*. The Soviet tug periodically closed on the U.S. ship and then backed off to maintain her vigil at a distance.

The *Glomar Explorer*'s captain repeatedly warned the tug to keep her distance, by radio and by flag hoists. When the tug persisted in closing on the drill ship day after day, and at night, Captain Gresham radioed Global Marine headquarters asking that a formal protest be made to the Soviet

The *Chazhma* was relieved in keeping watch on the *Hughes Glomar Explorer* by the naval salvage tug *SB-10*. With limited surveillance capabilities, the *SB-10* had no better success in detecting the lift ship's clandestine activity. Standard Soviet naval tugs of this type were designated MB; the salvage tugs were designated SB.

The *SB-10*, a naval salvage tug, had two women in her crew. They may have been responsible in part for the *Glomar Explorer*'s crewmen keeping close watch on their "watchers." As shown here, the women often wore dresses; the male crewmen wore a variety of semi-uniform and civilian clothing. One engineer aboard the *Glomar Explorer* observed that the "two women . . . seemed to trade off dresses among themselves."

government, through diplomatic channels, to stop the tug's harassing of the seafloor mining operation. Eventually the tug backed off, but remained in the area.

The lowering of the capture vehicle did not go smoothly. The plan had been to move pipe at the rate of six feet per minute, but the actual rate was much slower because the system encountered numerous problems. Most were minor problems. For instance, on July 22 there was a breakdown in the pipe-handling system that halted operations for almost two hours. Furthermore, the grabbers were losing pressure and beginning to "fold in"; if the loss continued and the grabbers closed on themselves the capture vehicle would have to be brought back up to the ship and, hopefully, repaired. Problems continued.

At 25 minutes after midnight on July 26 the command-control van reported that the capture vehicle's sonar had contact with the seafloor. At this stage the pipe-string consisted of 211 "doubles"—the capture vehicle was at a depth of 12,690 feet. It was about 3,600 feet above the seafloor.

Suddenly, at 3:45 AM on the 26th a cable broke on board the *Glomar Explorer*, dropping a 30,000-pound counterweight attached to the pipe conveyor onto the deck—sending a shock vibration through the entire ship. The Lift Log Book noted that it "made a hell of a bump." That stopped operations until 1:24 AM on the 27th. Later that morning, at 8:15, another cable broke and there was a hold at 15,008 feet until 5 PM; there was another hold at 7:52 PM with another pipe-handling problem. The deputy mission director for recovery reported, "The heavy lift system is operating marginally."[12]

Meanwhile, at the end of the pipe-string, the capture vehicle was being maneuvered in an effort to locate the target object—the *K-129*. The capture vehicle–mounted sonar detected the submarine and, at 7:52 PM on the 28th, the Lift Log Book recorded, "ARRIVED OVER T.O. [Target Object]." As the closed-circuit television cameras revealed the target object, engineer Feldman was in the control van:

> it was very impressive how clear it was . . . we could see all sorts of detail.
>
> We could see crabs crawling about . . . we could see rattail fish.
>
> We could see much detail of the sub; in fact we were able to imme-

diately pick out the towing eye at the bow, which was one of our aligning points and also the crack at the aft end [another alignment point].

We could see the missile tubes . . . what was left of them; they were
pretty well crushed up.

Someone said they could see something down in one of the
tubes . . . perhaps a warhead.[13]

The capture vehicle was rotated by use of the hydraulic thrusters to align
with the submarine. Pipe running was continued. At 1:02 PM on July 29 the
capture vehicle was 217 feet from the seafloor. At 11 PM it was 90 feet from
the seafloor.

On July 30 the decision was made on board the *Glomar Explorer* to move
the capture vehicle about 800 feet "down hill," away from the target, to permit
a full, 60-foot "double" to be added to the pipe-string. This was done to allow
sufficient pipe length in the ship's pipe-string to attach hydraulic pumps. The
capture vehicle's movement began at 11:24 PM and was completed at 1 AM
on the 31st, when the last pipe was added to the pipe-string. Two hours later
the capture vehicle was maneuvered back over the submarine. At 4:36 AM the
Lift Log Book noted, "Back Over T.O."

Carefully the recovery team rotated the capture vehicle to align it with the
K-129's remains. The capture vehicle had been designed to align with three
points on the submarine—a towing eye on the crumpled bow, a stanchion
just forward of the sail structure, and a fracture in the hull at the after end
of the forward section of the submarine. The capture vehicle was carefully
aligned with the *K-129*. Although problems persisted, at 9:13 AM on July 31
the log book recorded, "TOUCHDOWN." With the exact alignment of the
capture vehicle over the submarine, at 9:33 AM the controllers began to dig
the eight beams and davit tips into the soil beneath the submarine with the
assistance of water jets attached to the davit arms. Numbers 2, 4, 5, 6, and
8 were on the port side, and numbers 1, 3, and 7, plus the missile containment system, were on the starboard side. The unbalanced arrangement was
necessitated by the submarine lying on her starboard side, with the "missing"
starboard grabbers leaving space for the sail structure. The beams and davit
tips were pushed into the ocean floor with two million pounds of force. This

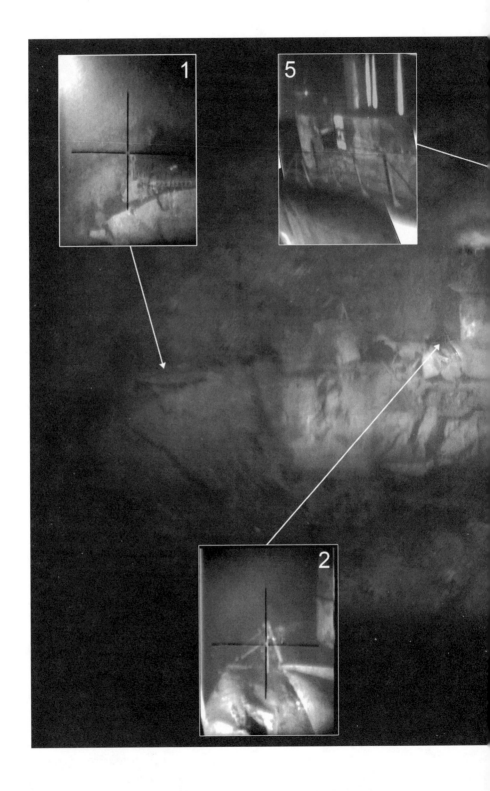

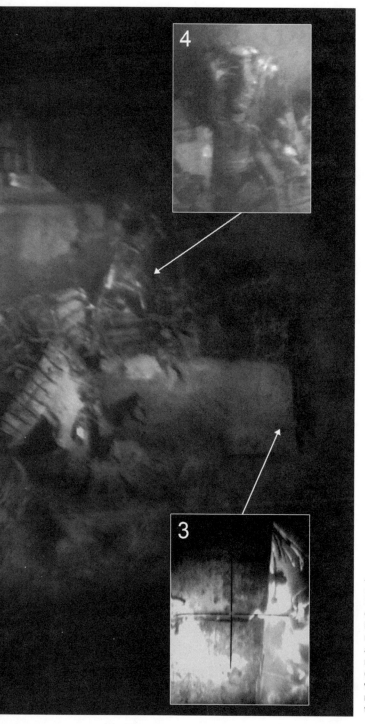

A mosaic of the wreckage of the *K-129* showing: No. 1, No. 2, and No. 3 the alignment points for the capture vehicle; No. 4 the surviving missile tube; and, No. 5 the raised periscopes, snorkel intake, and mast, confirming that the submarine was at periscope depth (approximately 50 feet keel depth) when the fatal events occurred, not at missile-launch depth (130 to 165 feet).

was accomplished by offloading weight onto the pipe-string as the heavy lift system continued to lower pipe. That released the "stretch" in the pipe-string to increase the weight on the capture vehicle.

It was immediately obvious that the soil was harder than anticipated. Another one million pounds of weight was offloaded onto the pipe-string to drive the grabbers deeper into the soil. The decision to offload the additional weight to drive the capture vehicle's "fingers" deeper into the soil was not supported or agreed to by the capture vehicle's support contractor on board nor by many of the senior people. According to one observer, "I think we all became very nervous and very concerned."[14]

The beams were closed in sequence, followed by the davits, capturing the submarine in their grasp. At 4:18 PM the missile containment net was partially deployed, to contain the hoped-for missile in the No. 1 tube. It would be fully deployed immediately after breakout. At 11:48 PM the four breakout legs were extended to jack the capture vehicle and submarine off the bottom, obviating the need to stress the pipe-string, possibly to the breaking point.

On August 1, at 25 minutes after midnight, the breakout occurred. At that point the submarine's remains shifted in the capture vehicle's grasp, possibly breaking one of the capture vehicle's beams.

The extending of the legs continued, and at 2:48 AM the *K-129* was completely free of the bottom—six years and four months after she had struck the ocean floor. At 5:15 PM the Lift Log Book recorded, "Legs OFF—ON the way UP." The breakout legs had been jettisoned because they were no longer needed. Later it was learned that, about this time, beam No. 4, on the port side opposite the front edge of the sail, had cracked and completely broken off. But there was no discernable strain on the lift system.

Slowly, surely, the pipe-string was recovered, raising the capture vehicle and the submarine toward the surface. Problems persisted, but the pipe kept coming up. At 3:30 AM on August 3 the *Glomar Explorer* had recovered 53 "doubles," raising the submarine more than 3,000 feet above the seafloor. Also on the 3rd, in accordance with the Azorian cover plan, a radio message went out over an open commercial channel saying that the ship had a problem with the "nodule collector vehicle" and requested permission from the Navy to enter Midway Atoll to perform repairs to the vehicle. This would

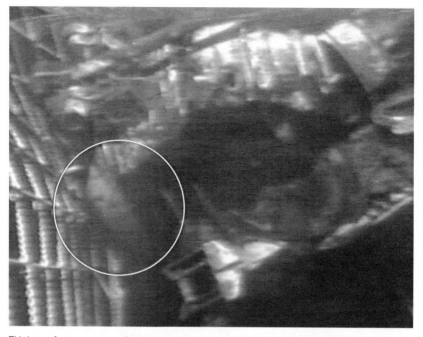

This image from a camera on the capture vehicle shows the surviving, albeit damaged, R-21 missile tube on the *K-129* and the deployed containment net (left). The cap on the missile tube is the light hemisphere pressed against the net that was intended to hold the missile, should it begin to slide from the tube as the submarine was lifted.

permit technicians—the B mission crew—to be flown out from the United States and board the ship.

At 6:25 AM on August 4 the Lift Log Book declared, "Pipe going like a son-of-a-bitch." But at 6:30 there was shut down for 1½ hours to repair a hydraulic leak.

At 6:53 AM the capture vehicle suddenly took a nose-down attitude as grabber No. 6 lost all pressure. The sail of the *K-129* began to rotate. "We were in the galley, a bunch of us having an impromptu meeting [with] a cup of coffee and the ship just shook slightly like a small earthquake," recalled Sherman Wetmore. "That wasn't right—something had gone wrong somewhere on the ship."[15]

The *Glomar Explorer*'s massive heave compensator had reached its limit, indicating that a tremendous amount of weight had been lost. Could the pipe-string have broken? Could the *K-129* have broken loose? The Lift Log Book recorded, "Heavy Lift shut down . . . CV took Nose down attitude to

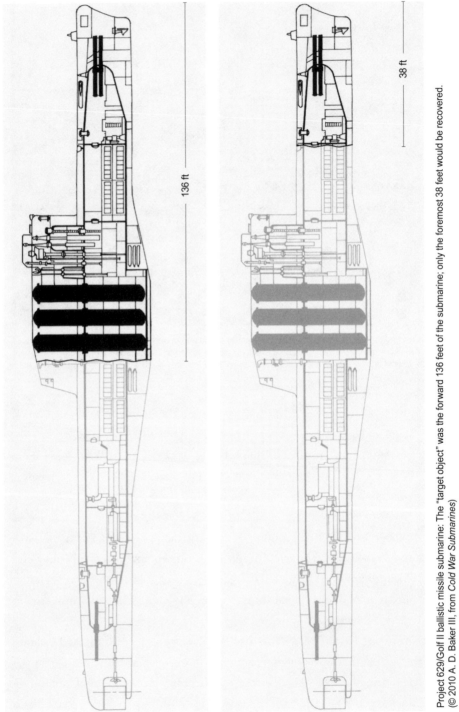

136 ft

38 ft

Project 629/Golf II ballistic missile submarine: The "target object" was the forward 136 feet of the submarine; only the foremost 38 feet would be recovered. (© 2010 A. D. Baker III, from *Cold War Submarines*)

-2.7° trim . . . Davit [grabber] 6 came to 0 PSI [pounds-per-square-inch pressure]. . . . Possibility is the T.O. broke up or rolled over?"

The capture vehicle at that moment was 6,720 feet above the ocean floor.

There was confusion in the control vans. As engineers checked the gauges and controls, it was obvious that the pipe-string was all right and that the capture vehicle was still attached to it. The capture vehicle control van was advised that the pipe-string had lost a considerable amount of weight. Inside the van the indications were that all 12 closed-circuit television cameras on the capture vehicle were working and everything appeared normal.

About 20 minutes later the capture vehicle control center had figured out the problem. The television system used multiplex video signals whereby images from the 12 cameras on the capture vehicle were transmitted sequentially up to the *Glomar Explorer*. Ironically, the real-time transmission of the video was disabled in order to save film tape during what appeared to be a quiescent period. The system engineers were thus looking at images of something that was not there. When the video system was switched back to "real time" the cameras revealed that most of the *K-129*'s hull had fallen away.

Only the foremost 38 feet of the submarine remained within the grasp of the capture vehicle. The remainder of the target object—almost 100 feet—had fallen back to the ocean floor, with its one remaining missile, fire control system, and cryptologic material.

THE BOUNTY

With the realization that most of the forward section of the *K-129* was lost there was shock, concern, and consternation aboard the *Hughes Glomar Explorer*. Within the approximately 100 feet of the submarine that the capture vehicle had lost were the possible R-21/SS-N-5 missile and the submarine's cryptologic material.

For an instant the thought came to some of the men on the ship that they should immediately go back down to the ocean floor and recover that section of the submarine *if* it were intact. That thought existed for only a fraction of a second: First, the extent of the problem with the capture vehicle's grabbers could not be ascertained until the device was retrieved in the moon pool and examined. Second, if the capture vehicle and the remaining 38-foot section were brought into the moon pool it would be impossible to lower the device without jettisoning the recovered section of the *K-129*—if the vehicle could be repaired on board, a practical impossibility. Third, there was no way of knowing the condition of the missile section after it fell back to the seafloor. The "bounty" of Project Azorian was thus limited to those 38 feet of *K-129* that had been recovered.

Of more immediate concern was the Soviet naval tug *SB-10* that was watching the salvage operation. When the submarine's hull tore apart debris began floating up into the moon pool. Was it also floating up around the ship? If so, it could be easily observed from the *SB-10*. But there was no reaction from the tug, nor was there any reaction the following day, August 5, when, that afternoon, the *Glomar Explorer* lowered the twin docking legs to a depth of

90 feet, tilted them inward, and then moved them back up to their previous position. The drill attempted to elicit any reaction from the *SB-10* that would indicate knowledge of the operation and possibly a plan for action when the submarine was brought into the ship. Although the *SB-10* started to close the distance to the *Glomar Explorer*, there was no change in her demeanor.

The decision had been made earlier that if the tug was in the area when the submarine was raised, the pipe-string would hold at a depth of about 500 feet during daylight hours—too deep for divers on board the tug to investigate the operation. Slowly the capture vehicle and its remaining prize came up toward the open moon pool. As the claw reached a depth of a couple of hundred feet beneath the ship, U.S. divers were sent down to survey the situation. They had to make certain that there were no pieces of wreckage hanging down that could impede the closing of the moon pool gates; they took underwater cutting equipment with them on their dive, just in case. There were such obstructions.

On August 6 the *SB-10* again maneuvered close aboard the salvage ship, coming to within 75 yards as the larger ship signaled the tug to stand clear. Meanwhile, the capture vehicle was raised slowly and carefully, although problems continued to occur with the lift system. At 5:11 PM the last pipe was retracted and the capture vehicle docking procedure began. At 9:17 PM the Lift Log Book recorded, "CLEMIE IS HOME! CV IS DOCKED WITH A PIECE OF T.O.!"

As if on prompt, at 9:35 PM the *SB-10* again approached the *Glomar Explorer*, again coming within 75 yards. And again the ship signaled the tug to keep clear. The Soviet ship backed off, sounded three long blasts of her whistle, and sailed off toward the horizon, heading back to her base at Petropavlovsk. By 10:30 PM she had disappeared from the *Glomar Explorer*'s radar screen. Thus ended just over 13½ days of close surveillance of Project Azorian by Soviet naval ships. The CIA report noted, "One can only conjecture the reaction and chagrin of Soviet authorities when they later realized that two Soviet Navy ships were on the scene and, in effect, witnessed the recovery operation against their lost submarine."[1]

The recovery phase of Project Azorian was finished on August 9. In a commercial message sent to Summa headquarters, the mission director on board the *Glomar Explorer* advised that "Event 36-A" had been completed, the prearranged code for the recovery phase. That same day, in Washington, D.C., President Nixon resigned and Gerald R. Ford was sworn in as the nation's 38th president. The following day, according to Secretary of State Henry Kissinger, he and Secretary of Defense James Schlesinger briefed the new president on Project Azorian. Interestingly, Kissinger would later write—incorrectly—that Ford was told on the day that he became president that the *Glomar Explorer* "was in place and all set to lift the submarine . . . and [he] ordered the salvage to begin."[2]

The closing of the moon pool gates on August 7 brought relief to the crew of the *Glomar Explorer*. GMDI engineer Charlie Johnson explained,

> The raising operation was the most dangerous part of the whole mission because we had maximum load. But mainly the stress on the pipe was continually in the back of our minds because if the pipe did break we were gonna have a sudden upward movement.
>
> There were thoughts that if something like that did happen that we could split the ship at the wing walls [of the moon pool] and sink . . . not to say we weren't thinking we were gonna die or anything but probably thought we would be on some life boats if something like that happened and so it was tense.[3]

For 15 hours on August 7–8 the water was pumped out of the moon pool. As the capture vehicle and then the remains of the *K-129* were revealed, crewmen installed wooden shoring to prevent the wreckage from rolling over. Immediately an inspection team in protective suits with respirators checked the *K-129* remains for nuclear contamination. Radiation was detected, primarily from one or both of the nuclear torpedoes carried by the submarine. The CIA believed that one or both of the torpedoes' high-explosive components had detonated without creating a nuclear explosion.[4] The plutonium[210] of the warheads was in a hydroxide form and thus there was little danger of airborne particulates; it was dangerous only if inhaled or digested. Whenever acetylene-cutting torches were used on the submarine during the next few days everyone in the area initially wore breathing devices because the plutonium could vaporize if heated and could then be inhaled. But that precaution was soon abandoned. Otherwise, personnel working on the submarine in the moon pool wore only industrial hard hats and disposable white coveralls.

As the wreckage was checked for radiation, a few mission specialists stood on balconies overlooking the moon pool and viewed the crumpled wreckage resting below them—amid flotsam, puddles, and a number of *manganese nodules that had come up with the wreckage.* As the capture vehicle released the wreckage, of the eight grabbers they saw that No. 4 and No. 5 were broken halfway up their length, and that No. 6 had its hydraulic cylinder torn away. It became obvious that the amidships section of the *K-129* broke away and fell through the gap created by the missing No. 4 and No. 5, carrying away the containment net attached to No. 7 grabber and damaging No. 6.

As for the submarine herself, she lay crumpled at the bottom of the moon pool. Without a sail of after section, the wreckage bore little resemblance to a submarine. Still, although only 38 feet had been salvaged, to many of the crew the submarine looked huge. Raymond Feldman recalled, "Looking into the opening of the piece [of the submarine] that we had it looked pretty much like a dump. There were no bulkheads that I could see. There were no fixtures that I could recall . . . , I don't remember seeing anything attached to the hull on the interior. There seemed to be a solid pile of material of maybe two or three feet in height that was very dense and very compacted. . . . There was nothing I could recognize as the interior of a submarine." And, "Immediately exploitation of the sub was started . . . people enthusiastically going in and digging like they were at an archeological site; it's the closest I can describe it."[5]

While the outer hull of the submarine was torn up, the inner or pressure hull appeared relatively intact.

As mission specialists sifted through the debris that had been the bow section of the *K-129*, appalling sights—and smells—awaited them. Several mutilated bodies were found, one recovered in what remained of his bunk; he had apparently been studying a manual related to the submarine's torpedoes when—in an instant—death came to all 98 men in the submarine. Details of the interior condition of the submarine are vague, but one other corpse was found that was relatively intact. The incomplete remains of other bodies were found in the debris, and smaller body parts had spilled out of the submarine and were found on the floor of the moon pool. At her resting depth the bodies within the submarine had been preserved because the

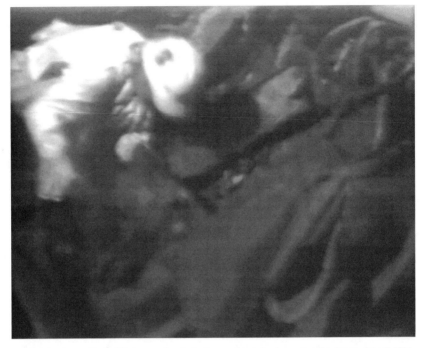

A technician dressed in a white jump suit and wearing a safety helmet searches the debris of the *K-129* in the moon pool. Participants compared working in the debris of the submarine to working in an archeological "dig." The debris yielded some items of value as well as the remains of several Soviet submariners.

near-freezing water and intense pressure had inhibited decay. Now, with the submarine on the surface and exposed to air, the bodies immediately started to deteriorate.

The feelings of many of those on board the *Glomar Explorer* were reflected in a later comment by Feldman: "You had to feel a great sense of respect and also feel sadness because they were young . . . very young men for the most part and you knew that their families were grieving for them."[6]

A "production line" of tables was set up in the moon pool where each item removed from the *K-129* was meticulously cleaned, photographed, entered into a log, and placed in preliminary packages. Subsequently, items that were identified as having no intelligence value were broken into small pieces and prepared for disposal. One of the items removed from the submarine—that would later become significant in U.S.-Soviet relations—was the submarine's bell. It had apparently been removed from the sail structure and stowed in the bow compartment when the *K-129* went to sea.

Papers, documents, and the few manuals that were found were rushed to vans that had special paper preservation facilities and materials. Letters and photographs were also found.

"One of the ironic aspects of the recovery of the sub was that during its exploitation we found manganese nodules lodged between the pressure hull and the outer hull, apparently as the *K-129* was sliding down the slope . . . it just happened to scoop up some manganese nodules," observed Feldman. He quickly added, "Since the manganese nodules are rather porous they were very highly contaminated . . . very hot."[7]

The *Glomar Explorer*'s crew was told "in no uncertain terms" that no souvenirs would be taken from the submarine. Two items that disappeared during the exploitation process were a submarine badge and a belt buckle with the hammer-and-sickle-and-anchor insignia. The crew was told that if the two items were not returned no one would ever leave the ship! The next day both items reappeared. Still, some small pieces of the submarine's hull and some of the manganese nodules "disappeared."

The ship sent another commercial message on August 10, ostensibly to Summa Corporation headquarters, stating, "every effort was being made to determine whether repair of the nodule collector vehicle could be made at sea." At the time—while the wreckage of the *K-129* was being examined— the *Glomar Explorer* was sailing toward a prearranged site near Midway where, under the cover plan, a decision would be made whether it would be necessary to enter Midway Atoll's lagoon where mission crews could be exchanged. The next day another message was sent, indicating that the ship was changing direction to a new destination because repairs to the vehicle would require at least 30 days. At CIA headquarters the decision was made to send the ship to Lahaina Roads, a passage off the northwest coast of the Hawaiian island of Maui. There a special team—the B crew—would come on board to "clean up" the remains of the *K-129*. The cover story for the members of the B crew would be that they were mining vehicle technicians and inspectors.

When the ship was some 500 nautical miles northwest of Oahu she came to a stop and drifted for several days. Using packaging supplies that had been stowed aboard the ship, the material from the *K-129* that was considered of intelligence value was crated for transfer to a "secret facility" where it would

		STORAGE/SHIPPING	SYSTEM	IDENT	WGHT	CUBE
		IL ST SD XY	SN	SQ	WT	CU
		CRA		0	4250	196

08/25/74   1 0   00   Y   3   7   08/25/74 1
ITEM DESCRIPTION(ID)- TORP TUBE

09/27/74   1 0   00   Y   3   7   08/25/74 1
ITEM DESCRIPTION(ID)- TORP TUBE

08/27/74   1 0   00   Y   3   3   7   08/25/74 1
ITEM DESCRIPTION(ID)- SONAR PENETRATION

| | | CRA | | 0 | 4250 | 196 |

08/27/74   1 00   Y   3
ITEM DESCRIPTION(ID)- SONAR PENETRATION

| H00L5250 00108 CRA | | 0 | 5250 | 167 |
| REMARKS(RE)- FWD PORT/3' LONG |

08/27/74   1 0   00
ITEM DESCRIPTION(ID)- VALVE PENET ??

| H00L5250 00108 CRA | | 0 | 5250 | 167 |
| REMARKS(RE)- PRESS. HULL PENET. |

08/27/74   1 0   00   Y   3
ITEM DESCRIPTION(ID)- HATCH DOOR

| H00L5250 00108 CRA | | 0 | 5250 | 167 |
| REMARKS(RE)- FWD HULL |

| H00L5250 00108 CRA | | 0 | 5250 | 167 |
| REMARKS(RE)- FWD HULL |

08/28/74   1 0   00   R
ITEM DESCRIPTION(ID)- PR

| H00L5250 00108 CRA | | 0 | 5250 | 167 |
| REMARKS(RE)- |

3   7   PRESSURE HULL SEC.

| H00L5200 00108 CRA | | 0 | 5250 | 167 |
| REMARKS(RE)- FAILED & RUPTURED |

08/28/74   1 0   00   R   3   1
ITEM DESC   DESCRIPTION(ID)- PRESS. HULL PENETR.

08/25/74   1 0   00   R   3
ITEM DESCRIPTION(ID)- PRESS. HULL PENETR.

| H00L5250 00108 CRA | | 0 | 5250 | 167 |
| REMARKS(RE)- |

H0105'   .00/24/74 o0 00   R   3   1
H01051   ITEM DESCRIPTION(ID)- PRESS. HULL PENET

| H00L3750 00109 CRA | | 0 | 3750 | 167 |
| REMARKS(RE)- |

H01040   08/23/74   1 0   00   R   3
ITEM DESCRIPTION(ID)- PIPING & FRACTURE SAMPLE

| H00L3750 00109 CRA | | 0 | 3750 | 167 |
| REMARKS(RE)- FM PRESS. HULL |

H01041   08/28/74   1 0   00   R   3
ITEM DESCRIPTION(ID)- WELD SAMPLE

| H00L3750 00109 CRA | | 0 | 3750 | 167 |
| REMARKS(RE)- FM PRESS. HULL |

An excerpt from the massive CIA list of items recovered from the *K-129*, indicating the date and location where each item was found in the wreckage; its description and condition; how it was cleaned; if it was to be retained, and if so how it was to be stored or packaged; weight; cube; and so on.

This photo of an unidentified Soviet sailor was found in the wreckage of the *K-129* when technicians went through the 38-foot section inside of the *Glomar Explorer*'s moon pool. Other documents and a manual, believed to be about torpedoes, were recovered from the submarine and, after being immersed in water for six years, were "recovered" through special processes. (Central Intelligence Agency)

be carefully examined and its final disposition decided. All other material was packaged, weighted, and disposed of over the side as the ship lay dead in the water.

After getting under way again, the *Glomar Explorer* sailed to Lahaina Roads, dropping anchor at 2:30 PM on August 16. The A mission crew was relieved by the B crew that evening, the latter having been flown out to Hawaii in two charter jets. The A crewmen from Global Marine and various other firms as well as government personnel had been at sea for two months, carrying out an intense, difficult, and productive operation. In Hawaii the *Honolulu Advertiser* newspaper featured a page one article on the ship and the seafloor-mining venture. The Azorian cover story was still holding. With the B crew on board to further analyze the material removed from the submarine and to make preparations for either disposal or retention of the remaining material and to "clean up" the ship, the *Glomar Explorer* now steamed toward her home port of Long Beach.

One of the most important matters concerning the CIA and the men on board the American ship was the handling of the remains of the crew of the *K-129*. Scrupulous examinations aboard the *Glomar Explorer* had identified the remains of three of the sailors that were found in the forward section of the submarine:

> Vladimir Kostyushko, seaman
> Viktor Lokhov, senior sonarman
> Valentin Nosachev, senior torpedoman

All three men were age 20; none was married. There were also the remains of other, unidentified sailors.

The Soviet seamen were buried at sea in a ceremony that was carefully scripted and filmed. William Colby, the Director of Central Intelligence at the time, subsequently stated, "We had to come up with a proper ceremony. We thought someday we might have to give this [information] to the Russians and we wanted to assure them that we treated their people with due respect and honors."[8] A statement presented by then–Director of Central Intelligence Robert Gates to Russian President Boris Yeltsin in October 1992, in Moscow, explained,

> From the time of their recovery from the submarine's hulk until the burial ceremony, the remains were handled with the utmost care and respect. A heavy steel box, 8 x 8 x 4 feet in dimension, was chosen for the burial ceremony and six individual shelves were installed to support the bodies.
>
> On the appointed day, 4 September 1974, two rehearsals were held to ensure that the actual ceremony would proceed smoothly and with the appropriate dignity. A six-person Honor Guard was selected from among the volunteers. Immediately prior to the ceremony, the Honor Guard transported each body to the burial vault individually. During transportation, a Soviet Naval Ensign, carried for this purpose by the *Glomar Explorer*, was draped over each body. The same ensign shrouded each body.

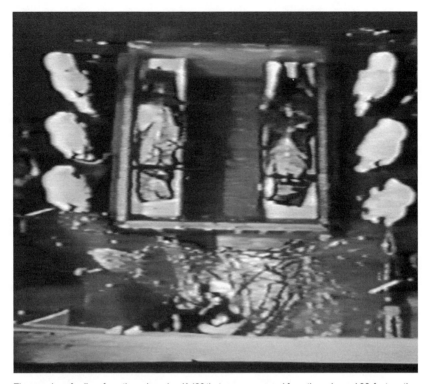

The remains of sailors from the submarine *K-129* that were recovered from the salvaged 38-foot section of the submarine were buried at sea with reverence and honors. This view is from the CIA film made of the burial service. The remains of only three sailors were positively identified by specialists aboard the *Hughes Glomar Explorer.* (Central Intelligence Agency)

After all bodies were placed in the burial vault, together with a representative portion of the vessel on which they served and perished, the ensign was mounted alongside the US National Flag behind the vault.

The ceremony, attended by some 75 of the ship's company, began with the National Anthem of the United States and of the Soviet Union. It continued with what was thought to be the closest ceremony approaching the actual Soviet Navy burial at sea ceremony. In addition, the US Navy ceremony for the burial of the dead at sea followed. An interpreter translated the Soviet service and the US Navy Service into Russian.

After the vault doors had been bolted shut, the vault was slowly hoisted over the side while the Committal and Benediction were read and the US Navy Hymn was played. At 1921 [7:21 PM] local time, during the final light of the evening twilight, the vault, now completely flooded, was released into a calm sea and fell free to the ocean floor.

The *Glomar Explorer* had come to a halt and the burial procedures took place approximately 90 nautical miles southwest of the island of Hawaii, at latitude 18°29' N and longitude 157° 34' W.

The respectful handling of the remains of those sailors from the *K-129* was disputed by some. Seymour Hersh, writing in *The New York Times* in late 1976, declared,

> Many crew members, in direct violation of C.I.A. orders, quickly stripped the bodies and the submarine of souvenirs and items of value—rings, watches, coins and bracelets, according to the Collier brothers [who were on board the *Glomar Explorer*].[9]

That report, however, is the opposite of what many other crewmen have told the authors of this book, and is contradicted by the careful packaging and logging of such items by technicians on board the *Glomar Explorer.*

The historic meeting of Gates and Yeltsin occurred less than a year after the collapse of the Soviet regime in December 1991 that ended the 45-year Cold War with its nuclear confrontation between the United States and the Soviet Union. In addition to the statement describing the procedure, Gates presented Yeltsin with the film of the burial ceremony and the Soviet naval ensign used in the ceremony.[10] It would be two more years before the Russian government released the names of those men lost in the *K-129* disaster.

Later, as the details of the submarine's loss and the burial ceremony were revealed, several Soviet officials and family members voiced strong objections to the handling of the sailors' remains. Rather, they declared, the remains should have been returned to the Soviet Union in 1974. As a precedent for such action they pointed to the British submarine *L-55* that had been sunk in the Bay of Kopor'ye (Gulf of Finland) in 1919 as a result of mine damage following an action with Bolshevik ships. All 41 men on board the British undersea craft had died. Nine years later the submarine was salvaged by the Soviet Navy and the bodies of the crew returned to Britain. But such action would have been impossible in 1974—during the Cold War, especially in the aftermath of a clandestine operation that may have violated international law. Also, the remains of the *K-129*'s crewmen had some level of nuclear contamination. In reality, the solemnity of the burial on board the *Glomar Explorer* was an event unprecedented during the 45 years of the Cold War.

Another gesture after the Cold War occurred when James Woolsey, then–Director of Central Intelligence, authorized Ambassador Malcolm Toon to present the bell from the *K-129* to the Russian government. The handover, on August 30, 1993, took place in Moscow during a meeting of the U.S.-Russian commission to look into personnel from both sides taken prisoner or missing during the Cold War. When this book went to press neither the authors nor their Russian contacts were able to determine the disposition of the bell—it seemed to have disappeared.

Revelation that the bell had been recovered led some individuals— suspicious of any CIA activity and statements—to conclude that the amidships section of the submarine, with the sail and its remaining missile, had been recovered along with the sail-mounted bell. In all navies a submarine's crew going to sea on "combat duty" would remove such accessories that produce noise and leave them ashore or stow them. In addition to the bell, subsequently, a photograph of an unidentified sailor found in the *K-129* wreckage was turned over to the Russian government (see page 129).

There was another burial at sea from the *Glomar Explorer*. From the outset of Global Marine's participation in Project Azorian, John Graham, the firm's chief engineer and principal naval architect, had a leading role in the design of the ship and key systems. He passed away, succumbing to lung cancer at age 59, on August 2, 1974. His ashes were flown to Hawaii and then transferred to the ship. The *Glomar Explorer* again came to a halt on September 10 and his ashes were passed over the side.

The *Glomar Explorer* reached her berth at Long Beach on September 21, 1974. At Long Beach the specialized mission vans were removed and the crates containing material from the *K-129* that would be the subject of further examination and assessment were brought ashore and shipped to an undisclosed location. There are indications that the location was the fabled Area 51, some 80 miles northwest of Las Vegas, Nevada.[11] The location is cited in numerous accounts of U.S. government activities related to Unidentified Flying Objects (UFO). More to the point, Area 51 was the scene of testing for several top-secret projects. By 1974 it contained a variety of technical facilities that could certainly perform examinations of the *K-129*'s remains. The final resting place of the submarine's remains that were deemed significant enough to retain were packed up and—according to unofficial but creditable statements made to the authors of this volume—are stored in a nondescript building, known simply as Building 7717, set back from Trigger Avenue, on the naval submarine base at Bangor, Washington.

The odyssey of the forward 38 feet of the submarine was over. But another deep-ocean salvage operation was being planned—to recover the lost amidships section of the *K-129*.

EXPOSURE AND REVELATION

Even as the *Hughes Glomar Explorer* sailed toward Long Beach, officials at CIA headquarters in Langley, Virginia, and at Global Marine head-quarters in Los Angeles evaluated the feasibility of returning to the site of the *K-129*'s remains to salvage the missile section and its hoped-for R-21/SS-N-5 missile and cryptologic material. And, a postmortem had to be held on the failure to lift the 130-foot forward section of the submarine.

The capture vehicle had failed while lifting the *K-129*. The fault was considered to be two-fold: first, the additional *million* pounds of weight that was offloaded onto the pipe-string and capture vehicle to drive the beams and davit tips deeper into the bottom soil, and second, the maraging steel that was used in the manufacture of the grabbers. The additional pressure was deemed necessary by the recovery director because the seafloor was deter-mined to be harder than expected. However, that decision was opposed by several senior personnel in the control room since it conflicted with the approved recovery plan. The additional weight, forcing the beams and davit tips into the soil and causing the shift of the *K-129* hull, was undoubtedly the cause of the fracture in No. 4. This action could possibly also have damaged beam No. 5.

Related to this situation was Lockheed's choice of maraging steel for the capture vehicle's beams and davits. Other steels would have allowed more deflection or "bending," permitting a better distribution of the load among the beams.[1] Lockheed had selected maraging steel for those components because it has superior strength and toughness compared to ordinary struc-tural steels. However, maraging steel is also relatively brittle, especially at low temperatures, as are encountered at great ocean depths. Thus its selection has been criticized as not being the proper material for use in Project Azorian.

Recently, information on Lockheed's selection of maraging steel has come to light. It has been revealed that the CIA provided a last-minute lift estimate that had increased the target object's weight by 500 tons. Since the capture vehicle's beams and davits were sized and the drawings released, Lockheed had no choice but to select another steel with a higher yield strength and equal ease of machining and workability in order to meet schedules.

The capture vehicle failure thus appears to have been caused by both the last-minute offloading of another million pounds of weight onto the vehicle and the basic decision to employ maraging steel.

The first step in an attempt to recover the amidships section of the *K-129* was to survey the site where the section had been dropped. While unclassified details are sparse, it appears that the U.S. nuclear-propelled submarine *Seawolf* (SSN 575) was employed to survey the site.

The *Seawolf*, completed in 1957, was the U.S. Navy's second nuclear submarine. The *Seawolf*'s original nuclear reactor plant used liquid-sodium as a heat exchange medium, in contrast to pressurized water employed in all other U.S. naval reactors. That original reactor plant was replaced with a pressurized-water reactor in 1958–1960, after which she saw limited service until the late 1960s, when she was modified to support saturation divers and to carry out other clandestine operations; her modifications gave her capabilities similar to those of the *Halibut*.

According to *Blind Man's Bluff,*

In late 1974 . . . the Navy had sent the USS *Seawolf* back to the Golf's grave site. . . . Using electronic "fish" to carry cameras down to the lost sub, *Seawolf* had collected photographs that showed the Golf had shattered after *Glomar* dropped it and lay in tiny unidentifiable pieces, a vast mosaic decorating the sand.

"It dissolved just like that, like an Alka-Seltzer in water," one former high-ranking naval officer says. "It spread all over acres on the ocean floor." Said another former Navy official: "It shattered. The judgment was made that there was no possibility to recover anything more."[2]

The USS *Seawolf* (SSN 575) was the world's second nuclear-propelled submarine. Her original sodium-cooled reactor plant was replaced by a pressurized-water plant, and she was rebuilt for deep-ocean search and saturation diving. The openings for her thrusters that permitted precise position keeping are visible forward and aft. (U.S. Navy)

This description of the wreckage seemed unlikely, however, since the CIA planned to rebuild the capture vehicle and return to the North Pacific site during the summer of 1975, when sea and weather conditions permitted. But the Navy officials involved in the planning, especially Captain James Bradley, the Navy's underwater intelligence expert, and Rear Admiral Bobby Ray Inman, the recently appointed Director of Naval Intelligence, voiced the opinion that the condition of the *K-129* remains would prevent effective recovery of either cryptologic material or the missile, if the latter still survived.

The CIA persisted and Project Azorian officially ended on October 20, 1974; the following day, Project Matador was initiated. Meanwhile, Global Marine, Lockheed, Honeywell, and other contractors involved in the *Glomar Explorer* and her lift systems began to rehabilitate the ship and to rebuild the capture vehicle. Not only would the damaged systems be repaired, but the grabbers and certain other components had to match the new configuration of the wreckage, that information being derived from the seafloor photographs taken by the *Seawolf*'s towed fish.

An unusual event occurred in December 1974 at the U.S. Navy's holiday party for foreign naval attachés, held in Bethesda, Maryland. At the party the Soviet naval attaché approached the U.S. Navy captain who served as liaison officer for foreign naval attachés. The Soviet officer, reportedly, said that it was known that the United States had tried to raise the submarine *K-129* and, "if you go back there it would mean war."[3]

Was the Soviet officer making an "official" statement? Had he had too much to drink at the party? And, did his statement reveal that the Soviets knew that the entire submarine had not been raised? Or that another salvage effort was being prepared? The conversation was reported to Admiral Inman the next morning.

Project Matador was short-lived. The break-in at the Summa Corporation offices just after midnight on June 5, 1974, had netted the burglars $68,000 in cash and some company papers. Summa executives told the CIA that the missing documents included a memo from a senior official at Hughes that outlined the submarine salvage project. The CIA alerted the Federal Bureau of Investigation (FBI) and the Los Angeles Police Department to watch for the sensitive document. Journalist James Phelan later wrote,

> The FBI, working through its Los Angeles office, urgently requested Los Angeles Police Chief Ed Davis to try to contact the burglars and retrieve the stolen papers, using a million dollars in federal funds for bait. In order to justify this highly unorthodox police effort, top officials in the Los Angeles Police Department were let in on the *Glomar* secret.[4]

In reality, the *Glomar Explorer*–related document never left the Summa headquarters building; apparently it was found by a security guard, who absent-mindedly put in his pocket and later simply destroyed it. None of the stolen documents was ever recovered when the Summa Corporation refused to pay the ransom of one million dollars demanded by the thieves.[5]

From either their contacts in the FBI or the police, Jerry Cohen and William Farr, investigative reporters for the *Los Angeles Times*, heard of the top-secret effort to salvage a Soviet submarine. Their article—albeit inundated with inaccuracies—appeared on page one of the *Los Angeles Times* on February 8, 1975, as the CIA and Global Marine were developing the plan and equipment to return to the *K-129* site. Immediately, William Colby, the Director of Central Intelligence, contacted the paper and asked that the story be killed. The story was not killed, but was pushed to a less-prominent location—page 18—in the next day's edition, and was then dropped altogether.

Phelan, who had long tracked Howard Hughes–related happenings, also learned some of the inside story. He had contacted Seymour Hersh of

A rare view of the barge HMB-1 with its sliding roof open and the massive capture vehicle visible. This photo, taken at Redwood City, California, in 1976, shows the capture vehicle as partially reconfigured for Project Matador, the planned recovery of the 100-foot section of the submarine *K-129* that fell away during the 1974 lift effort. (Reginald McGovern Collection/San Mateo County History Museum)

The New York Times. Hersh, a Pulitzer Prize–winning investigative reporter, was concentrating on the Watergate story, but the reports of a clandestine "snatch" of a Soviet submarine got his interest. Tapping various sources, he uncovered the cover-story code name "Jennifer." He then "dropped" the name whenever he could talk with his Navy or CIA contacts.

Colby spoke with the senior editors at *The New York Times* and convinced them to print only a digest of the *Los Angeles Times* story, and convinced Hersh to withhold his story in return for the CIA providing him with additional information on the salvage effort. Next, learning that journalist-muckraker Jack Anderson was onto the story, Colby spent a half-hour with him attempting to stop his revelations. On March 18, Anderson revealed much of the story—again with reasonable accuracy—on his national radio show. And, he labeled the effort a government "boondoggle." The following day, Hersh's more comprehensive story ran on page one of *The New York Times*, telling of the CIA's attempt to salvage a Soviet *nuclear* submarine.[6] Interestingly, Hersh told of how a *Times* reporter learned some details of the salvage operation in late 1973, when the *Glomar Explorer* was conducting tests in the Atlantic. He stopped his research on the matter after a request from Colby.

Also on March 19, the *Los Angeles Times* ran a page-one story about the salvage, with a photo of the Hughes mining barge No. 1 (HMB-1). It claimed, "The barge, longer than a football field, was lowered to the ocean floor where it its hangar-like roof was rolled back to free a huge claw. The claw, then connected by pipe fed down from a recovery ship, grabbed the submarine. The barge then resurfaced."[7] *Newsweek* magazine even showed a diagram of how the barge was suspended beneath the *Glomar Explorer* during the salvage, but not lowered to the ocean floor.[8] The HMB-1, of course, throughout the salvage operation was anchored some 350 miles northwest of Los Angeles, at Redwood City.

The *Los Angeles Times* article also stated,

> The *Times* is publishing the story now because of its partial disclosure Tuesday night [March 18] by Jack Anderson on the Mutual Broadcasting System.
>
> After the story broke in several publications following Anderson's radio broadcast, William Colby, director of the CIA, told the *Times*: "We blew [it]. I have no comment on this. I did my best."

Asked if he could not at least make some comment about the various news reports, Colby said, "Let me wait and see what it looks like tomorrow. There are a lot of diplomatic aspects of it and I can't talk about it now."[9]

Also in the late morning of March 19, Colby met with President Ford at the White House and urged that the government say nothing about Project Azorian—which was constantly referred to in the press as Jennifer.[10] The head of the CIA argued that no official should confirm or deny the effort, provide no background briefings, and no fact sheets. The president agreed. The CIA still hoped to go forward with Project Matador. Indeed, in contradiction of his own policy of no statements, in April *The New York Times* quoted Colby saying that the CIA had been preparing to attempt to salvage the rest of the submarine when the operation was revealed.[11]

The world press was now running stories—filled with errors—about the salvage effort. Some press reports had the bathyscaph *Trieste II* locating the sunken submarine, others had the Navy's oceanographic research ship *Mizar* (which had located the sunken submarine *Scorpion* [SSN 585] later in 1968). Neither, of course, the *Trieste II* nor *Mizar* had participated in the Azorian effort. *The Washington Post* noted,

[O]ne report was being circulated by intelligence sources on the fringe of the CIA that the *Glomar Explorer* had in fact retrieved the entire lost submarine, not just one-third of it. This report had the *Glomar Explorer* bringing up so many pieces of the lost boat that they comprised just about all of the 2,800-ton submarine.

If true, this would mean the CIA recovered the warheads on the torpedoes, the warheads on the three ballistic missiles the submarine carried and the code machine that unscrambled all the secret naval messages in the submarine would have received.[12]

The mystique of the *Trieste*, which undertook both white and black recovery operations, became a constant factor in books and articles about "what really happened" in the *K-129* story. Kenneth Sewell, who had served in a U.S. nuclear submarine, in a later edition of his book *Red Star Rogue*, reported, a U.S. Navy bathyscaph, *Trieste II* (DSV-1), made six dives on the wreck of a Soviet ballistic missile sub between November 1971 and August 1972. One of these dives earned the crew of the bathyscaph and its two support ships a meritorious unit citation for the recovery of an object of extreme value from the ocean floor adjacent to the wreckage—probably the warhead from the sub's number two missile silo. Importantly, these clandestine dives were conducted in Hawaii's Northwest Leeward Islands, near the location . . . posited was the most likely spot where the Russian submarine met its ultimate fate.[13]

Unfortunately for that account, the *Halibut* photos show the after portion of the sail of the *K-129*, where the two after missile tubes were housed, torn away, with no evidence of the missiles in the area—if they still existed. Could Sewell have meant the No. 1 missile tube, which was relatively intact? Still, the video from the *Glomar Explorer*'s capture vehicle showed the cap still in place on that tube in July 1974. If the warhead had already been recovered by the *Trieste II* in 1972, why the containment net apparatus to "catch" the missile if it slid out of the tube while the submarine was being raised in 1974? Indeed, why the time, cost, and political risks of going forward with Project Azorian if the *Trieste II* had recovered the warhead in 1971–1972? (Or could the cryptologic material really have been the primary objective of Project Azorian?)

Sewell's account also fails to consider the implications of employing the *Trieste II* to recover a missile warhead. First, requiring surface support and operating from the surface, the bathyscaph could not operate in the North Pacific except for possibly a brief period in the summer because of sea and wind conditions. Second, the *Trieste II* dives in the North Pacific would have attracted the attention of the Soviet Navy, as had the various phases of Project Azorian. The *Trieste II* and her support ships were U.S. Navy vessels, making them much more suspect than a commercial ocean mining venture sponsored by Howard Hughes.

Third, the *Trieste II* dive log does show six dives from November 1971 to August 1972. Dives No. 37 on November 4, 1971, and No. 38 on April 25, 1972, were at approximately 25°N and 167°W—about 300 nautical miles from Oahu. By coincidence, the depth of both of those dives was 16,400 feet, approximately the depth of the *K-129* wreckage. But the *K-129* was not at that location! The location of the *K-129* sinking has been verified—the *Glomar Explorer* recovery location has been documented, by those who were on board the ship at the time, by the British merchant ship *Bel Hudson*, and by several Soviet ships that observed the salvage operation. Rather, on dive No. 38 the *Trieste II*—with surface support ships, the floating dry dock *White Sands* (ARD 30), and the fleet tug *Apache* (ATF 67)—recovered a satellite film package or "bucket." These were normally "deorbited" and parachuted to earth over the mid-Pacific, to be captured while descending by a specially equipped U.S. Air Force recovery aircraft flying from Hickam Air Force Base on Oahu. That package missed midair capture and fell into the sea. After a preset time, the bucket sank to prevent it being recovered by foreign forces.

This package, weighing several hundred pounds, was recovered on April 25, 1972, on the bathyscaph's third dive at that location. (This was the largest object to be recovered by one of the *Trieste* bathyscaphs, except for the submersible being used to help salvage a crashed World War II aircraft.) The object recovered on April 25 was certainly not a nuclear warhead from the submarine *K-129*.[14]

On March 29, 1975, the Soviet ambassador to the United States, Anatoly Dobrynin, sent a lengthy note to Secretary of State Kissinger:

> Moscow paid attention to the reports in foreign press, including the American press, regarding the fact that certain U.S. services have conducted for some time the work of raising the Soviet submarine that sunk in 1968 in the open sea in the area northwest of Hawaii. According to these reports, the operation had been carried out by a special U.S. ship, the *Glomar Explorer*. It was reported, in particular, that a part of the submarine has been recovered some time ago with the bodies of the crew members, that were thrown out into the sea.
>
> It goes without saying that we cannot be indifferent to any operation of raising any parts and property of the submarine belonging to the USSR.
>
> Special concern is caused by the fact that the bodies of the crew members of the sunken submarine, according to the press reports, were recovered and then thrown back into the sea. The matters related to the

submarine and to the submarine and the dead seamen are the preroga-
tives of the Soviet Union alone.

We expect from the U.S. side explanations with regard to the above
mentioned reports, including complete information about the crew
members of the sunken submarine and also information on the discon-
tinuance of any operations connected with the submarine.[15]

Kissinger, on April 2, sent a memorandum to the president—SECRET/
SENSITIVE/EYES ONLY—telling him of Dobrynin's note and of his intention
to make an oral statement to the Soviet official informing him that no comment would be made on the matter. "This conforms to your standing instruc-
tion not to comment," concluded Kissinger.

The Secretary's oral response, as provided with his note to President
Ford, was,

> The United States has issued no official comment on the matters
> related to the vessel *Glomar Explorer*. It is the policy of this government
> not to confirm, deny or otherwise comment on alleged intelligence
> activities. This is a practice followed by all governments, including the
> USSR. Regardless of press speculation, there will be no official position
> on this matter.[16]

There was no comment—it is questionable if the Soviet government
expected one. As noted by Secretary Kissinger, the Soviet regime rarely
if ever commented on its intelligence activities, even after they had been
exposed by the West.

Also, in March 1975 the Soviet naval tug *MB-11* was reported in the
general area where the *K-129* sank. (Earlier the tug was reported to have
sailed within 35 miles of the entrance to Pearl Harbor.)

Project Matador was cancelled.

The *Glomar Explorer* and her related systems were highly specialized and
unique. They were intended for a single mission and, unless heavily modified,
could not be adopted for other missions. But with the revelation by the press
of the *Glomar Explorer*'s true purpose, there could not be more clandestine lift
operations. Accordingly, the capture vehicle, brought back to Redwood City

for repairs and reconfiguration for Project Matador, was simply dismantled and the remarkable pipe-string was scrapped.

The HMB-1, however, would have a future role in another top-secret project: The Lockheed "skunk works," which had developed the U-2 spyplane, SR-71 Blackbird, and F-117 stealth fighter, among other black projects, had developed and built a stealth test ship for the Navy, the *Sea Shadow* (IX 529). She was a test platform for several surface ship technologies, among them ship control, automation, structures, sea keeping, and—especially—signature reduction, i.e., stealth. The 563-ton, 164-foot ship was constructed within the HMB-1 from 1983 to 1985. Subsequently, after her *nighttime* trials and evaluation, the *Sea Shadow* was placed in reserve in the HMB-1 from 1986 until 1993, when at-sea testing resumed—this time in daylight. She was again laid up from 1995 to 1999, then again reactivated, for tests of signature-reduction techniques.

The *Glomar Explorer* herself had a less interesting "second career." Following the press exposure of the submarine salvage operation, there were officials in the Navy and CIA who looked at potential roles for the large ship. None materialized: she was too large, too specialized, and too "obvious" for the roles suggested. In September several newspapers "revealed" that the Navy was planning to employ the ship in "neutralizing Soviet sensors planted near a U.S. Navy-run island 50 miles off California."[17] Such a mission, however, was highly unlikely for the ship, since she was ill-fitted for such a search and recovery operation; several other Navy ships would have been far more capable—and easier to employ—in that role. The *Glomar Explorer* was not used for that mission, if it was in fact undertaken. Instead, the ship remained idle.

From March to June 1976 the U.S. General Services Administration attempted to lease the ship, but even interest initially coming from Lockheed failed to develop because of the costs to modify and operate the ship. On September 30, 1976, she was "legally" acquired by the U.S. Navy, designated as a miscellaneous auxiliary (AG 193), and her name changed, deleting the prefix "Hughes." While a Navy ship, she was transferred to Maritime Administration custody so that she could be "laid up"—anchored and preserved—in Suisun Bay near San Francisco. There she was readily identifiable from the scores of naval auxiliaries and merchant-type ships at nearby anchor, many rusting away. The *Glomar Explorer* was moored at some distance from

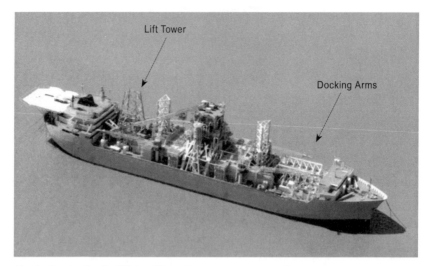

After Project Azorian the *Hughes Glomar Explorer* was laid up at Suisun Bay, near San Francisco, California. The top of the derrick tower had been dismantled and placed amidships, and the twin docking legs were removed and stowed forward. The ship was moored away from the other merchant ships and naval auxiliaries in reserve at Suisun Bay.

other ships; the reason can no longer be ascertained—perhaps someone at the Maritime Administration was concerned about residual radiation.

During this period there were attempts to sell the ship to a private operator. Instead, in 1978 she was leased (time chartered) to Global Marine Development, Inc., for a commercial seafloor mining venture on behalf of a consortium called the Ocean Minerals Company of Mountain View, California. Lockheed was to operate the ship. The lease was for a 13-month period, to begin about June 1, 1978, with additional lease options. Global Marine was to pay $300,000 for the original lease, and $25,000 per month during option periods.[18] For this project the *Glomar Explorer* was fitted with a tethered, self-propelled mining vehicle to harvest seafloor minerals.

At about the same time it was revealed that the National Science Foundation (NSF) had requested four million dollars in its fiscal year 1979 budget for feasibility studies on how to convert the *Glomar Explorer* for use as a deep-sea drill ship, to replace the older *Glomar Challenger*.[19] Subsequently, the NSF decided on the conversion, with the ship to be fitted for drilling in water depths to 25,000 feet; while drilling in half that depth she would be able to drill 23,000 feet into the Earth's crust. She was to be capable of drilling for oil and gas in addition to drilling in a scientific capacity. In the event, the NSF project was never funded.

The *Glomar Explorer* departed Suisun Bay under tow on July 1, 1978, en route to San Pedro (Long Beach) for reactivation and conversion at the Bethlehem Steel shipyard. The conversion was completed in late October and the ship subsequently carried out systems tests off the Santa Cruz Islands in water 6,000 feet deep. The ship's master, James Drabos, wrote of those trials,

> Although numerous equipment problems were encountered, the min-ing system was deployed successfully to the bottom and operated in spite of poor bottom conditions.
>
> We departed the [first] site on 15 November for the mining site and returned to San Pedro on 9 December. Although no nodules were collected on this trip, a great deal was learned about conditions in the area and equipment requirements which will make our next voyage to the mining site quite productive.[20]

But the mining project was cancelled, and the ship was returned to Navy control on April 25, 1980, and again assigned to the Maritime Administra-tion, abandoned, and laid up in Suisun Bay. In 1997 the ship was again heav-ily modified for use as a deep-sea drill ship for oil and gas exploration. The unique moon pool was sealed off as she was modified to drill in water 11,500 feet deep. The GlobalSantaFe Corporation leased the ship from the Navy in 2001 on a 30-year agreement to operate as the *GSF Explorer*.[21] In July 2007 Transocean announced that it was merging with GlobalSantaFe, the new entity to retain the name Transocean.[22]

Transocean, in March 2010, purchased the *GSF Explorer* outright from the U.S. government for 20 million dollars. The ship works on contracts for various oil corporations, drilling around the world. In 2010 the ship was drill-ing off Angola. In a way, the ship is performing the role for which she was originally publicized—exploiting the resources of the ocean floor.

ELEVEN

CONSPIRACIES AND CAUSES

W hat caused the loss of the submarine *K-129*?

The Soviet Navy's concerns were both general and specific. They were general because submarines and land-based aircraft were the principal war-fighting component of the Soviet Navy. At the start of 1968 the Soviet Navy was operating more than 300 submarines, including 23 of the Project 629/Golf-class ballistic missile submarines. That same year the Soviets had completed the first Project 667A/Yankee ballistic missile submarine (SSBN). The 16-tube, nuclear-propelled craft was analogous to the U.S. Navy's Polaris submarines. Series production was under way and a major portion of the Soviet Union's strategic missiles would be placed in these SSBNs.

Could the *K-129* have been trailed and then intentionally sunk by the U.S. Navy with some secret weapon? Was this the test of a new weapon that could destroy the Soviet SSBN force in time of war? Could such a weapon locate, track, and destroy a submarine without itself being detected? Periodically during the Cold War the U.S. Navy believed that the Soviets were working on just such a breakthrough in anti-submarine warfare.

The early 1960s were violent, with several confrontations between the Soviet Union and the United States: the shootdown of a U-2 spyplane over the USSR in 1960, the Berlin crisis of 1961 that saw U.S. and Soviet tanks facing off, the nuclear confrontation during the Cuban missile crisis of 1962, the ongoing Vietnam War with Soviet weapons (including jet fighters) being supplied to the forces fighting the United States, and the North Korean capture of the U.S. spy ship *Pueblo* in January 1968, an act that many Americans believed was encouraged if not directly supported by the Soviet Union. Thus, there was some Soviet concern that the loss of the *K-129* could be a harbinger of some new American anti-submarine capability, with such an attack being completely believable with the U.S.-Soviet animosity of the time.

The Soviet Navy's concern was also specific. There might have been a flaw in the *K-129*: something electrical or mechanical, or possibly structural, had failed. She was the first Project 629/Golf-class submarine of the Pacific Fleet to be converted to launch the R-21/SS-N-5 Serb ballistic missile and fitted with the new D-4 fire control system; there were other changes, as well. After her loss the second Golf II conversion, the *K-126*, upon returning from the search for her sister submarine, entered the No. 202 Dalzavod yard at Vladivostok where the conversions had taken place. Technicians and engineers carefully examined the submarine to determine if some fault had been introduced during the conversion.

Many potential causes for the *K-129* disaster were considered: a battery explosion, missile accident, snorkel failure, collision with a surface ship (while snorkeling), and more. The Soviet naval officers with whom the authors have discussed the issue indicate that a snorkel valve float failure was officially blamed for the casualty. But nothing in the Soviet Navy's investigations could be conclusively demonstrated as the definitive factor in her loss.

Soon a definite cause was advanced for the loss of the *K-129*: collision with a U.S. nuclear-propelled submarine, specifically the USS *Swordfish*. Completed in 1959, the U.S. submarine was already outdated by 1968 because new generations of nuclear submarines were being rapidly introduced in the U.S. and Soviet fleets. A submarine–submarine collision was not suggested in the initial meetings and discussions at various Soviet naval headquarters. In later years Rear Admiral Dygalo, commander of the 29th Submarine Division to which the *K-129* had belonged, put forth the theory that the submarine had been trailed by the *Swordfish* and accidently rammed by the American craft.

According to Dygalo, writing after the Cold War had ended, the *K-129* was sailing at periscope depth with her snorkel mast extended, using diesel engines for both propulsion and battery charging. In this condition the submarine's sonar was "deaf" because of the noise of the diesels. When in that condition the submarine relied on visual (periscope) detection and the hostile radio or radar emissions signals intelligence for warning that another submarine or an aircraft or ship was nearby. In this situation, the *Swordfish* maneuvered close aboard and struck the *K-129*'s hull as the Soviet submarine was turning on a new course.[1]

Dygalo later declared,

> It should be noted that the *Swordfish* belonged to the *Skate* [SSN 578] class type and had a specific design that provided a particularly reinforced sail structure so it could be possible to be able to ram underwater.[2]
>
> It should not be excluded that these submarines were not only prepared for accidental collisions, but could also sink ships of the Soviet fleet on purpose.
>
> Here I can say that the Americans are not that foolish to resort to ram submarine intentionally in peacetime . . . this action would be rather reserved for wartime.
>
> The fact they used to approach extremely close in order to record the acoustic signature of a submarine as clear as possible was later confirmed by the Americans and their specialists and was to be read in the press, also.
>
> Obviously, the *Swordfish* got very close to the *K-129* trying to record her [acoustic] signature. The *K-129* was maneuvering . . . on a new course and she did not notice that the *K-129* exposed her hull. The *Swordfish* wanted to plunge under her but collided with [her] sail structure between the second and third sections of the *K-129*.

Dygalo then described the damage to the *K-129*:

> The only thing that disturbed the general appearance of the submarine was a large hole in the [bow] part—as it was later reported—between the second and the third sections that looked like it had been struck by a gigantic hammer and the sail structure of a *Skate* looked exactly like that.
>
> It was also discovered that the metal edging around the hole was bent not outside but inside, which meant that the strike came from outside.

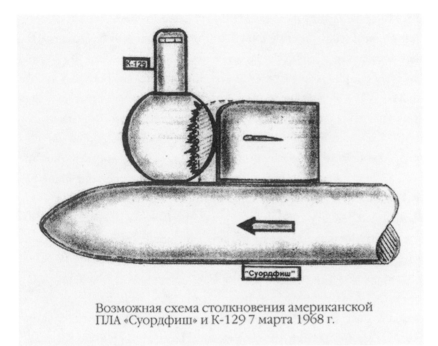

Возможная схема столкновения американской
ПЛА «Суордфиш» и К-129 7 марта 1968 г.

Rear Admiral Dygalo, like many Soviet naval officers, was convinced that the U.S. submarine *Swordfish* rammed—possibly intentionally—and sank the submarine *K-129*. This sketch of the "event" appears in Dygalo's book, *A Rear Admiral's Notes* (2009). The photographed damage on the two submarines does not support Dygalo's theory. (From *A Rear Admiral's Notes*)

The form matches the sail structure of a *Skate*, the subject of the decoded communications about the need to repair [the *Swordfish*] in Japan.[3]

Of course, Dygalo had not seen the photos of the *K-129* wreckage until well after the Cold War had ended. To corroborate this account, Dygalo stated that a Soviet intelligence ship "had intercepted shortly after the loss of the *K-129*, communications that were decoded between the multipurpose nuclear-propelled submarine *Swordfish* and her base stating that she had set course for Yokosuka [Japan] after an accident at sea."[4] And, Dygalo, in his articles and book, provides a sketch of how the *Swordfish* rammed the *K-129*.[5] But a careful review of both the *Halibut* photos and those taken by the capture vehicle show no damage as described by Dygalo.

This account was oft repeated by Soviet naval officers, submarine designers, and journalists, sometimes with creative and imaginative elaborations describing damage to the *Swordfish* that resulted in her being out of commission for periods variously touted as from six months to three years. Had they bothered to research the Japanese newspapers at the time, they would have found a photo of the *Swordfish* entering the Japanese port of Yokosuka on March 17. There is no damage evident to her large sail structure, only a bent periscope that, according to U.S. officials, was smashed by an ice floe in the Sea of Japan. On March 8 the *Swordfish* was on station off the port of Vladivostok, keeping watch on Soviet ships entering and departing the port, and serving as a picket for two U.S. carrier groups operating in the Sea of Japan in the aftermath of the North Korean seizure of the U.S. spy ship *Pueblo* in late January 1968. In reaction to the *Pueblo* seizure, the U.S. Navy sent nine submarines into the Sea of Japan, including the *Swordfish*. By February 29—one month after the seizure—all had departed except for the *Swordfish* and two diesel-electric submarines.

In 2010, in response to a request in conjunction with the preparation of this book, the U.S. Navy Department released the chart showing, "Submarine Positions as of 11 March 1968," originally classified "Top Secret/Limdis" (Limited Distribution) and, subsequently, additional charts for the period of concern. The U.S. Navy's then-secret plots of submarine operations show the same, three-submarine deployment. On March 12 the plot shows the single nuclear attack submarine (SSN) moving eastward from Vladivostok toward the Tsugaru Strait, and on March 13 the plot shows the *Swordfish* south of the strait. On the 14th the submarine has moved about 100 nautical miles to the east, and on the 15th she has passed through the strait and into the Pacific Ocean. (Two diesel-electric submarines remained in the Sea of Japan.) The *Swordfish* had been scheduled to enter Yokosuka on March 15; however, the American Embassy in Tokyo requested a delay of two days because of the possibility of strikes by local naval base workers along with the inevitable anti-SSN demonstration.[6]

On March 16 the Navy plot shows the *Swordfish* east of Tokyo; the following day she arrived at Yokosuka. With the end of the Cold War, the Navy released the deck log of the *Swordfish* for the month of March 1968, presenting a copy to the Soviet government on September 11, 2007. The log shows the submarine on "special operations" from March 1 through 16, 1968.

Perhaps more significant, in response to a request from U.S. Senator Robert C. Smith in 1999, the U.S. Director of Naval Intelligence, Rear

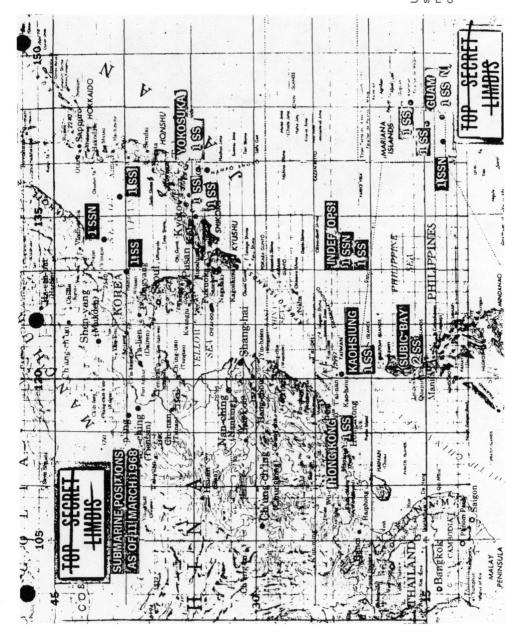

U.S. Navy flag plot representation of the deployment of U.S. submarines on March 11, 1968.

The nuclear-propelled attack submarine *Swordfish* (SSN 579) arrives at the U.S. naval facility at Yoko-suka, Japan, on March 17, 1968. Note the bent periscope, probably damaged on an ice floe off the Soviet port of Vladivostok. The lack of other damage visible during her daylight arrival in port gives lie to Russian charges that the *Swordfish* had rammed the submarine *K-129*, causing the loss of the latter.

Admiral P. M. Ratliff, stated that on March 2, 1968, the *Swordfish* "struck an iceberg while operating in the Sea of Japan and as a result sustained damage to one of her periscopes. The damage did not require an immediate return to port and the SSN completed its previously assigned operations prior to arriving in Yokosuka." Ratliff also noted, "a thorough review of U.S. Navy operational records from that time frame indicate that at the time the GOLF II sank, no U.S. submarine was operating within 300 nautical miles of the lost GOLF datum."[7]

However, the *Swordfish* story continues to be told, and in the post–Cold War era it has been reinforced by a U.S. naval officer, Captain Peter Hucht-hausen, a former U.S. naval attaché in Moscow. In his account of Cold War intelligence operations, Huchthausen wrote,

Until 1997, the identity of the U.S. submarine involved in that [*K-129*] incident was closely guarded as a politically sensitive and potentially damaging secret. (The Soviets claimed that it was the USS *Swordfish*.) In October 1997, a witness, who wished not to be named, told me that he had been on board a U.S. ship and that the loss indeed

The photo of the *Swordfish* with a bent periscope but no other damage to her sail structure was published in the Japanese newspaper *Asahi*. Such "evidence" of the lack of damage to the U.S. submarine thus was readily available to the public as well as to Soviet intelligence operatives in Japan.

resulted *from a collision or an accidental weapons launch by an unnamed U.S. Navy ship.*[8] [Emphasis added.]

In addition to his lack of precision—a weapon or a collision, a surface ship or a submarine—Huchthausen's account of the *K-129* sinking contains numerous factual errors: He has the U.S. Navy research ship *Mizar* being used in the search for the *K-129*, and the *Halibut* not only obtaining photographs of the wreckage, but also having "retrieved some items from the hull."[9]

An even more bizarre explanation of the *K-129* loss has been put forward by a principal American source: Dr. John P. Craven, a key figure in the U.S. Navy's development of underwater search and recovery capabilities, who served as chief scientist of the Polaris–Poseidon program (see Chapter 4). Craven described the *K-129* as a "rogue submarine," writing,

> To put it succinctly, there existed a possibility, small though it might be, that the skipper of this rogue submarine was attempting to launch or had actually launched a ballistic missile with a live warhead in the direction of Hawaii.
>
> There is also a small possibility that this launch attempt doomed the sub. Whatever happened, something in the missile's warhead may have exploded, causing the initial damage and possibly kicking off a chain of other events. Given the fact that the sub was armed with highly flammable liquid-fueled missiles, an explosion was certain to produce a conflagration in the command and control area [just forward of the missile tubes]. It would certainly have killed everyone in the vicinity. The surviving crew members would have made efforts to get on deck and put out the fire or failing that, abandon ship. And those fighting the fire would be dressed in protective garb—like the clothing and boots on the skeleton.[10]

The *Halibut* photos of the wreckage did show a skeleton with boots— but not with clothes or foul-weather gear, as would be worn on the surface. Even after only a month or two on the ocean floor the clothing material would have disappeared. More important, why would Captain Kobzar have attempted a missile launch? And could he have initiated the launch himself?

Or were there operatives of the KGB state security service on board who attempted the missile launch? In *The Silent War*, Craven noted that there is a "small" possibility that the commanding officer attempted to launch a missile, and "a small possibility" that the launch attempt doomed the submarine. According to one review of his book, "Craven then dismisses other scenarios for the loss, leaving—Sherlock Holmes-style—one possible answer for the conundrum, which then becomes a probability."[11]

The book *Red Star Rogue* by Kenneth Sewell, a former U.S. Navy submariner, postulates that the launch would have been part of a conspiracy, centered on the KGB to initiate a war between the United States and China by making it appear that a Chinese submarine had launched the missile.[12] In 1968 the Chinese Navy did posses a single ballistic missile submarine—a Golf SSB. The No. 199 shipyard at Komsomol'sk in the Far East—where the *K-129* was built—had fabricated components for two Golf submarines for transfer to China, with one assembled at Darien in the mid-1960s and designated Type 035. (The second submarine was never assembled.) The Chinese submarine was to have been armed with the Soviet R-11FM missile, but no missiles were delivered and the submarine has served as a test platform for Chinese-developed missiles. Furthermore, the Chinese submarine has never deployed, i.e., travelled out of coastal areas, and there was no submarine-launched ballistic missile available in the 1960s, and U.S. naval intelligence knew that.

The Soviet Navy had developed major safeguards to prevent a one-man launch of submarine missiles, as had the U.S. Navy. To again quote Admiral Dygalo,

> If the situation was getting tense the captain kept the so-called eight-hour communication schedule. That means he surfaced [*sic*] according to [communication] documents every eight hours parallel to Moscow time and not local time and received information. If the signal [from Moscow] was to increase readiness and the submarine switched on the one-hour readiness . . . by the one-hour readiness the ship had to be prepared to use nuclear missile weapons and torpedoes.
>
> In order to make sure the instruction was right the captain had four addressed envelopes to issue [to] commanders of the combat unit

1 (navigation), combat unit 2 (missiles), combat unit 3 (mines and torpe-does), and the deputy for political training.

The envelopes were renewed every mission. Everyone took an envelope. An envelope contained one piece of paper with three or four figures. . . . [T]hese envelopes together made up a code. This code was then entered into a machine and allowed the start key to be engaged and thus able to launch the missile.[13]

It would have been highly unlikely for officers of the *K-129* to carry out such a "rogue" launch of nuclear-armed missiles. These men were hardly likely to carry out a "rogue" missile firing that could lead to World War III. Of the fourteen officers aboard the *K-129* on her final voyage, twelve were married and two were divorced; all but one of them had children. All were career naval officers, the youngest, Senior Lieutenant Vladimir Mosyachkin, having served in the Navy for eight years. The other officers had served longer. Mosyachkin was in charge of the SIGINT detachment aboard the submarine and was thus involved in "special operations," but as one of the most junior officers on board, it is unlikely that he could have led a "coup." None of the officers is known to have had a state security (KGB) background. Even the submarine's political officer, Captain 3rd Rank Fedor Lobas, had served in the Navy for sixteen years, a significant portion of that time in ships.

Another widely circulated fiction related to the demise of the *K-129* is that an attempted missile firing—as well as her sinking—was detected by the Navy's SOSUS and by satellites. But SOSUS did not detect the submarine when she was at sea, nor did it identify her loss. The AFTAC system is not mentioned by Sewell nor by other authors addressing Project Azorian.

With respect to satellite detection, Sewell has written,

there have been published acknowledgments that satellite spy photography was used in the search for the *K-129* site. A number of U.S. Air Force and intelligence spy satellites were operational in that period.

* * *

Another, and probably the most likely, source of satellite intelligence that could have been used to pinpoint the *K-129*'s location at the time of the explosion was a dual-purpose program that disguised orbital spies as part of the Defense Meteorological Satellite Program—ostensibly for weather forecasting. This system, codenamed TIROS, began in 1965, and employed heat-reading infrared, multispectral scanners that could both track the heat in storms and pinpoint the heat trails of missile launches, from ignition and liftoff through the complete flight of the missile.

* * *

These satellites were in constant orbit over the earth's oceans, as well as the landmasses of Europe and Asia. In 1968, a Pacific Ocean-orbiting TIROS would have easily spotted and recorded the heat generated by the missile explosion in the middle of the cool waters of the northern Pacific. The Soviet submarine would have had to be riding on the surface at the time of the mishap for the infrared television camera to detect the heat image.[14]

Employing satellite photography to locate a submarine on the ocean floor, at a depth of three miles, clearly was—and remains—a technical impossibility. The Tiros was a civilian weather satellite, with full access to its findings available to the public. The Tiros satellites launched after 1966 were placed in near-polar orbits with an altitude of about 860 miles. Because the Tiros had an orbital period of 113 minutes, the orbital plane would shift about 28 degrees with each revolution. It would have been extremely fortuitous for the satellite to have been in the exact location to observe the alleged *K-129* event.

Sewell also cites the Corona, a photographic satellite, and Midas, a ballistic missile launch detection satellite, as having possibly sighted the *K-129*'s attempted missile launch. The Corona's KH-4A camera systems used film that was parachuted from the satellite to be "captured" by Air Force recovery aircraft. The system was preprogrammed to photograph specific "denied" areas of the Soviet Union and certain other countries. Unless there was some forewarning, it is inconceivable that the limited film available in Corona flight 123 (orbited on January 24, 1968) would be consumed in random photographing of the North Pacific.

The Midas—Missile Defense Alarm System—satellites could detect land- and sea-based missile launches, but that program was cancelled in 1966. Project 949 satellites, its geosyncronous replacement, was not launched until August 1968. The alleged missile launch from the *K-129* could not have been detected by a U.S. satellite.

Thus, material related to the *K-129* in *Red Star Rogue* is still another wild and teetering edifice built on factual errors, contrived conspiracies, and false reasoning. The book, however, was a *New York Times* "nonfiction" best seller.

Many of these same errors of fact appear in the more recent (2010) book by Craig Reed, *Red November*.[15] Beyond repeating the faults and flaws of Sewell and others writing about the *K-129* and Project Azorian, Reed introduces several additional errors to the story, such as having the *Glomar Explorer* carry the barge HMB-1 to the salvage scene and lower the barge over the *K-129*, with the claw extending from the barge to capture the submarine.[16] In addition, Reed attempts to "dramatize" each event in his book with virtually every U.S. submarine operation during the Cold War almost ending in disaster. With respect to Project Azorian, he states that 11 "strangers" walked across the gangplank onto the *K-129* just before she sailed and, "To this day, aside from a few Soviets in command at the time, no one knows who these strangers were or why they were on board."[17] In Reed's tale, those 11 men were responsible for the attempt to launch the submarine's missiles against Pearl Harbor. But in 1993 the Russian government published a list of all 98 men on board the *K-129* for her final cruise, with details of their ranks and positions, while Admiral Dygalo and others have written extensively about who was on board for her final cruise.

There is one more major conspiracy theory related to the loss of the *K-129*. If the Soviet regime believed that the United States had intentionally sunk the *K-129*, then did the Soviet Navy intentionally sink the USS *Scorpion* in retribution on May 22, 1968—less than three months later in the Atlantic, some 400 nautical miles southwest of the Azores? All 99 men on board went down with the U.S. submarine.

The *Scorpion* was en route back to the United States after a deployment in the Mediterranean. She had been diverted on a "special mission"—which might have been to ensure that a Soviet attack submarine was not trailing a U.S. ballistic missile submarine. She sent a last message on May 21 that reported her position, course of 290°, and speed-of-advance of 18 knots, and sailed on toward Norfolk . . . for one more day.

As Sewell wrote in *Red Star Rogue*—about the loss of the *K-129*—that the *Scorpion*,

> was diverted to investigate a strange assembly of Soviet warships near the Azores in the eastern Atlantic. The *Scorpion* disappeared on May 24, 1968, [*sic*] while returning from that clandestine mission.
>
> Speculation was rampant among submariners in both the United States and the Soviet Union that the *Scorpion* had been sunk by a Soviet torpedo.[18]

Based on Canary Island hydrophone detections of *Scorpion*'s breaking-up sounds and then a search by the Navy's research ship *Mizar*, Sewell notes, "To this day, articles in Russian publications and on Internet sites suggest that the Soviets deliberately sank the *Scorpion* in an act of revenge for the Americans' sinking the *K-129*."[19] Picking up this theme, in *Hide and Seek* author Huchthausen wrote that he was told by a U.S. deep submergence expert who had visited the wreckage in the bathyscaph *Trieste II* that "the photos of *Scorpion*'s hull show twisted metal with Cyrillic writing enmeshed in the hull."[20] Craig Reed, in his book *Red November*, picks up on that theme: "Theories and speculations abound and have been addressed ad nauseam in several books, but most concur that the evidence points to an external explosion."[21]

Then, after describing SOSUS paper recordings related to the *Scorpion* sinking, Reed wrote,

> the scribbles verified a high-speed screw. The targeted submarine's signature shifted in width and size, indicating evasive actions as the torpedo neared. Seconds later, the paper filled with black ink as the high-speed screws caught up with the evading submarine and ended her life.
>
> Students [at a Navy SOSUS training class in 1982] were told that the recoding was made during *Scorpion*'s encounter with an Echo II submarine.[22]

But SOSUS detected neither a Soviet Submarine, torpedo propeller noises, nor any explosive sounds that were external to the *Scorpion*'s pressure hull. According to Bruce Rule, the Navy's senior acoustic analyst at that time, and his reevaluation in 2008–2009 of the original acoustic data,

The initiating events responsible for the loss of the SCORPION were two small explosions that occurred one-half second apart . . . and were contained within the submarine's pressure hull. The source of these explosions, which are estimated to have been equal to the explosion of not more than about 20 lbs of TNT each, has been determined to be battery associated.

Scorpion sank to a depth of 1,530 feet, where the pressure hull collapsed in less than one-tenth of a second.

Scorpion was lost because of an on board problem (the battery explosions) that the crew could not overcome; there was no Soviet involvement.[23]

The theory that a Soviet torpedo sank the *Scorpion*, like the theory of the USS *Swordfish* ramming and sinking the *K-129*, defies logic, evidence, and circumstances. It is another conspiratorial theory—that has a half-life of "eternity."

The officer-of-the-deck aboard the USS *Swordfish* when her periscope was damaged by the ice flow, Lieutenant Commander Richard Lee, later wrote, "For those of us actually on board *Swordfish* (about 115 people), it's interesting how a writer (of historical fiction) can take separate events and draw whatever conclusion he wants."[24]

What sank the *K-129*?

The first American knowledge of a possible problem with a Soviet submarine in the North Pacific came from the Navy cable ship *Albert J. Myer*, which detected and taped two acoustic events on March 11, 1968—the first at 12:36:04Z and the second at 12:42:05Z. Correcting the data for the sound-travel times, the *Myer*'s detections were essentially midnight and six minutes later at the location of the *K-129*. A subsequent review of the naval facilities (NavFacs) for any SOSUS detections of the events and the AFTAC arrays showed that only the latter had identified those acoustic events. The AF-TAC tapped into one SOSUS hydrophone line out of Adak, Alaska. It was probable that other SOSUS arrays in the Pacific did detect those events, but the short duration of the signals and the system operators, probably looking for extended-duration signals, led to failure for those operators to recognize them. The AFTAC recorders, seeking subtle indications of nuclear detonations, were more than ten times more sensitive than the SOSUS displays.

There were two major sequences of acoustic events, both of 155 seconds duration with an interval of six minutes.

Detailed analysis in 2009 of the AFTAC data identified three lower-amplitude "precursor" acoustic events, at 11:58:58Z, 11:59:43Z, and 11:59:47Z. Each of these events contained multiple energy pulses of, respectively, 1.5, 0.7, and 0.7 seconds. These signals were produced by small, explosive-like events contained within the submarine's pressure hull. Had these events breached the *K-129*'s pressure hull and produced energy within the water column they would have exhibited longer durations because of a phenomenon known as "bubble-pulse." That condition would have been more easily recognized by SOSUS operators.

It is probable that the three precursor events were directly related to the first of the two major acoustic events that occurred a few seconds later. If the precursor events had been some form of explosive detonation of a conventional or nuclear torpedo in the *K-129*, the force would certainly have breached the pressure hull, or at least forced open the outer torpedo tube door to create a bubble-pulse. The submarine's six torpedoes—two with nuclear warheads—were normally kept in the torpedo tubes, not stowed within the pressure hull. While they may have been withdrawn from the tubes for checks or maintenance, such action was most likely conducted infrequently, probably on the order of once a month.

The most reasonable interpretation of this information is that an R-21 missile's rocket engine ignited at 12:00Z on March 11 and burned for 96.5 seconds until fuel exhaustion in its launch tube. Precisely six minutes after the ignition of the first missile engine, a second R-21 missile ignited within its tube and burned for 95.8 seconds until fuel exhaustion. These burn durations and the six-minute interval between firings are consistent with known values for the R-21 missile system—the burn of their engines and the missile launch interval.

Dr. Eugene Miasnikov, a senior Russian research scientist specializing in nuclear weapons, has written, "According to data published recently, the burn time of the R-21 at maximum distance was about 94 s[econds]. . . . Six minutes between the launch of the first and second missiles was demonstrated at one of the first test launches from a Golf SSB."[25]

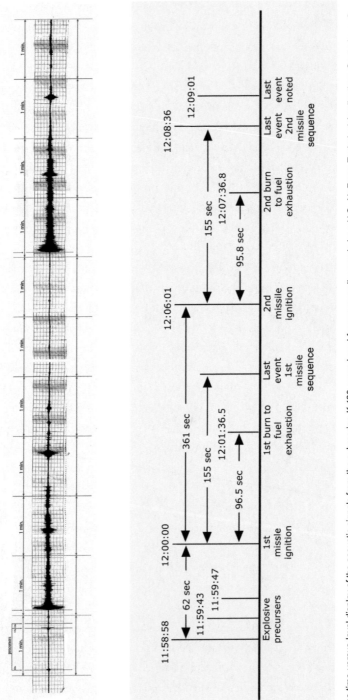

The time-versus-level display of the acoustic signals from the submarine *K-129*, reproduced from a recording made by a U.S. Air Force Technical Applications Center's seafloor sensor from 11:58:58Z to 12:09:01Z on March 11, 1968. The time line (bottom) is not to scale.

The small, explosive-type events beginning seconds before 12:00:00Z strongly suggest a scheduled event. Most probably, the missile-launch team was conducting a planned systems check or a training "dry" launch event. Something went terribly wrong, possibly because of the new crewmen being trained. The No. 3 missile engine most likely ignited within its tube. Six minutes later the No. 2 missile engine ignited.

The almost precise repeatability of the two sequences of events—each with a similarity in component signal amplitudes— indicates that they were produced by a fully automated (programmed) sequence (see figure on previous page). This indicates that, once initiated, an electromechanical system— as would occur with the submarine's D-4 missile launch control system—had control of the launch process. The three small acoustic events that occurred seconds before the first of the two major events may have resulted from the sequencing of the D-4 launch system. The actual launch of missiles may have been prevented *only* by the failure of the launch-control sequencer to automatically open the missile tube caps and (outer) hatches. Some manually controlled lock-down devices, not under control of the D-4 sequencer, could also have prevented the release of the two R-21 missiles.

The submarine was near the surface, operating the snorkel (as determined from the wreckage), hence all internal compartments were most likely open for ventilation. The extremely high-temperature exhaust plume of one or both missiles probably burned through the launch-tube liners and exhausted into the *K-129*'s still-intact pressure hull. The crew suffered explosive (burning) injuries as well as pressure-induced (crushing) injuries. This condition was consistent with observations by the medical personnel on board the *Hughes Glomar Explorer* who examined the remains of the *K-129* crewmen recovered from the bow section.

The catastrophic effects of the burning of the No. 2 and No. 3 missile engines also tore away the after portion of the sail structure as well as the bottom of the fourth compartment, beneath the missile tubes. The submarine, with her crew dead, was now open to the sea and plunged downward, before the intense heat or the D-4 sequencing, could similarly ignite the engine of the No. 1 missile. There are data suggesting that the after section of the sail was ripped open within 30 seconds of the first major acoustic event, or about 12:01Z. The 98 men on board the *K-129* would have undoubtedly been exposed to the intense heat and poisonous fumes from the rocket fuel and would have died by that time.

Because the submarine was using her snorkel, with internal compartments open, the submarine flooded during her descent. There was no implosion of the pressure hull that, like the *Thresher* and *Scorpion* sinkings, would have been detectable by SOSUS as a major acoustic event.

Significantly, despite the intense heat from the missile burns, there was no detonation of the conventional "triggers" of the missile's one-megaton nuclear warheads. In order to detonate a plutonium device the high explosives around the core need to be precisely detonated to "focus" the shockwave and symmetrically compress the plutonium to achieve criticality. This precise detonation can only be achieved by electronic detonation of the explosive primers down to a couple of nanoseconds of simultaneous detonations. Intense heat could set off some explosives, but a fission reaction is impossible. The plutonium contamination of the wreckage was most likely due to the crushing of the two nuclear torpedoes in their bow tubes and the physical damage to their warheads. Whatever happened to the R-21 missiles, both still fired to their fuel exhaustion.

There are possible, albeit less likely, alternative explanations as to what happened aboard the *K-129*. For example, the R-21 fuel (dimethyl hydrazine) and the oxidizer (red fuming nitric acid) have a violent reaction when mixed, producing combustion chamber temperatures as high as 5,250°F. There could have been leaks in one of the missiles that resulted in the two liquids mixing within the confined space of the missile tube. That could be disastrous. This kind of accident happened on board the Project 667A/Yankee submarine *K-219* north of Bermuda in 1986. That submarine reached the surface but sank after several days because the damage was irreparable.

But unlike the *K-219* disaster, aboard the much smaller *K-129* a rocket booster ignition in the missile tube would have breached the interior bulkheads and the toxic exhaust would pass into the pressure hull. Had the exhaust plumes not been released into the submarine it is unlikely that the R-21 engines would have fired until fuel exhaustion.

Again, the time of the acoustic events on board the *K-129* and their sequence make it far more likely that it was a failure of the R-21/D-4 launch control system. That failure could have been electromechanical or crew-initiated, the latter a training exercise that went terribly wrong.

One other factor needs to be considered in determining the cause of the *K-129* sinking. Following his communications check on February 26, Captain Kobzar had failed to meet his radio transmission schedule, and failed to respond to several demands from Soviet radio stations to acknowledge their calls. The submarine may have also been, again, trying to send a transmission on the 12:00Z schedule on March 11. With communications problems probably extending over several days, and the AFTAC acoustic recordings revealing small, explosive precursor events in the range of the equivalent of 10 to 20 pounds of TNT, it is possible that an antenna coupler explosion could have contributed to the chain of events leading to the live booster burns within the *K-129*'s missile tubes. While such a scenario is unlikely, it has been suggested to the authors by knowledgeable persons.

Regardless, analysis of the AFTAC acoustic data indicate that the *K-129* and her entire crew were lost to the sequential ignition of two missile engines while confined within their launch tubes within the hull and sail of the submarine. Catastrophic and unrecoverable damage was almost immediate when those missile engines ignited.

TWELVE

FAILURE AND FRUSTRATION

T wo aspects of the *K-129* disaster would frustrate the Soviet government. First, a submarine with five nuclear weapons on board—three strategic missiles and two torpedoes—had been lost. The Soviet Navy had been unable to locate the wreckage while the Americans had succeeded in not only locating the submarine, but also in raising a portion of the *K-129* with Soviet naval ships watching the endeavor. Further frustrating the government, a note had been delivered to the Soviet Embassy in Washington before the operation warning that the Americans would attempt to salvage a sunken submarine. That note had been brought to the Soviet Navy's attention, but the probable depth of the remains and the perceived impossibility of deep-ocean salvage led to the warning being ignored except for the surveillance of the *Glomar II*'s survey operation.

After the salvage effort was revealed in mid-1975, Admiral Gorshkov, the CinC of the Soviet Navy, established a panel to determine "what the Americans could possibly get if they [had] access to nuclear weapons, codes, torpedoes and mechanisms inside the submarine, welding technology, composition of metals," according to Rear Admiral Dygalo.[1] "They came up with the following," he continued,

[L]et's start with the most important; if Americans did in fact lift the nose part then they should get the nuclear weapons, I mean, the special combat payloads of two torpedoes. It goes without saying, the torpedoes were crushed by the pressure of 570 atmospheres . . . but for specialists even debris can say a lot about the level of our nuclear technologies and the way they could be upgraded and enhanced. Secondly . . . they would know the composition of steel, welding technology and other specific shipbuilding details.

The Soviet Navy's summary of its formal analysis of the *K-129* episode stated,

> Considering that the submarine was lost at a depth of more than 5,000 m[eters], the special [nuclear] ammunition should have been destroyed and it is impossible to determine from it its complete characteristics.
>
> If U.S. specialists succeeded in raising warheads, the maximum information, with incomplete destruction of the special ammunition, will be the following:
>
> • general level of Navy munitions as of the early 1960s
> • physical and technical solutions contained in warhead design
> • designs of individual assemblies and special ammunition
>
> It should be taken into account that at the moment of the *K-129*'s loss the majority of special ammunition assemblies had been removed from production and were not being used in new types of weapons.

With respect to cryptologic material, the report noted, "Concerning ciphers and encryption units: all Fleet documents were changed following the loss of *K-129*."

Second, the Soviet government knew unequivocally by mid-March that the *K-129* and her entire crew of 98 were lost. There was a *local* ceremony honoring the dead at Rybachiy on May 5, but the government could not admit to the loss and hence could not acknowledge how the crew died. Dygalo recalled,

> The families of the perished officers and re-enlistees [senior petty officers] that wished to leave from Kamchatka were provided with [apartments] in their new places of residence. They were granted a compensation payment but the allowance of pensions was delayed for bureaucratic reasons in Moscow. . . .

> Despite the prohibition of the Commander-in-Chief [Gorshkov] to inform the relatives of the death of the *K-129* crew officially, I sent the relatives of the deceased a personal letter of death notification, from the end of May to the beginning of June.[2]

Dygalo relates that he had a heart attack on June 10 as he signed the 98th letter. He spent the next month in a hospital. His letters, of course, had no legal standing in the Soviet regime with respect to benefits for the families of the men lost in the *K-129*.

Bureaucratic red tape and the Soviet refusal to publicly acknowledge the loss led to delays and major problems for the survivors as they sought payment due for the loss of their loved ones. Based on a decree issued by the Navy Commander-in-Chief on September 12, 1968, the families of the men lost in the *K-129* were each given 1,500 rubles—roughly equivalent to that amount of dollars, but with more buying power—and certificates were at last issued saying the individuals were "deemed deceased." The wording was similar to their having accidently drowned. Only after the end of the Cold War, in November 1993, did the Russian government finally allow the list of men who died on board the *K-129* to be published (see Appendix B). And the Order of Valor award was presented posthumously to each member of the submarine's crew in 1996.

A very different kind of frustration was felt in the United States—by the several hundred civilian contractors, *Hughes Glomar Explorer* crewmen, CIA officers, and government officials who knew of Project Azorian. They had found the wreckage of the *K-129*, designed and built a ship and systems to lift a 136-foot section, and had undertaken the lift operation. All of this was accomplished over a six-year period, with continued press attention—because of the cover story—and with the actual lift attempt made under the eyes of Soviet naval "watchers."

Yet, the Americans failed. Only some 38 feet of the submarine were recovered. While that section did have intelligence value, the principal targets of the effort—an R-21/SS-N-5 ballistic missile and cryptologic material—were not brought into the *Glomar Explorer*'s moon pool. (Of course, rumors and press reports continue to ascribe the recovery of the entire submarine or, at least, the missile and the crypto material.)

The recovery of two crushed nuclear torpedoes, a few documents, and some basic knowledge of Soviet submarine construction—for a dated, non-nuclear design—was a pretty thin "take" compared to the envisioned haul. Lee Mathers, a former U.S. Navy intelligence officer, wrote, "Azorian was a great gamble, displaying the actions of a confident country with the wealth and the will to make such a gamble if the potential gain would make the effort worthwhile."[3]

He continued,

> If successful, the effort would have potentially provided a long-term look into Soviet cryptologic systems and established a solid data-point in our understanding of the Soviet technological development curve concerning both missiles and nuclear weapons. However, such a gain—especially in the area of cryptographics—would be fleeting unless the [secret recovery] mission could be kept completely secure for a long, indeed an indefinite, time.

The total cost of Project Azorian was on the order of $500 million in early-1970s money, including about $200 million for constructing the *Glomar Explorer*. The cost of a manned mission to the moon at the time was on the order of $500 million. The CIA has carefully withheld all cost data on the project, even to the date of this book's publication. Could such data be useful—several decades after the event—to a potential enemy? Or even to the Congress?

The cost was significant. Was the effort "worth it"? Here is Admiral Dygalo's evaluation of the project:

> I said it many times: one must judge fairly his adversary. It goes without saying that the USA made a breakthrough in technology and had [a] successful economy—both became possible exclusively thanks to highly qualified human resources. Just the fact that they managed to build a ship of 60,000 tons of displacement, to install equipment to sustain such a [submarine] load, to make provision of how to accommodate the submarine under the ship and finally to lift it up. It seemed to us something unreal, fantastic, I can compare it with a mission to the moon in regard of technology and invested money. And another point—the ship was

built in two years [*sic*] and we were fooled these two years—the disin-
formation was organized outstandingly.[4]

Thus did the "enemy" judge Project Azorian. That judgment was
shared by many Americans, and was "made official" in July 2006 when the
American Society of Mechanical Engineers awarded its prestigious Historic
Mechanical Engineering Landmark award to the *Hughes Glomar Explorer*. The
citation noted,

> The success of the *Hughes Glomar Explorer* proves that the impossible
> is, indeed, possible when talented engineers with the courage to take
> prudent risks are provided an incentive to stretch the state-of-the-art.

The *Hughes Glomar Explorer* and Project Azorian—history's most ambitious ocean engineering effort—thus took its place among such remarkable
American engineering achievements as the Wright Flyer III, the Hughes Flying Boat HK-1, the hydrodynamic research submarine *Albacore* (AGSS 569),
the Saturn V rocket, and the Apollo command module. Project Azorian was
certainly a remarkable and audacious engineering achievement—even if not
fully successful.

While the engineering accomplishments of Azorian were considerable,
on another level the operation was a major intelligence achievement. The
decision to go ahead with the salvage effort despite questions if not actual
opposition from several senior members of the defense and intelligence com-
munities demonstrated a commendable attitude to undertake "acceptable"
risks and expend resources for potential and unique intelligence gains at the
height of the Cold War. Further, the operation was undertaken with a cover
story—Howard Hughes–sponsored seafloor mining—that actually attracted
press and public attention. And, an overt and unique salvage platform—the
Hughes Glomar Explorer—that was easily observed by the Soviets was constructed with major publicity. These aspects of the operation demonstrated
a high degree of imagination.

Project Azorian *failed* in its primary goal in that neither the R-21 missile and its nuclear warhead, nor cryptologic material were recovered. Yet
the project was *successful*: Soviet intelligence agencies were unable to detect
the U.S. salvage effort—despite the warning that the United States would

The *Hughes Glomar Explorer*, renamed the *GSF Explorer*, continues to sail the oceans as an oil-drilling exploration ship. This is her current configuration: a different oil-derrick "tower" has been installed and the distinctive docking legs are gone, as are the numerous vans that housed her "black" activities. (GlobalSantaFe/Transocean)

attempt to salvage a sunken Soviet submarine and the Soviet Navy's close surveillance of U.S. activities at the *K-129* site. Material recovered from the wreck, including two nuclear torpedoes and documents, did have intelligence value.

Today U.S. intelligence agencies continue to undertake clandestine underwater missions, including search and recovery efforts for small objects—American and foreign—that fall into the ocean. But none are known to have reached the scale or the originality demonstrated in Project Azorian.

APPENDIX A

THE KAMCHATKA FLOTILLA

The Petropavlovsk-Kamchatka submarine complex was one of the world's largest submarine bases in 1968 with almost 40 submarines based at "Petro" at that time.[1] At any time some 20 percent of the submarines were in the No. 202 Dalzavod shipyard at Vladivostok or other nearby shipyards for conversion, overhaul, or maintenance, or were on post-overhaul shakedown cruises in the Sea of Japan, or conducting weapons training in the Sea of Okhotsk. About 10 percent of the submarines would also be deployed out-of-area on "combat duty" (deployments) or special missions. Thus, at any given time some 70 percent of the submarines would be in port or under way on local training operations.

While this deployment ratio was significantly lower than that for U.S. submarines during the Cold War, Soviet submarines in port were generally kept at a higher level of readiness to deploy on short notice than were their American counterparts.

Submarine deployments of 60 days or more occurred infrequently prior to the 1970s. "Strategic" patrols were initiated in 1968, with deployments of 70 days or longer.

Kamchatka Flotilla, February 1968
(Rear Adm. Boris Yefremovich Yamkovoy)

15th Submarine Squadron
(Rear Adm. Yakov I. Krivorochenko)

182nd Submarine Brigade[2]
(Rear Adm. Igor V. Karmadonov)

12	SS	Foxtrot		
		K-8	*K-55*	*K-133*
		K-15	*K-85*	*K-135*
		K-33	*K-101*	*K-143*
		K-50	*K-112*	*K-164*

Note: Five of these submarines were forward deployed to the isolated base code-named "Finval" some 45 miles northeast of Petropavlovsk at Bechevinskoy Bay.

5	SS	Zulu		
		B-66	*B-72*	*B-90*
		B-71	*B-88*	

1	SSR	Whiskey-Canvas Bag		
		S-73		

10th Submarine Division
(Capt. 1/R V. Arkady)

8	SSGN	Echo II		
		K-10	*K-108*	*K-184*
		K-48	*K-116*	*K-189*
		K-94	*K-175*	

29th Submarine Division
(Rear Adm. Viktor Ananevich Dygalo)

4	SSB	Golf II[3]		
		K-99	*K-126*	*K-129*
		K-136		
4	SSB	Golf I		
		K-75	*K-139*	*K-163*
		K-83		
2	SSB	Zulu		
		B-62	*B-89*[4]	

45th Submarine Division
(Rear Adm. N. B. Chistyakov)

5	SSGN	Echo I		
		K-45[5]	*K-66*	*K-151*
		K-59[5]	*K-122*[5]	
4	SSN	November		
		K-14	*K-115*	
		K-42	*K-133*	

APPENDIX B

THE CREW OF THE *K-129*

The submarine *K-129* sank on March 11, 1968, with 98 officers, warrant officers, and enlisted men on board. All were lost. The Soviet government did not announce the names of those lost with the submarine until a list was published in the official military newspaper *Krasnaya Zvezda* on November 13, 1993. The following list is abridged from the official roster, which also included the names of the wife or parents of the crewman, date of birth of wife if married, names and dates of birth of children, and address of residence.

Position	Military Rank First Name LAST NAME	Year of Birth Year Entered Navy	Nationality
Commanding officer	Captain 1st Rank Vladimir Ivanovich KOBZAR	1930 1948	Ukrainian
Executive officer	Captain 2nd Rank Aleksandr Mikhaylovich ZHURAVIN	1933 1951	Jewish
Deputy commander for political affairs	Captain 3rd Rank Fedor Yermolayevich LOBAS	1930 1952	Ukrainian
Senior watch officer	Captain 3rd Rank Vladimir Artemyevich MOTOVILOV	1936 1954	Russian

Position	Military Rank First Name LAST NAME	Year of Birth Year Entered Navy	Nationality
Navigation department head	Captain-Lieutenant Nikolay Ivanovich PIKULIK	1937 1957	Ukrainian
Head of navigation department electro- navigation group	Lieutenant Anatoliy Petrovich DYKIN	1940 1959	Russian
Missile-gunnery department head	Captain 3rd Rank Gennadiy Semenovich PANARIN	1935 1953	Russian
Missile-gunnery department control group officer	Captain-Lieutenant Viktor Mikhaylovich ZUYEV	1941 1958	Russian
Torpedo department head	Captain 3rd Rank Yevgeniy Gigoryevich KOVALEV	1932 1952	Belorussian
Engineering department head	Captain 3rd Rank Nikolay Nikolayevich OREKHOV	1934 1953	Russian
Engineering department motor group officer	Engineer Captain-Lieutenant Aleksandr YEGOROVICH	1934 1953	Russian
Chief of electronics service	Senior Lieutenant Aleksandr Fedorovich ZHARNAKOV	1939 1957	Russian
Chief of medical service	Medical Service Major Sergey Pavlovich CHEREPANOV	1932 1952	Russian
Group officer	Senior Lieutenant Vladimir Alekseyevich MOSYACHKIN	1940 1960	Russian
Helmsmen/signalmen team leader	Warrant Officer Vyachcslav Semenovich BORODIJLIN	1939 1958	Russian

Position	Military Rank First Name LAST NAME	Year of Birth Year Entered Navy	Nationality
Helmsmen/signalmen squad leader	Petty Officer 2nd Class Petr Tikhonovich LOPSAR	1945 1964	Russian
Helmsman/signalman	Senior Seaman Leonid Vasilyevich TOKAREVSKIY	1948 1967	Russian
Helmsman/signalman	Seaman Sergey Nikolayevich TRIFONOV	1948 1967	Russian
Helmsman/signalman	Senior Seaman Yuriy Fedorovich KARABZHANOV	1947 1966	Russian
Helmsman/signalman	Seaman Vitaliy Pavlovich OVCHINNIKOV	1944 1965	Russian
Electrician/navigation team leader, navigation department	Petty Officer 2nd Class Mansur Gabdulkhanovich KHAMETOV	1945 1964	Tatar
Senior electrician, navigation department	Senior Seaman Mikhail Ivanovich KRIVYKH	1947 1966	Russian
Electrician apprentice, navigation department	Seaman Gennadiy Semenovich KASYANOV	1947 1966	Russian
Control squad leader	Senior Seaman Nikolay Ivanovich GUSHCHIN	1945 1964	Russian
Senior electrician operator	Senior Seaman Viktor Ivanovich BALASHOV	1946 1965	Russian
Senior electrician operator	Seaman Anatoliy Sergeyevich SHUVALOV	1947 1966	Russian

Position	Military Rank First Name LAST NAME	Year of Birth Year Entered Navy	Nationality
Control team leader	Petty Officer 2nd Class Aleksey Georgiyevich KNYAZEV	1944 1964	Russian
Gyroscope operators team leader	Petty Officer 1st Class Vladimir Vladimirovich LISITSIN	1945 1964	Russian
Senior gyroscope operator	Seaman Viktor Vasilyevich KOROTETSKIKH	1947 1966	Russian
Engineers team leader	Petty Officer 2nd Class Nikolay Ivanovich SAYENKO	1945 1964	Russian
Senior engineer	Seaman Yuriy Ivanovich DUBOV	1947 1966	Russian
Senior engineer	Petty Officer 2nd Class Valeriy Mikhaylovich SURNIN	1945 1964	Russian
Torpedomen team leader	Petty Officer 2nd Class Valeriy Gcorgiyevich CHUMILIN	1946 1965	Russian
Senior torpedoman	Seaman Valeriy Grigoryevich NOSACHEV	1947 1966	Russian
Torpedoman	Seaman Vladimir Mikhaylovich KOSTYUSHKO	1947 1966	Russian
Torpedo electricians team leader	Petty Officer 2nd Class Viktor Andreyevich MARAKULIN	1945 1964	Russian
Radiotelegraphers team leader	Warrant Officer Vitaliy Ivanovich TERESHIN	1941 1965	Russian

Position	Military Rank First Name LAST NAME	Year of Birth Year Entered Navy	Nationality
Radiotelegraphers team leader	Petty Officer 2nd Class Valeriy Stepanovich NECHEPURENKO	1945 1964	Russian
Radiotelegrapher	Seaman Anatoliy Andreyevich ARKHIPOV	1947 1966	Chuvash
Machinists team leader	Petty Officer 1st Class Aleksandr Vasilyevich KUZNETSOV	1945 1964	Russian
Senior machinist	Senior Seaman Yuriy Ivanovich TELNOV	1946 1965	Russian
Machinist	Petty Officer 2nd Class Petr Ivanovich GOOGE	1946 1965	Russian
Machinist team leader	Petty Officer 2nd Class Viktor Dmitnyevich PLYUSNIN	1945 1964	Russian
Senior machinist	Senior Seaman Mikhail Vladimirovich ZVEREV	1945 1964	Russian
Senior machinist	Petty Officer 1st Class Gennadiy Mikhaylovich SHPAK	1945 1964	Russian
Machinist	Seaman Yuriy Vasilyevich SHISHKIN	1946 1965	Russian
Machinist	Seaman Aleksandr Sergeyevich VASILYEV	1944 1966	Russian
Machinist	Seaman Sergey Vladimirovich OSIPOV	1947 1966	Russian

Position	Military Rank First Name LAST NAME	Year of Birth Year Entered Navy	Nationality
Machinist	Seaman Gennadiy Ivanovich KRAVTSOV	1947 1966	Russian
Machinist	Seaman Nikolay Andreyevich REDKOSHEYEV	1948 1967	Russian
Machinist	Seaman Anatoliy Semenovich KABAKOV	1948 1967	Russian
Machinist	Seaman Ivan Ivanovich ODINTSEV	1947 1966	Russian
Machinist	Seaman Vladimir Valentinovich KOLBIN	1948 1967	Russian
Machinist	Seaman Anatoliy Ivanovich RUDNIK	1948 1967	Russian
Electrical team leader	Warrant Officer Ivan Tikhonovich KOTOV	1939 1959	Russian
Team leader	Petty Officer 2nd Class Nikolay Nikolayevich BAZHENOV	1945 1964	Udmurt
Team leader	Chief Petty Officer Nikolay Dmitriyevich ABRAMOV	1945 1964	Russian
Team leader	Petty Officer 2nd Class Vladimir Grigoryevich OSHEPKOV	1946 1965	Russian
Senior electrician	Seaman Vladimir Alekseyev POGODAYEV	1946 1965	Russian

Position	Military Rank First Name LAST NAME	Year of Birth Year Entered Navy	Nationality
Senior electrician	Senior Seaman Leonid Konstantinovich BOZHENKO	1945 1965	Russian
Senior electrician	Seaman Ivan Aleksandrovich DASKO	1947 1966	Russian
Electrician	Seaman Aleksandr Nikiforovich OZHIMA	1947 1966	Russian
Electrician	Seaman Vladimir Matveyevich GOSTEV	1946 1966	Russian
Electrician	Seaman Boris Petrovich TORSUNOV	1948 1967	Russian
Electrician	Seaman Aleksandr Nikolayevich TOSHCHEVIKOV	1947 1966	Russian
Electrician	Seaman Anatoliy Afanasyevich DYAGTYAREV	1947 1966	Russian
Electrician	Seaman Vladimir Vasilyevich SOKOLOV	1947 1966	Russian
Machinist team leader	Chief petty officer (extended service) Valentin Pavlovich INANOV	1944 1963	Russian
Machinist team leader	Petty Officer 2nd Class Aleksandr Dmitriyevich POLYANSKIY	1946 1965	Russian
Machinist team leader	Petty Officer 2nd Class Mikhail Seliverstovich SAVITSKIY	1945 1964	Russian

Position	Military Rank First Name LAST NAME	Year of Birth Year Entered Navy	Nationality
Machinist team leader	Senior Seaman Gennadiy Innokentyevich KOBELEV	1947 1966	Russian
Bilgeman	Senior Seaman Vladimir Mikhaylovich SOROKIN	1945 1964	Russian
Bilgeman	Seaman Yevgeniy Konstantinovich PESKOV	1947 1966	Russian
Bilge machinist	Seaman Aleksandr Ivanovich YARYGIN	1945 1964	Russian
Bilge machinist	Seaman Aleksandr Stepanovich KRYUCHKOV	1947 1966	Russian
Bilge machinist	Seaman Vladimir Nikolayevich POLYAKOV	1948 1967	Russian
Radiotechnical team chief	Warrant Officer (extended service) Vladimir Yulianovich SPRISHEVSKIY	1934 1953	Russian
Sonar leader	Senior Seaman Aleksandr Petrovich KULIKOV	1947 1966	Russian
Senior sonarman	Senior Seaman Viktor Aleksandrovich LOKHOV	1947 1966	Russian
Senior sonarman	Seaman Aleksandr Aleksandrovich PICHURIN	1948 1967	Russian
Radiometer team leader	Senior Seaman Anatoliy Sergeyevich NAYMISH	1947 1966	Russian

Position	Military Rank First Name LAST NAME	Year of Birth Year Entered Navy	Nationality
Senior radiometer operator	Seaman Nikolay Dmitriyevich **KOSHIKAREV**	1947 1966	Russian
Radiometer operator	Seaman Oleg Vladimirovich **ZUBAREV**	1947 1966	Russian
Chemist orderly	Petty Officer 2nd Class Valeriy Mikhaylovich **BAKHIREV**	1946 1965	Russian
Senior cook instructor	Chief Petty Officer Viktor Mikhaylovich **LABZIN**	1941 1960	Russian
Senior cook	Senior Seaman Leonid Vladimirovich **MATANTSEV**	1946 1965	Russian
Senior cook	Seaman Gennadiy Viktorovich **CHERNITSA**	1946 1965	Russian
Radiometer senior instructor	Petty Officer 2nd Class Aleksandr Ivanovich **KUCHINSKIY**	1946 1965	Belorussian
Radio telegraph team leader	Petty Officer 1st Class Aleksandr Vladimirovich **KHVATOV**	1946 1965	Russian
Radio telegraph team leader	Petty Officer 2nd Class Anatoliy Semenovich **CHICHKANOV**	1946 1965	Russian
Radio telegraphist	Seaman Vladimir Vasilyevich **KOZIN**	1947 1966	Russian
Radio telegraphist	Seaman Oleg Leonidovich **KRUCHININ**	1947 1966	Russian

Position	Military Rank First Name LAST NAME	Year of Birth Year Entered Navy	Nationality
Apprentice radio telegraphist	Seaman Vladimir Mikhaylovich PLAKSA	1947 1967	Russian
Radiometer team leader	Senior Seaman Timur Tarkhayevich MIKHAYLOV	1947 1966	Buryat
Sonar team leader	Senior Seaman Aleksey Vasilyevich ANDREYEV	1947 1966	Russian
Torpedoman	Seaman Aleksandr Vladimirovich KOZLENKO	1947 1966	Russian
Cypher specialist	Chief Petty Officer Gennadiy Fedorovich GUSHCHIN	1946 1966	Russian
Bilge machinist	Seaman Georgiy Ivanovich BASHKOV	1941 1966	Russian

APPENDIX C

THE SUBMARINE *K-129*

T he *K-129* was one of 23 Project 629 ballistic missile submarines commissioned in the Soviet Navy from 1959 to 1962.[1] Of these, 16 were constructed at shipyard No. 402 at Severodvinsk on the White Sea, and seven were built at shipyard No. 199 at Komsomol'sk-on-Amur in the Far East. The last Severodvinsk submarine—the *K-142*—was completed as Project 629B with two tubes for the submerged-launch R-21/SS-N-5 Serb missile. Components for two additional submarines were fabricated at Komsomol'sk and transferred to China, with one assembled at Darien in the mid-1960s (designated Type 035); the second submarine was never assembled.

These submarines remained in Soviet service as SSBs until 1989 with the last units retired after almost 30 years of continuous service. Some units continued briefly in missile test and communications roles. The Project 629 missile test configurations were

PROJECT	NAME	NATO SYSTEM	MISSILES
601	*K-118*	Golf III D-9	6 R-29/SS-N-8
605	*K-102*	Golf IV D-5	4 R-27K/SS-NX-13
619	*K-153*	Golf V D-19	1 R-39/SS-N-20

In addition, under Project 629E the *K-113* was to have been converted to a specialized minelayer (cancelled). Under Project 629R three submarines were converted to communication relay ships (SSQ): *B-42*, *K-61*, and *K-107* (renamed *BS-83*, *BS-167*, and *BS-107*, respectively).

The *K-129* was converted to the Gulf II configuration from March 1964 to June 1966 at shipyard No. 202 Dalzvod at Vladivostok.

Design: Nikolai Isanin was the chief designer of Project 629, which was designed at Special Design Bureau No. 143, later named "Malachite."

The design was based on the contemporary torpedo submarine of Project 641 (NATO Foxtrot). An additional section was added, aft of the control spaces, to house three missile tubes. The tubes penetrated the pressure hull upward through the sail, and extended down into the extended pressure hull "step-down" beneath the keel.

Section 1	torpedo room, crew berthing
Section 2	forward batteries; crew berthing
Section 3	control-navigation
Section 4	missile section
Section 5	after batteries, galley, officers
Section 6	diesel engines
Section 7	electric motors, switchboard
Section 8	torpedo room, crew berthing

Engineering: All submarines were built with a snorkel installation. (The TsKB-16 design bureau had proposed fitting Golf missile submarines with a small nuclear power plant to provide a means of keeping the electric batteries charged without employing a snorkel. This modification to the Golf class, known as Project 629M, was not pursued.)

Missiles: The first five Project 629 submarines were armed with the R-11FM ballistic missile (NATO SS-1B Scud-A). These submarines were later rearmed with the R-13 missile (NATO SS-N-4 Sark), which were fitted in all subsequent submarines except the last unit. The final submarine of this class was completed with the R-21 (NATO SS-N-5 Serb) missile. Subsequently, 13 earlier submarines were converted to the Project 629A configuration with the R-21 missile, including the *K-129*. (See Appendix D for details on NATO missile designations.)

The R-11FM and R-13 missiles were surface launched. The submarine came to the surface and the missile was elevated up and above the tube for launching. The R-21 underwater launched from the missile tube. The missile could be launched from (keel) depths of 130 to 165 feet with the submarine traveling up to 4 knots.

Submarines rearmed with the R-21 were fitted with the D-4 missile system in place of the earlier D-2 system.

Operational: The world's first launch of a submarine missile armed with a thermonuclear warhead occurred on October 20, 1961, when a Project 629 submarine launched an R-13 missile carrying a one-megaton warhead that detonated on the Novaya Zemlya (Arctic) weapons range in test "Rainbow." (The first U.S. test launch of a Polaris missile with a nuclear warhead occurred a half year later when a Polaris A-1 missile with a warhead of just over one megaton was fired from the submarine *Ethan Allen* [SSBN 608].)

The 23 submarines served in the fleet areas where they were constructed until 1976. The six submarines of the 16th Submarine Division were transferred from the Northern Fleet to the Baltic Fleet in September–October of that year to serve in the sea-based theater nuclear strike role.

Torpedoes: No spare/reload torpedoes were carried in these submarines. Two nuclear-armed torpedoes were normally carried on "combat duty" deployments.

SEVERODVINSK UNITS		KOMSOMOL'SK UNITS	
Completed 1959–1962		Completed 1959–1962	
B-40	(later *K-72*)	*B-93*	(later *K-126*)
B-41	(later *K-79*)	*B-103*	(later *K-129*)
B-42	(later *K-83*)	*B-109*	(later *K-136*)
B-92	(later *K-96*)	*B-113*	(later *K-139*)
B-121	(later *K-102*)	*K-75*	
K-36	(later *K-106*)	*K-99*	
K-61		*K-163*	
K-88			
K-91			
K-93			
K-107			
K-110			
K-113			
K-142			
K-153			

The *B-103* (later *K-129*) was laid down on March 15, 1958; launched on May 8, 1959; and commissioned on December 31, 1959.

Displacement	
surface	2,820 tons
submerged	3,610 tons
Length	324 ft 5 in (98.9 m)
Beam	26 ft 11 in (8.2 m)
Draft	26 ft 7 in (8.1 m)
Diesel engines	3 Kolomna 37-D (2,000 hp each)
Electric motors	1 PG-102 center shaft (2,750 hp)
	2 PG-101 outboard shafts (1,350 hp each)
Shafts	3
Speed	
surface	14.5 knots
submerged	12.5 knots
Test depth	985 ft (300 m)
Missiles	3 R-21/SS-N-5 Serb ballistic missiles
Torpedo tubes	4 21-inch (533-mm) bow
	2 21-inch (533-mm) stern
Torpedoes	6
Radar	Albatross
	Chrom
	Nakat
Sonar	Arktika-M
	MG-10
Missile system	D-4
Complement	83 (13 officers + 70 enlisted men)

APPENDIX D

THE R-21/SS-N-5 SERB MISSILE

The R-21 missile was developed to provide an underwater launch capability to Soviet ballistic missile submarines.[1] The decision to begin development of the missile was made on March 20, 1958, and was intended for rearming 14 diesel-electric Project 629/Golf and 7 nuclear-propelled Project 658/Hotel submarines. A new, nuclear-propelled missile submarine—Project 667—was initiated to carry the R-21 missile. Developed under the direction of chief designer A. S. Kassatsier, the Project 667 design was highly complicated because of the proposal that the R-21 missile undergo final assembly within the submarine and provision of a rotating launcher for the missile.[2] Several designs were considered for Project 667; one design model, now located in the Central Naval Museum (St. Petersburg), shows a cruise-missile launcher firing forward through the sail with ballistic missiles fitted amidships.

In the event, the R-21 missile was only carried by the Project 629A/B and Project 658M submarines.

In March 1958—just prior to completion of the first Project 629 SSB—work began at the Special Design Bureau No. 586 under chief designer M. K. Yangel on the R-21 submerged-launch ballistic missile (NATO SS-N-5 Serb).[3] A year later the missile project was transferred to Special Design Bureau (SKB) 385 under chief designer Viktor P. Makeyev.

The new missile had a maximum range of 755 nautical miles, i.e., twice that of the previous R-13 submarine (surface-launched) missile. The R-21 could be launched from submarine keel depths of 130 to 165 feet, providing

A Project 629/Golf I submarine launches an R-13/SS-N-4 Sark missile from the surface. Seven Golf submarines initially carried the earlier R-11FM missile. The Soviet Navy developed the world's first ballistic missile submarines, but they were soon outdated by the U.S. Navy's development of the Polaris system. (Malachite Design Bureau)

enhanced survivability for the submarine, with the submarine traveling up to 4 knots at the time of launch. The D-4 system for the R-21 missile provided for the launch tubes to be flooded prior to missile launch.

The R-21 used a cold-launch, solid-propellant rocket to eject the missile from the launch tube prior to ignition of the main rocket motor. The rocket employed inhibited red fuming nitric acidamine (AK-271) as an oxidizer and unsymmetrical dimethylhydrazine as a fuel. These compounds ignited upon contact (hypergolic) to produce combustion-chamber temperatures as high as 5,250°F. Initially the R-21 missile could be fueled and maintained ready to launch for six months; this period was later extended to two years.

The development of the R-21 was delayed because of technical problems. Initial underwater launches of R-21 dummy missiles took place in 1961 from the Project 613D4/Whiskey test submarine *S-229*; that submarine was fitted with a single missile launch tube aft of the conning tower. A year later *two* R-21 launch tubes were installed in the *K-142*, the last Project 629 submarine being built at Severodvinsk (redesignated Project 629B). Completed in 1961, that submarine made the first underwater test launch of an R-21 missile on February 24, 1962.

TABLE D.1 Submarine-Launched Ballistic Missiles

	R-11FM NATO SS-1b Scud-A	R-13 NATO SS-N-4 Sark	R-21 NATO SS-N-5 Serb
Operational	1959	1961	1963
Weight	12,050 lb (5,466 kg)	30,322 lb (13,745 kg)	36,600 lb (16,600 kg)
Length	34 ft 1 in (10.4 m)	38 ft 8 in (11.8 m)	42 ft 4 in (12.9 m)
Diameter	34⅔ in (0.88 m)	51 in (1.3 m)	55 in (1.4 m)
Propulsion	liquid- propellant 1 stage	liquid- propellant 1 stage	liquid- propellant 1 stage
Range	80 nautical miles (150 km)	350 nautical miles (650 km)	755 nautical miles* (1,400 km)
Guidance	inertial	inertial	inertial
Warhead**	1 RV conventional or nuclear 10 KT	1 RV nuclear 1 MT	1 RV nuclear 1 MT

Notes: There were several variants of each missile.
  * A later version of R-21 carried an 800-kiloton warhead to a range of 865 nautical miles.
  ** KT = Kiloton; MT = Megaton; RV = Reentry Vehicle.

Through 1972, 13 additional Project 629 submarines and 7 Project 658 submarines were converted to the D-4 system with three R-21 missiles, becoming Projects 629A and 658M, respectively.

Operational: The R-21 missile was in service in Soviet submarines from March 1963 until late 1989. During that period there were 228 launches of the R-21 missile, of which 193 were successful (i.e., 85 percent).

APPENDIX E

THE SUBMARINE *HALIBUT*

The *Halibut* was designed and constructed as a guided (cruise) missile submarine (SSGN 587) to launch the Regulus strategic attack missile.[1] After serving in that role from 1960 to 1964, with the end of the Regulus missile program in 1964 the *Halibut* was employed as a special-mission submarine. For that role she underwent two extensive conversions, in the 1960s and again in the 1970s, to enable her to support saturation diving, undertake deep-ocean search, and to perform other clandestine activities (see Chapter 3). She was reclassified as an attack submarine (SSN 587) on July 25, 1965.

This was the U.S. Navy's only nuclear-propelled guided (cruise) missile submarine until the start of the twenty-first century, when four converted Trident ballistic missile submarines were converted to the SSGN role. Those submarines, armed with the Tomahawk land-attack cruise missile, were changed from SSBN to SSGN 726–729, two ships in 2002 and two in 2004.

The *Halibut* was taken out of service in 1976 and laid up at Bremerton, Washington, until she was "recycled," i.e., reactor removed and mostly scrapped. Her disposal was completed in 1994.

The characteristics listed below are as a cruise missile submarine.

Design: The submarine was originally ordered as a diesel-electric SSG, but on February 27, 1956, the Navy announced that she would be provided with nuclear propulsion.

The *Halibut* had a conventional post–World War II hull design with a large missile hangar faired into her bow. The Regulus missiles were launched from a short launching rail between the hangar and the sail structure.

Subsequent nuclear-propelled Regulus submarines, the SSGN 594–596, 607, and eight or nine additional submarines, were to be of a different design, carrying four Regulus II missiles. In the event, these craft were built as torpedo-attack submarines (SSN).

Engineering: The S3W reactor plan was similar to that in the *Skate*-class SSNs.

During her conversion to a special mission submarine the *Halibut* was fitted with a single, trainable thruster atop the former missile hangar (a complete failure); subsequently she was fitted with four through-hull ducted thrusters for station keeping, installed between the pressure hull and the upper outer hull.

Missiles: As an SSGN the *Halibut*'s missile hangar could accommodate five Regulus I or two Regulus II missiles; she never carried the latter weapons.

Builder	Mare Island Naval Shipyard, Calif.
Keel laid	April 11, 1957
Launched	January 9, 1959
Commissioned	January 4, 1960
Decommissioned	June 30, 1976
Stricken	April 30, 1986
Displacement	
surface	3,845 tons
submerged	4,755 tons
Length	350 ft (106.7 m)
Beam	29 ft (8.84 m)
Draft	20 ft (6.1 m)
Reactors	1 Westinghouse S3W pressurized water-cooled
Turbines	2 Westinghouse (3,650 hp each)
Shafts	2
Speed	
surface	20 knots
submerged	20 knots

Test depth	700 ft (213 m)
Torpedo tubes	4 21-inch (533-mm) bow
	2 21-inch (533-mm) stern
Torpedoes	17
Sonar	AN/BQS-4
Fire control	Mk 101 Mod 12 torpedo fire control
Complement	123

APPENDIX F

THE LIFT SHIP *HUGHES GLOMAR EXPLORER*

The *Hughes Glomar Explorer* was designed and constructed specifically to lift the remains of the Soviet missile submarine *K-129* from the ocean floor. The ship was built under the "cover" of a seafloor mining ship sponsored by Howard Hughes.

The ship was designed by Global Marine and Sun Shipbuilding. Originally she was scheduled to be completed on or before September 30, 1972, to permit the salvage attempt to be made during the summer of 1973. However, technical problems and the decision to widen the ship to achieve greater stability delayed her completion for almost a year. She undertook the salvage of the *K-129* in July–August 1974.

After the decision not to proceed with a second lift attempt in 1975 (Project Matador), the ship was made available for commercial lease. She was then modified for commercial work (including seafloor mining) and at times was laid (mothballed) in the National Defense Reserve Fleet in Suisun Bay, California (see Chapter 10).

She was technically acquired by the U.S. Navy on September 30, 1976; at that time she was renamed *Glomar Explorer* and classified as a "miscellaneous auxiliary" (AG 193). She was stricken from the Naval Vessel Register on November 19, 2007.

Design: The major features of the ship (as built) included a heavy lift system with an almost 8,000-ton lift capacity: the flooded submarine section estimated to weigh up to 2,000 tons, the capture vehicle weighing almost 2,000 tons, and the 16,000-foot pipe-string weighing some 4,000 tons. The central derrick structure of the lift/pipe-string system towered 263 feet above the ship's keel and sat atop at 755-ton gimbal system that served to keep the derrick and pipe-string vertical as the ship heaved and rolled at sea.

The ship was provided with a massive interior docking well (moon pool) 199 feet long, 74 feet wide, with a minimum vertical clearance of 65 feet to accommodate the approximately 140-foot forward section of the *K-129* and the capture vehicle; the usable length of the moon pool was 179 feet because of the docking legs for the capture vehicle fitted at both ends of the opening. The well could be closed off with bottom doors (gates).

A small helicopter deck was fitted aft.

Engineering: The ship was provided with an automated dynamic-positioning system, with three through-hull bow thrusters and two stern thrusters.

Operational: The ship currently operates as a leased seafloor oil drilling ship.

Builder	Sun Shipbuilding, Chester, Pennsylvania
Launched	November 4, 1972
Completed	July 1973
Stricken	November 19, 2007

Displacement		
	light ship	21,000 tons (well closed and dry)
	full load	63,300 tons (well closed and flooded)
Tonnage		
	deadweight	39,705 tons
	gross register	27,445 tons
Length		618 ft 8 in (188.5 m)
Beam		115 ft 8½ in (35.16 m)
Draft		46 ft (14.02 m)
Propulsion		diesel-electric
		5 Nordberg diesel engines
		6 General Electric motors
		13,200 hp

Shafts		2
Speed		
	normal	10 knots
	maximum	12 knots
Radar		navigation
Complement		178

APPENDIX G

THE CAPTURE VEHICLE

The capture vehicle was constructed to match and lift the forward 136-foot section of the submarine *K-129* from the ocean floor. Suspended at the end of the 16,000-foot pipe-string from the lift ship *Hughes Glomar Explorer*, the capture vehicle was intended to remain positioned directly over the wreckage regardless of the motion of the ship more than three miles above.

The vehicle—referred to as Clementine by the crew of the *Glomar Explorer*—was built by Lockheed in Redwood, California, and assembled within the Hughes Mining Barge No. 1 (HMB-1). This enabled the barge to be towed to Catalina Island and submerged, and the *Glomar Explorer* moved over the barge and lifted the vehicle up into the ship's moon pool without any indication to outside observers of the configuration of the vehicle and hence its purpose.

The core of the capture vehicle was a strongback or "spine" that comprised two massive steel beams, 179 feet long and 31 feet wide. Mounted on the beams were a number of sensors, thrusters, cameras, and lights, along with the grabbers that would lift the submarine (see Chapter 7).

Intended to lift a submarine section approximately 136 feet long and weighing up to 2,000 tons, the capture vehicle was fitted with eight "grabbers"—beams and davits—to conform to the configuration of the submarine's hull. Because the *K-129* hull was lying on her starboard side, the grabbers were arranged with five on the left side and three on the right side, with a containment net provided that, when extended, could capture the single remaining R-21 missile should it begin to slide from the tube within the submarine's sail structure. Water jets were mounted along the sides of the grabbers to help excavate the soil and silt so that the davit tips could penetrate deeper into the soil, and under the submarine. It was critical that the grabbers not pierce the submarine's hull, which would have damaged the submarine.

The capture vehicle's four breakout legs were deployed (hydraulically lowered) when the vehicle approached the ocean floor; after alignment with the *K-129* wreck, the vehicle landed on the four legs. The legs were then retracted to allow the capture vehicle weight to drive the grabbers into the seafloor. After the grabbers were closed, encircling the submarine's hull, the legs were hydraulically activated to break the bottom suction and to jack the wreckage off the seafloor. Once their role was completed, the legs were jettisoned from the capture vehicle upon liftoff. They remain at the wreck site.

After Project Azorian the capture vehicle was returned to Lockheed—in the HMB-1—for reconstruction to enable it to lift the central section of the *K-129*, which broke away from the claw as the submarine was being lifted from the ocean floor. However, with the demise of Project Matador in 1975, the capture vehicle was stripped of its various components.

The basic strongback structure is now part of a device for testing high-strength structural assemblies with forces up to five million pounds, operated by the Coordinated Equipment Company in California.

Dry weight		2,390 tons
Wet weight		
	descent	2,055 tons
	without legs	1,489 tons
	ascent	3,449 tons (with *K-129* section)
Length		179 ft (54.57 m)
Width		31 ft (9.45 m)
	beams extended	110 ft 10 in (33.79 m)
Height		
	with breakout	
	legs extended	97 ft 2 in (29.62 m)
	breakout legs	35 ft (10.67 m)

APPENDIX H
THE HUGHES MINING BARGE NO.1

The Hughes Mining barge No. 1 (HMB-1) was constructed specifically to house the capture vehicle for Project Azorian. The barge was constructed by National Steel and Shipbuilding in San Diego, California. After offshore submergence trials, it was towed to Redwood City, where the capture vehicle was fabricated and then assembled within the HMB-1, which was towed to Catalina Island for the mating of the vehicle with the lift ship *Hughes Glomar Explorer*.

The craft's hull and dry-dock-type wing walls were subdivided into ballast tanks which, when flooded, submerged the barge to the seafloor. As the barge submerged, four air cylinders, normally nested at the four quarters of the barge, rose to a vertical position to assist the barge in sinking on an even keel. Subsequently they were flooded and reclined back into their nesting position. The roof of the HMB-1, when submerged, slid open to permit the *Glomar Explorer*, moored above the barge, to lift out the capture vehicle. The barge is non-self-propelled.

Early in the development of the HMB-1 it was envisioned that a crew would remain on board when the barge submerged. However, all controls were remote with a tow/support ship providing operational control, air (for blowing ballast), and electrical power through umbilicals.

The HMB-1 subsequently was used to support the U.S. Navy's stealth research ship *Sea Shadow*.

Displacement
empty	4,585 tons
loaded	10,875 tons

Length
overall	324 ft (98.78 m)
internal	276 ft (84.15 m)

Beam	106 ft 10 in (32.57 m)
Width internal	76 ft 8 in (23.37 m)

Height
overall	90 ft (27.44 m)
air cylinders raised	146 ft 6 in (44.66 m)
internal	62 ft (18.9 m)

NOTES

CHAPTER 1. THE BUBBLE

1. William Farr and Jerry Cohen, "CIA Reportedly Contracted with Hughes in Effort to Raise Sunken Soviet A-Sub," *Los Angeles Times* (February 8, 1975).

2. The authors are in debt for this account to John D. Gresham, author and former senior researcher for novelist Tom Clancy; Gresham was a student in Ocean Engineering 101 at the time.

3. Commission on Marine Science, Engineering and Resources, *Our Nation and the Sea: A Plan for National Action* (Washington, D.C.: 1969).

4. Ibid., p. ii.

5. Ibid., p. 130.

6. *Summa* is Latin for "peak" or "top." Previously almost all Hughes companies carried his name, such as the Hughes Sports Network and Hughes Tool Company. But the men now running the firm for the ill master of the domain overcame his objections and the name Summa remained.

7. Hughes Tool Company news release, November 29, 1972, Houston, Texas.

CHAPTER 2. SAILING ON COMBAT DUTY

1. The letter *K* indicated *Kruiser* (cruiser), the Soviet designation for large submarines.

2. The designation Type 53-58 indicates a torpedo of 53-centimeter (21-inch) diameter that became operational in 1958.

3. Dygalo had been notified of his promotion from captain 1st rank to rear admiral on the morning of February 23, 1968.

4. Rear Adm. Viktor A. Dygalo interview with Michael White, May 15, 2007, Moscow.

5. The officer, Snr. Lt. A. Vladimir Mosyachkin, was assigned to the intelligence staff of the 15th Submarine Squadron.

6. Dygalo interview with Michael White, May 15, 2007.

7. Ibid.

8. The "baffle" is the sound isolation material fitted behind a submarine's bow-mounted sonar equipment to isolate the hydrophones from the submarine's own noises.

9. Dygalo interview with Michael White, May 15, 2007.

10. The Soviets gained extensive knowledge of SOSUS as well as Navy communications because of Chief Warrant Officer John A. Walker, a U.S. Navy communications specialist who spied for the Soviet Union from at least 1968 until his arrest in 1985.

11. This military time group indicates March 26 at precisely 12 noon on prime meridian, i.e., Greenwich (England) Mean Time (GMT). The military uses the letter "Z" (Zulu) to indicate GMT; that was 12 midnight for the *K-129*, which maintained Kamchatka time while at sea.

12. Naval Security Group was the euphemism used for U.S. Navy's Bullseye intercept stations. In the northern Pacific they were located in Japan, Alaska, Midway, Oahu, and on the U.S. West Coast.

13. Reconnaissance satellites also may have been used for "fingerprinting," although this seems unlikely because of their orbits and the inability to match the radio intercepts with real-time satellite surveillance. See John Piña Craven, *The Silent War: The Cold War Battle Beneath the Sea* (New York: Simon & Schuster, 2001), pp. 203–204.

14. The *K-129*'s side number was often referred to as PL-722, the letters *PL* indicating *Podvodnaya Lodka* (Russian for submarine).

15. Dygalo unpublished manuscript.

16. Lee Mathers, e-mail to N. Polmar, November 12, 2009.

CHAPTER 3. TWO SUBMARINES

1. The description of submarines and their weapons is based primarily on I. D. Spassky (ed.), *Istoriya Otechestvennogo Sudostroeniya* (History of Indig-

enous Shipbuilding), vol. V, 1946–1991 (St. Petersburg, Russia: Sudostroenie, 1996); and N. Polmar and K. J. Moore, *Cold War Submarines: The Design and Construction of U.S. and Soviet Submarines* (Dulles, Va.: Potomac Books, 2004).

2. The Kapustan Yar test facility is located on the Volga River, near Volgograd (formerly Stalingrad).

3. The development of the first ballistic missile submarines is described in Spassky, *The History of Indigenous Shipbuilding*, vol. V, pp. 140–146; Malachite SPMBM, *Istoriya Sankt-Peterburgskogo Morskogo Buro Mashinostroenita "Malakhit"* (History of the Saint Petersburg Maritime Machinebuilding Bureau Malachite), vol. 2 (St. Petersburg: Malachite, 1995), pp. 150–166; A. A. Zapol'ski, *Raketi Startuyut s Morya* (Missiles Launch from the Sea) (St. Petersburg: Malachite, 1994); and V. I. Zharkov, "Creation of the First Submarines with Ballistic Missiles," *Gangut* (no. 14, 1998), pp. 103–117.

4. Soviet submarine missile systems had D-series designations.

5. Capt. 2nd Rank V. L. Berezovskiy, "Ballistic Missile Submarines on a Conveyor Belt," *Sudostroenie* (no. 6, 1977), p. 68. Berezovskiy later became the first commanding officer of the *Leninets (K-137)*, the first Project 667A/Yankee SSBN.

6. Spassky, *The History of Indigenous Shipbuilding*, vol. V, p. 146.

7. The dates of the Cuba visits were April 29 to May 6, 1972, and April 29 to May 7, 1974, respectively.

8. See, for example, Joseph Kraft, "SALT: A Time for Open Dealing," *The Washington Post* (June 25, 1974); and "Excerpts from Secretary Kissinger's News Conference on Missile Agreements," *The New York Times* (June 25, 1974).

   The Golf-class submarines were built with three missile tubes except for the last unit, which had two R-21/SS-N-5 Serb missile tubes; subsequently, several submarines were modified as missile test platforms with additional tubes providing a nominal 70 missile tubes in 22 submarines (see Appendix C).

   Nitze served as Assistant Secretary of Defense from 1961 to 1963, Secretary of the Navy from 1963 to 1967, and Deputy Secretary of Defense from 1967 to 1969. He was a member of the U.S. SALT delegation from 1969 to 1973.

9. Les Gelb, "Washington Dateline: The Story of a Flap," *Foreign Policy* (no. 16, fall 1974), pp. 174–175.

10. The only launching of a V-2 missile from a ship occurred on September 6, 1947, from the U.S. aircraft carrier *Midway* (CVB 41).

11. Two definitive works on the Regulus missile are David K. Stumpf, *Regulus: The Forgotten Weapon* (Paducah, Ky.: Turner Publishing, 1996), and Berend Derk Bruins, "U.S. Naval Bombardment Missiles, 1940–1956: A Study of the Weapons Innovation Process," PhD dissertation (New York: Columbia University, 1981). Also see N. Polmar and Robert S. Norris, *The U.S. Nuclear Arsenal: A History of Weapons and Delivery Systems Since 1945* (Annapolis, Md.: Naval Institute Press, 2009), pp. 191–195.

12. Gates served as Secretary of the Navy from 1957 to 1959 and Secretary of Defense from 1959 to 1961.

13. Capt. Peter L. Fullinwider, USN (Ret), "Recollections of Regulus," *The Submarine Review* (October 2009), p. 76.

14. N. Polmar, *Atomic Submarines* (Princeton, N. J.: Van Nostrand, 1963). The chapter "White Elephants" describes the submarines *Halibut* and *Triton* (SSRN 586), the latter a nuclear-propelled radar picket submarine (pp. 166–195).

15. Sherry Sontag and Christopher Drew, *Blind Man's Bluff: The Untold Story of American Submarine Espionage* (New York: PublicAffairs, 1998), p. 53. The *Halibut* was constructed on a building way at the Mare Island Naval Shipyard, and not in a dry dock.

CHAPTER 4. A SERIES OF EVENTS

1. This chapter is based in large part on Dygalo interview with Michael White, March 15, 2007.

2. The *K-126* was the second Golf-class submarine in the Pacific Fleet to be converted to the Project 629A/Golf II configuration. She completed the conversion in January 1968.

3. Aleksin quoted in Nikolay Burbyga, "The Submarine from 'Grave Bay,'" Part I, *Izvestiya* (July 4, 1992), p. 8.

4. Commanding Officer, Patrol Squadron NINE to Chief of Naval Operations (OP-05A5G), Subj: Command History for Calendar 1968; submission of (U), ser: 009/69, March 12, 1969, p. 2, p. 8.

5. Commanding Officer, Patrol Squadron NINE to Commander Naval Air

Force, U.S. Pacific Fleet, "Post Deployment Intelligence Report; Submission of," ser 0028, June 10, 1968, Annex A, "Patrol Squadron Nine Post Deployment Intelligence Report."

6. Citation for Meritorious Unit Commendation to Patrol Squadron Nine (1968).

7. Sontag and Drew, *Blind Man's Bluff*, pp. 75–76. The authors erroneously placed the *Barb* off Vladivostok, not Petropavlovsk.

8. Capt. Peter A. Huchthausen, USN (Ret); and Alexandre Sheldon-Duplaix, *Hide and Seek: The Untold Story of Cold War Espionage* (Hoboken, N.J.: John Wiley & Sons, 2009), p. 174.

9. Ibid.

10. Adm. Amel'ko was rotated from command of the Pacific Fleet in March 1968 and became the Deputy Commander-in-Chief of the Soviet Navy for anti-submarine warfare.

11. Alexandr Kandaurov e-mail to Michael White, May 12, 2010. Mr. Kandaurov spoke with Adm. Dygalo on May 11, 2010.

12. Four men survived the *Thetis* sinking in 160 feet of water with some 20 feet of her stern projecting above the surface. The worst submarine disaster in Soviet or Russian history occurred on August 12, 2000, with the sinking of the nuclear-propelled cruise missile submarine *Kursk*, with 118 men lost.

13. The Soviets believed that the submarine was lost by accident or even sunk by U.S. forces. In reality, the *L-16* was torpedoed and sunk by the Japanese submarine *I-25* on October 11, 1942. At that time Japan was at war with the United States but not with the Soviet Union.

14. Peter Almquist, *Red Forge: Soviet Military Industry since 1965* (New York: Columbia University Press, 1990), p. 23.

15. Quoted in Burgya, "The Submarine from 'Grave Bay,'" p. 8.

16. Dygalo interview with Michael White, March 15, 2007.

17. See N. Polmar, *Death of the USS* Thresher (Guilford, Conn.: Lyons, 2001).

18. Chief of Naval Operations memorandum to Navy offices Op-09a, Op-002, and Op-03, Subject: Soviet North Pacific Operation, 17 May 1968, serial 0047P32. "Op" indicated specific offices in the Office of the Chief of Naval Operations. The SOSUS "recordings" were a frequency-versus-time representation of an incoming sound "bite" on which the

time history of its spectral content was indicated by the blackening of specially sensitized paper by an electrostatic stylus that swept repeatedly along the frequency axis. In this way, the presence of distinctive submarine sound signatures could be discerned against the ocean background in the composite signal picked up by a seafloor array.

19. The establishment and development of AFTAC is well described in Charles A. Ziegler and David Jacobson, *Spying Without Spies: Origins of America's Secret Nuclear Surveillance System* (Westport, Conn.: Praeger, 1995).

20. Notes maintained by Capt. Joseph P. Kelly, USN, "Soviet SUBMIS [Submarine Missing] Golf 722 11 March 1968," p. 3. Capt. Kelly, at the time assigned to the U.S. Navy Electronic Systems Command, was the U.S. Navy's foremost SOSUS expert; he worked on SOSUS-related projects from 1951 until his retirement in 1973. (Hereafter referred to as "Kelly notes.")

21. In 2008–2009 an analysis of the AFTAC detected signals by Bruce Rule, formerly with NAVSTIC, identified at least 53 separate, weak-to-strong acoustic signals produced by the *K-129*.

22. Kelly notes, p. 3.

23. Ibid.

CHAPTER 5. FINDING THE TARGET OBJECT

1. See Jacques Piccard and Robert S. Dietz, *Seven Miles Down: The Story of the Bathyscaph Trieste* (New York: G. P. Putnam's Sons, 1961), and Capt. Don Walsh, USN (Ret), "A Dive to the Bottom of the Sea . . . 50 Years Later," U.S. Naval Institute *Proceedings* (January 2010), pp. 88–89. Walsh was officer-in-charge of the *Trieste* on her deep dive, being accompanied by Jacques Piccard, son of *Trieste* inventor Auguste Piccard.

2. Later in 1968 the *Mizar* would locate the hulk of the USS *Scorpion*.

3. Craven, *The Silent War*, p. 132. Craven served as director of DSSP from 1965 until the fall of 1969, when he was succeeded by a Navy captain; he remained with DSSP as chief scientist.

4. About 35,000 feet of cable were available, but was not carried for this mission.

5. One of the authors of this book was on board the *Halibut* in September 1961 and heard this comment on several occasions.

6. Craven, *The Silent War*, p. 140.

7. This incident is described—with some drama added—in Roger C. Dunham, *Spy Sub: A Top Secret Mission to the Bottom of the Pacific* (Annapolis, Md.: Naval Institute Press, 1996), pp. 172–181. This is a thinly disguised novel about the submarine *Halibut*, in which Dunham served as an enlisted reactor control operator.

8. Capt. Edward Moore, USN (Ret), e-mail to N. Polmar, March 2, 2010.

9. Dunham, *Spy Sub*, p. 160.

10. Ibid., pp. 160–161.

11. The Nixon presentation is cited in Sontag and Drew, *Blind Man's Bluff*, p. 85, and Craven, *The Silent War*, p. 220.

12. Capt. Moore, e-mail to N. Polmar, January 23, 2010.

13. Harlfinger had seen extensive combat in submarines during World War II, and was awarded the Navy Cross, the service's second-highest decoration. Before becoming the Assistant Chief of Naval Operations for Intelligence, Harlfinger had been assistant director for collection of the Defense Intelligence Agency, responsible for collecting enemy hardware as well as intelligence.

14. Sherman Wetmore interview with Michael White, June 8, 2007, Houston, Texas.

15. Sontag and Drew, *Blind Man's Bluff*, p. 190. The *K-129*'s hull broke immediately aft of the heavily damaged sail structure—immediately aft of the three missile tubes.

16. Raymond Feldman interview with Michael White, December 9, 2006, San Francisco.

CHAPTER 6. THE PLAN

1. Portions of this and subsequent chapters are based in part on the CIA-authored article "Project Azorian: The Story of the *Hughes Glomar Explorer*," *Studies in Intelligence* (Fall 1985), pp. 1–50. This publication was classified Secret/NOFORN (No Foreign), with the original manuscript written at the Top Secret/Compartmented level. When released to the public on January 4, 2010, the article was heavily censored, with about one-third of the words "blanked out," including the names of the CIA authors. Reportedly, one of the authors was the late Harry W. Hean, who worked on Project Azorian while with the CIA from 1951 to 1979. The CIA article and related materials are available on the web site

of the National Security Archives in Washington, D.C.: www.gwu. edu/~nsarchiv/.

2. Packard was cofounder of Hewlett-Packard, the highly innovative computer company.

3. William J. Broad, "Navy Has Long Had Secret Subs for Deep-Sea Spying, Experts Say," *The New York Times* (February 7, 1994), p. A1.

4. Capt. James Hay, USN (Ret), conversation with N. Polmar, Washington, DC, October 28, 2009.

5. CIA, "Project Azorian," p. 5.

6. Quoted in David S. Rosen, "Ship Has Berth in U.S. History," *Houston Chronicle* (July 20, 2006).

7. The name *Cuss I* was derived from the consortium of the oil firms that financed the endeavor—Continental, Union, Superior, and Shell. The non-self-propelled *YFN 730* was built in 1944 and served in the Navy until 1947.

8. *Glomar* was derived from *Global Marine*. The name *Challenger* recalled the highly successful British ocean survey ship of that name completed in 1872.

9. Vance Bolding interview with Michael White, June 9, 2007, Houston, Texas.

10. Feldman interview with Michael White, December 7, 2006.

11. The *Gidrograf* (SSV 480), displacing 2,300 tons full load, 256 feet long, was converted in 1967 from a salvage tug; the *SS-23*, displacing 930 tons full load, 235 feet, was a converted minesweeper.

12. "Memorial to the Crew of Submarine *K-129*, Rybachiy Settlement, City of Petropavlovsk-Kamchatskiy," *Krasnnaya Zvezda* (Red Star) (August 5, 1991).

13. Walker was arrested for espionage in 1985 and sentenced to life imprisonment.

14. Rear Adm. Dygalo interview with Michael White, May 15, 2007.

15. CIA, "Project Azorian," p. 35.

16. Curtis Crooke, speech at American Society of Mechanical Engineers ceremony, July 20, 2006, Houston, Texas.

17. U.S. Patent issued to Crooke et al., "Apparatus for Raising and Lowering Large Objects from a Surface Ship," No. 3,894,640, July 15, 1975.

18. CIA, "Project Azorian," p. 15.

19. Crooke, speech at American Society of Mechanical Engineers, July 20, 2006.

20. CIA, "Project Azorian," p. 16.

21. At the time the Forty Committee, chaired by Dr. Kissinger, was composed of the Director of Central Intelligence, Deputy Secretary of Defense, Chairman of the Joint Chiefs of Staff, and Under Secretary of State for Political Affairs.

22. CIA, "Project Azorian," p. 17.

23. Ibid.

24. Lee Mathers, e-mail to N. Polmar, April 2, 2010.

25. The panel consisted of representatives of the Director of Central Intelligence, Office of the Science Advisor to the President, Defense Contract Audit Agency, and the Assistant Secretary of Defense (Comptroller), plus another, unnamed agency—probably the National Security Agency.

26. CIA, "Project Azorian," p. 19.

27. American Society of Mechanical Engineers, "An ASME Historic Mechanical Engineering Landmark, July 20, 2006," brochure.

28. Charles Cannon, e-mail to M. White, November 23, 2009, corroborated by Stephen G. Kemp, e-mail to N. Polmar, January 12, 2010.

29. Although the moon pool was 199 feet in length, its useable space was restricted by the vertical docking legs to 179 feet.

30. Crooke, speech at American Society of Mechanical Engineers, July 20, 2006.

31. CIA, "Project Azorian," p. 24.

CHAPTER 7. GET READY, GET SET . . .

1. CIA, "Project Azorian," p. 28.

2. Ibid., p. 27.

3. Feldman interview with Michael White, December 8, 2006.

4. CIA, "Project Azorian," p. 36.

5. Rear Adm. Anatolyi Shtyrov at www.navy.ru/history/si58.htm (in Russian); accessed April 30, 2010.

6. Craven, *The Silent War*, p. 209.

7. Stephen E. Ambrose, *Eisenhower: The President* (New York: Simon and Schuster, 1984), p. 569; Michael R. Beschloss, *May-Day: Eisenhower, Khrushchev, and the U-2 Affair* (New York: Harper & Row, 1986), p. 10.

8. John Phelan, *Howard Hughes: The Hidden Years* (New York: Random House, 1976), p. 162.

CHAPTER 8. THE LIFT

1. Wetmore interview with Michael White, June 8, 2007.
2. Feldman interview with Michael White, December 7, 2006.
3. Wetmore interview with Michael White, June 8, 2007.
4. Feldman interview with Michael White, December 7, 2006.
5. Capt. John O'Connor, USN (Ret), discussion with N. Polmar, December 15, 2009, Arlington, Va. O'Connor was plans officer for Commander, Submarine Force Pacific Fleet, in the summer of 1974.
6. Wetmore interview with Michael White, June 8, 2007.
7. The *Chazhma* was converted in 1963 to a missile tracking ship, shortly after her completion as a bulk ore/coal carrier. She displaced 14,065 tons full load and was 459 feet long.
8. Shtyrov quoted in Nikolay Burbyga, "The Submarine from 'Grave Bay,'" *Izvestiya* (July 7, 1992), p. 6.
9. CIA, "Project Azorian," p. 39.
10. The *SB-10* displaced 925 tons full load and was 155 feet long.
11. Feldman interview with Michael White, December 7, 2006.
12. CIA, "Project Azorian," p. 42.
13. Feldman interview with Michael White, December 7, 2006.
14. Ibid.
15. Wetmore interview with Michael White, June 8, 2007.

CHAPTER 9. THE BOUNTY

1. CIA, "Project Azorian," p. 46.
2. Henry Kissinger, *Years of Renewal* (New York: Simon & Schuster, 1999), p. 38.
3. Charlie Johnson interview with Michael White, June 9, 2007, Houston, Texas.
4. CIA, "Project Azorian," p. 46.
5. Feldman interview with Michael White, December 7, 2006.
6. Feldman interview with Michael White, December 9, 2006.
7. Feldman interview with Michael White, December 8, 2006.
8. William E. Colby, ABC television, 1993.
9. Seymour M. Hersh, "Human Error Blamed in 1974 Failure of *Glomar*

Explorer to Retrieve Soviet Submarine," *The New York Times* (December 9, 1976), p. 1. Wayne Collier subsequently coauthored, with Roy Varner, *A Matter of Risk: The Incredible Inside Story of the CIA's Hughes Glomar Explorer Mission to Raise a Russian Submarine* (New York: Random House, 1978).

10. In his autobiography, Gates tells of making the presentation to Yeltsin, but gives no indication of the Russian president's reaction. Gates was the first Director of Central Intelligence to visit the Soviet Union or Russia. See Robert M. Gates, *From the Shadows: The Ultimate Insider's Story of Five Presidents and How They Won the Cold War* (New York: Simon & Schuster, 1996), pp. 553–554.

11. Area 51, a dry lake bed some $3\frac{1}{2}$ miles in circumference surrounded by mountains, became the flight-testing site for the U-2 spyplane in 1955. Subsequently it was used for other secret military projects. The location, just a few miles from the Atomic Energy Commission's Nevada test site, was known as Watertown Strip and Groom Lake before becoming known as Area 51.

CHAPTER 10. EXPOSURE AND REVELATION

1. The maraging steel issue was discussed in Feldman interview with Michael White, December 7, 2006; Wetmore interview with Michael White, June 8, 2007; and Bolding interview with Michael White, June 9, 2007. Also see Eugene Schorsch and Charles Garland, "Maraging Steel and Other Competitive Materials for Deep Submersibles," a paper presented to the Society of Naval Architects and Marine Engineers, Philadelphia, December 17, 1965. (Sun Shipbuilding and Dry Dock Company document No. S40-3.)

2. Sontag and Drew, *Blind Man's Bluff*, p. 197.

3. Rear Adm. Edward D. Sheafer Jr., USN (Ret), discussion with N. Polmar, September 13, 2010. Sheafer was Director of Naval Intelligence from August 1991 to September 1994.

4. James Phelan, *Howard Hughes*, p. 162.

5. Ibid., pp. 163–164.

6. Seymour Hersh, "C.I.A. Salvage Ship Brought Up Part of Soviet Sub Lost in 1968. Failed to Raise Atom Missiles," *The New York Times* (March 19, 1975), pp. 1, 48.

7. Jerry Cohen and George Reasons, "CIA Recovers Part of Russian Sub," *Los Angeles Times* (March 19, 1975), p. 1.

8. David M. Alpern, "CIA's Mission Impossible," *Newsweek* (March 31, 1975), p. 29.

9. Cohen and Reasons, "CIA Recovers Part of Russian Sub," p. 1.

10. Although Project Azorian had been "blown," for the next two decades almost all press articles and subsequent books on the subject called it Project Jennifer, which was a "compartment" name, of which Project Azorian was one part. Ironically, as early as 1978 the code name Azorian was revealed by Roy Varner and Wayne Collier in their book *A Matter of Risk;* Collier had been employed by Global Marine to recruit personnel for Project Azorian.

11. "Glomar Explorer to Sail This Month," *The New York Times* (April 4, 1975), p. 8

12. Thomas O'Toole, "A-Warheads Believed Recovered," *The Washington Post* (March 21, 1975), pp. A1, A5.

13. Kenneth Sewell, *Red Star Rogue: The Untold Story of a Soviet Submarine's Nuclear Strike Attempt on the U.S.* (New York: Pocket Books, 2005; paperback edition), pp. 409–410.

14. N. Polmar discussions with *Trieste* pilots at reunion of *Trieste* pilots, April 16–17, 2010, Washington, D.C. Also, e-mail from Beauford Myers to N. Polmar, May 10, 2010. The two previous *Trieste II* dives for the bucket were on November 4, 1971, and November 30, 1971.

15. Henry A. Kissinger memorandum to President Ford, April 2, 1975, Attachment Tab A.

16. Ibid., Attachment Tab B.

17. "Hughes Ship Said Ready for Mission," *The Washington Post* (September 4, 1975), p. 20.

18. Department of Defense news release, "Navy to Lease *Glomar Explorer*" (No. 44-78, January 27, 1978).

19. "*Glomar Explorer* Leased for Ocean Mining," *Sea Technology* (March 1978), p. 9.

20. "*Glomar Explorer* to Be Converted," *Sea Technology* (December 1978), p. 9.

21. James Drabos, comment on "The Recovered Sunken Warship: Raising a Legal Question," U.S. Naval Institute *Proceedings* (March 1979), p. 22.

22. GlobalSantaFe Corp. was a merger of Global Marine Drilling and Santa Fe International Corp.

CHAPTER 11. CONSPIRACIES AND CAUSES

1. Rear Adm. V. A. Dygalo, *Zapiski Kontr-Admirala* (A Rear Admiral's Notes), (Moscow: Kuchkovo Pole, 2009), p. 260.

2. The four submarines of this class did have strengthened sail structures for under-ice operations. The *Skate* herself was the world's first submarine to surface at the North Pole, on August 11, 1958.

3. Dygalo interview with Michael White, May 15, 2007.

4. Ibid.

5. Rear Adm. Dygalo, *Zapiski Kontr-Admirala*, photo section.

6. Chief of Naval Operations Briefing Notes, March 14, 1968, Item 6, "*SWORDFISH* YOKO VISIT(S)."

7. Rear Adm. P. M. Ratliff, USN, Director of Naval Intelligence, letter to Sen. Robert C. Smith, December 13, 1999.

8. Huchthausen and Sheldon-Duplaix, *Hide and Seek*, p. 172.

9. Ibid., p. 176.

10. Craven, *The Silent War*, pp. 217–218.

11. "The Learning Curve," *African Armed Forces* (October 2008), p. 37.

12. Sewell, *Red Star Rogue*, p. 180.

13. Dygalo interview with Michael White, May 15, 2007.

14. Sewell, *Red Star Rogue*, pp. 181–182.

15. W. Craig Reed, *Red November: Inside the Secret U.S.-Soviet Submarine War* (New York: HarperCollins, 2010).

16. Ibid., p. 224.

17. Ibid., p. 205.

18. Sewell, *Red Star Rogue*, p. 176.

19. Ibid., p. 177.

20. Huchthausen and Sheldon-Duplaix, *Hide and Seek*, p. 173.

21. Reed, *Red November*, p. 213.

22. Ibid., p. 214.

23. Bruce Rule, letter to the Director of Naval Intelligence, August 6, 2010.

24. Capt. Richard Lee, USN (Ret.), e-mail to Lee Mathers, May 8, 2010.

25. Dr. Eugene Miasnikov, e-mail to Bruce Rule, May 12, 2008.

CHAPTER 12. FAILURE AND FRUSTRATION

1. Dygalo interview with Michael White, May 15, 2007.

2. Rear Adm. Dygalo, *Zapiski Kontr-Admirala*, p. 258.

3. Lee Mathers, e-mail to N. Polmar, April 16, 2010.

4. Dygalo interview with Michael White, May 15, 2007.

APPENDIX A. KAMCHATKA SUBMARINE FLOTILLA

1. This appendix was compiled by Mr. Lee J. Mathers.

2. SS/SSN   = torpedo attack submarine
   SSB/SSBN = ballistic missile submarine
   SSGN   = guided (cruise) missile submarine
   SSR   = radar picket submarine

3. The submarines *K-99* and *K-136* were in shipyard No. 202 at Vladivostok undergoing conversion to the Project 629/Golf II configuration.

4. The *B-89* was in shipyard No. 202 at Vladivostok undergoing conversion to a Project AV611E/SSB configuration. After completion in March 1969, she was assigned to the 19th Submarine Brigade at Ulysses Bay near Vladivostok.

5. These three submarines were in the Zvezda shipyard, northeast of Vladivostok, undergoing conversion to Project 659T torpedo attack submarines; the other two Project 659/SSGNs were out of service in preparation for conversion to that configuration.

APPENDIX C. THE SUBMARINE *K-129*

1. This appendix is based on Spassky, *History of Indigenous Shipbuilding*, vol. V, pp. 142–146; Polmar and Moore, *Cold War Submarines*, pp. 107–111; and Zharkov, "Creation of the First Submarines with Ballistic Missiles," pp. 104–119.

APPENDIX D. THE R-21/SS-N-5 SERB MISSILE

1. This appendix is based, in part, on Pavel Podvig (ed.), *Russian Strategic Nuclear Forces* (Cambridge, Mass.: MIT Press, 2001), pp. 315–319; Polmar and Moore, *Cold War Submarines*, pp. 110–112; and Zharkov, "Creation of the First Submarines with Ballistic Missiles," pp. 104–119.

2. V. P. Semyonov discussion with N. Polmar, St. Petersburg, May 6, 1997. Semyonov was longtime principal deputy to Sergei Kovalev, chief designer of the various Project 667 derivatives (NATO Yankee and Delta) and Project 941 (NATO Typhoon) ballistic missile submarines.

3. In the NATO designation system, SS indicated surface-to-surface missile, the letter N indicated a naval weapon, with a sequential number; all surface-to-surface missiles were assigned code names beginning with the letter S.

APPENDIX E. THE SUBMARINE *HALIBUT*

1. This appendix is based, in part, on Stumpf, *Regulus: The Forgotten Weapon;* Polmar and Moore, *Cold War Submarines*, pp. 90–93; and various editions of N. Polmar, *Ships and Aircraft of the U.S. Fleet* (Annapolis, Md.: Naval Institute Press).

BOOK LIST

The first books to address Project Azorian were *The Jennifer Project* by Clyde Burleson (1977) and *A Matter of Risk* by Roy Varner and Wayne Collier (1978), with the latter using the code name Azorian in the text and as the title of the French-language edition. Although these books contained numerous errors about both the *K-129* and the salvage effort, their publication shortly after the event was revealing and certain material in them makes both efforts useful to a study of this subject.

The next significant book to address Project Azorian was *Blind Man's Bluff* by Sherry Sontag and Christopher Drew (1998). That book introduced a new genre to readers—Cold War submarine espionage. Project Azorian did involve submarine espionage in the context of the submarine *Halibut* seeking the wreckage of the submarine *K-129*, and hence the attempted salvage of the *K-129* is addressed in *Blind Man's Bluff* (albeit called Project Jennifer). This book, despite several shortfalls, was highly successful and is still strongly recommended for everyone with an interest in Cold War–era submarines and intelligence.

Blind Man's Bluff has been followed by a flotilla of books that sought to reveal the "true" stories of Cold War submarine espionage. The first was *The Silent War* (2001) by John Craven. A key player in this field, Craven was head of the Navy's Deep Submergence Systems Project, which developed "black" and "white" capabilities for deep-ocean search, recovery, and salvage operations. However, his book, with a surprising number of factual errors as well as unusual theories, is primarily a personal memoir.

Subsequent books have been seriously flawed, all of them being inundated with factual errors and misinterpretations even though some of their authors had served in submarines. These were: Kenneth Sewell, *Red Star Rogue* (2005); Gary Weir and Walter Boyne, *Rising Tide* (2006); Peter A. Huchthausen, a former U.S. naval attaché in Moscow, and Alexandre Sheldon-Duplaix, *Hide and Seek* (2009); and Craig Reed, *Red November* (2010).

Two Soviet memoirs have been useful to the authors of this book, especially Rear Admiral Viktor Dygalo, *A Rear Admiral's Notes* (2009), and Admiral Nikolai Amel'ko, *In the Interest of the Fleet and the State* (2003).

The submarine data in the present volume are based primarily on the Russian-language reference work edited by Academician Igor Spassky, *The History of Indigenous Shipbuilding*, vol. V, *1946–1991* (1996), and N. Polmar and K. J. Moore, *Cold War Submarines* (2004). Several other books are cited below that provide data on the development of Soviet ballistic missile submarine development. Spasky was head of the Rubin submarine design bureau in St. Petersburg at the time and worked closely with the authors of *Cold War Submarines*. The story of "life aboard the *Halibut*" is told by Roger Dunham in *Spy Sub* (1996), a well-written, thinly disguised novel about the USS *Halibut's* search for the remains of the *K-129*. And, David Stumpf's *Regulus* (1996) provides an excellent description of the development of that weapon and the *Halibut*.

Russian-language books are indicated by an asterisk.

Amel'ko, Nikolai N. *In the Interest of the Fleet and of the State: Memoirs of Admiral N. N. Amelko*. Moscow: Nauka, 2003.*

Burleson, Clyde W. *The Jennifer Project: Howard Hughes . . . the CIA . . . A Russian Submarine . . . The Intelligence Coup of the Decade*. Englewood Cliffs, N.J.: Prentice-Hall, 1977.

Craven, John Piña. *The Silent War: The Cold War Battle Beneath the Sea*. New York: Simon & Schuster, 2001.

Dunham, Roger C. *Spy Sub: A Top Secret Mission to the Bottom of the Pacific*. Annapolis, Md.: Naval Institute Press, 1996.

Dygalo, Viktor A. *A Rear Admiral's Notes*. Moscow: Kuchkovo Pole, 2009.*

Huchthausen, Peter A., and Alexandre Sheldon-Duplaix. *Hide and Seek: The Untold Story of Cold War Naval Espionage*. Hoboken, N.J.: John Wiley & Sons, 2009.

Karpyenko, A. B. *Russian Missile Weapons, 1943–1993*. St. Petersburg, Russia: PEKA, 1993.*

Krutein, Eva, and Manfred Krutein. *Amerika? America! From Immigration to Espionage*. Albuquerque, N.Mex.: Amador Publishers, 1997.

Malachite SPMBM. *History of the Saint Petersburg Maritime Machinebuilding Bureau Malachite*, vol. 2. St. Petersburg, Russia: Malachite, 1995.*

Polmar, Norman, and K. J. Moore. *Cold War Submarines: The Design and Construction of U.S. and Soviet Submarines*. Washington, D.C.: Brassey's/Potomac Books, 2004.

Razlyotov, Boris K. *History of Bureau "Malachite,"* vol. 2. St. Petersburg, Russia: Gangut, 1995.*

Reed, Craig W. *Red November: Inside the Secret U.S.–Soviet Submarine War*. New York: William Morrow, 2010.

Sewell, Kenneth, and Clint Richmond. *Red Star Rogue: The Untold Story of a Soviet Submarine's Nuclear Strike Attempt on the U.S.* New York: Simon & Schuster, 2005.

Sontag, Sherry, and Christopher Drew. *Blind Man's Bluff: The Untold Story of American Submarine Espionage*. New York: PublicAffairs Press, 1998.

Spassky, Igor D., ed. *The History of Indigenous Shipbuilding*, vol. V, *1946–1991*. St. Petersburg, Russia: Sudostroenie, 1996.*

Stumpf, David K. *Regulus: The Forgotten Weapon*. Paducah, Ky.: Turner Publishing, 1996.

Varner, Roy, and Wayne Collier. *A Matter of Risk: The Incredible Inside Story of the CIA's* Hughes Glomar Explorer *Mission to Raise a Russian Submarine*. New York: Random House, 1978.

Weir, Gary E., and Walter J. Boyne, *Rising Tide: The Untold Story of the Russian Submarines That Fought the Cold War*. New York: Basic Books, 2006.

Zapol'ski, A. A. *Missiles Launch from the Sea*. St. Petersburg, Russia: Malachite, 1994.*

INDEX

Ranks listed are the highest used in the text. Ship designations are listed on pages xvii–xviii; non-U.S. ships are identified by nation.

AUTHOR BIOGRAPHIES

NORMAN POLMAR is an internationally known analyst, consultant, and author specializing in naval, aviation, and intelligence issues. Since June 2008 he has been the senior consultant for National Security Programs at Gryphon Technologies, where he has supported Navy ballistic missile defense, cyber operations, and shipbuilding programs. Until May 2008 he served as the senior policy advisor in the Center for Security Strategies & Operations within General Dynamics/Information Technology; he previously held that position with the Anteon and Techmatics firms prior to corporate buyouts.

From 1982 to 1986 and from December 2002 until June 2008, he served as a member of the Secretary of the Navy's Research Advisory Committee (NRAC). He also served on a subpanel of the Defense Science Board' s study of transition to and from hostilities (2004) and was a member of a Defense Advanced Research Projects Agency's advisory panel looking at future warfare requirements (2007).

He has worked extensively as an analyst and consultant in the submarine area for the U.S. Department of Defense and the U.S. Department of the Navy, U.S. and foreign commercial firms, and government agencies, and for members of the U.S. House of Representatives and Senate. He spent four years with the Navy's Deep Submergence Systems Project (DSSP) while an employee of Northrop Corp.

Mr. Polmar has written or coauthored 50 books in the naval, aviation, and intelligence fields, and coauthored one about the city of Washington, with his daughter-in-law, Brigette Polmar. From 1967 to 1977 Mr. Polmar was editor of the United States sections of *Jane's Fighting Ships*, and was completely responsible for almost one-third of that annual reference work. He is currently a columnist for the *Proceedings* and *Naval History* magazines, both of which are published by the U.S. Naval Institute.

He is a resident of Alexandria, Virginia.

MICHAEL WHITE is a film director and producer specializing in highly technical and documentary films. He has worked in the feature film, television, and advertising industries since 1976.

Born in London, he left school at age 15 and served for five years in the British merchant marine before finding a job in the newspaper media. His career in special and visual effects began in 1976 on the set of "Superman: The Movie." Subsequently, he worked on 16 international films for various studios in England and Europe. From 1988 onwards his career expanded into directing commercials for television and cinema throughout Europe, and in 1990 he established his workplace and home in Vienna. In 1996 he expanded into producing technical films for the international defense industry.

In 2002 Mr. White additionally turned to making full-length documentary films; in 2006 he completed his first television documentary, "On a Wind and a Prayer." This award-winning film tells the remarkable story of the Japanese balloon bomb offensive against the North American continent during World War II.

His latest documentary—"Azorian: The Raising of the *K-129*"—provides the most accurate film account yet produced of the incredible covert operation and partial recovery of the Soviet submarine *K-129* by the CIA.

He works and resides in Vienna, Austria.

LIFT SHIP *HUGHES GLOMAR EXPLORER*

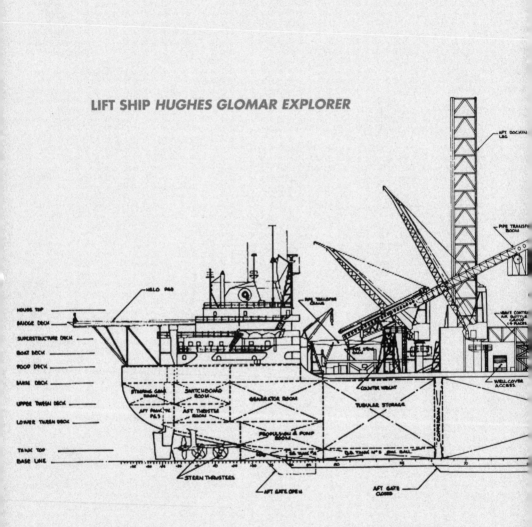

(BELOW